A Tablespoon of
LOVE,
A Tablespoon of
DISCIPLINE

MAXGAN ASSOCIATES

RICE, VA

**Publishing that addresses a higher level
of moral, social and ethical values.**

A Tablespoon of
LOVE,
A Tablespoon of
DISCIPLINE

The Recipe for Raising a Child

by

Donald L. Gandy

A Tablespoon of Love,
A Tablespoon of Discipline:
The Recipe for Raising a Child

ISBN-13: 978-0-9792791-0-2
ISBN-10: 0-9792791-0-0

Printed in the United States

Published by:

MAXGAN Associates
Rice, Virginia 23966-2674
www.maxganassociates.com

Credits: Shirley Caesar, from a tape entitled Shirley Caesar's Trea-
sures, a song entitled, "King Heroin." Vera Hildebrand, from *Introduction to
Early Childhood Education*, Education (page 36), Direct Guidance (page 96),
Goals for Early Childhood, Michigan State University, Second Edition,
MacMillan Publishing Co., NY, 1976. Modern Maturity, an article entitled,
Cults—Let Us Prey, June, 1994. Dr. Charles Stanley, from *The Business
Man's Bible™, New King James Version*, Priority Profiles for Today's Work-
place. Ladies Home Journal, an article entitled "Ask Any Woman" by
Marcelene Cox. Jacob M. Brande, from *Speaker's Encyclopedia*, Prentice
Hall, 1955, Englewood Cliffs, NJ. Unless otherwise noted, all Bible quota-
tions are from the King James Version. References marked "NKJ" are from
The New King James Version of the Bible, copyright © 1979, 1980, 1982, by
Thomas Nelson, Inc., Nashville, Tennessee.

Dedication

I dedicate this book to my granddaughter Carla, to give her a lasting memory of her granddad

and to

the memory of Dave, Carla's father and the person who was so much a part of Celeste, the central theme of this book.

ACKNOWLEDGMENTS

I would first like to acknowledge God, my Savior, who gave me the knowledge and inspiration to write this book. If and whatever success this writing achieves, I owe it all to Him because He set the stage for all the things that had to come together to make it happen.

The knowledge had to be there; the memory had to be there; and God gave them to me. The right timing had to be there, and God set the timing. The accomplishment had to be there in order for me to be able to write these words of advice. God kept us on track in our role as parents so we could help bring our child to a point whereby she could be declared (in our opinion) a child-raising success story. So all that I have, all that I am and all that I hope to be is and will be only by God's grace.

I'm the type of individual who has his own mind about most things, but the encouragement I get from others certainly adds to my belief in myself. I want to thank all of those various individuals who encouraged me as I progressed in this endeavor.

First, I would like to acknowledge my daughter, Celeste, who is the subject of this writing and the primary reason why I did this book. She is the child who this book speaks mostly about, and she believes in my ability to accomplish what I set out to do. She helped to make my parenting experience easy.

I would like to acknowledge Clara Gandy, Celeste's mother and the other half of the parenting equation. She loved and disciplined as the circumstance required and was always there with her presence.

I also would like to acknowledge my wife and friend who gave assistance where needed with professional advice and knowledge garnered from study in her field, which is related to this writing. My wife thinks I can do many things well and especially those of an intellectual nature. She always refers to me as "the guy who wears many hats."

And let me not forget our friend Shirley, who in her role as a professional counselor gave insight that helped to add validity to many of my thoughts and premises.

Then there's my high school buddy Joseph, who gave me his parents' slant on how they were raised. That slant is embedded in the pages of this book.

Along with Joseph's contribution is that of my former church sister and dear friend Rose, who is always eager to add a positive spin to any worthwhile endeavor. She critiqued and encouraged. Her excitement over this endeavor fueled me the more to complete it. She has been a continuous source of encouragement, support and inspiration. She is a catalyst for igniting any worthwhile endeavor.

Let me also acknowledge Beverly Delgado who added finishing touches and editing to the overall manuscript where she saw a need and formatted the file for printing. She is one of those highly organized individuals who always contributes valuable input. She's been a client of mine over the years, and whenever I received paperwork from her, it was always in order. She is the height of efficiency, and I have always believed in her ability.

In addition to those mentioned above and those not mentioned, I would also like to acknowledge anyone else who so much as spoke an encouraging word or said he or she will buy the book when it is published. I thank God for all of them, and I thank Him for seeing me through to the completion of the book.

Last, but not least, I would like to acknowledge the tireless efforts of Dr. Harold McDougal who edited, advised, taught and corrected and was the unbroken thread between my manuscript and the printer's completion. Without him this could not have happened.

CONTENTS

My Survey 13

Preface 17

A Literary Agent's Comments and My Rebuttal 29

Introduction 34

I: Before the Beginning and in the Beginning 53

1. Things You Eat, Drink and Ingest 53

2. Get Ready, Your Child Is Coming 56

3. The Way You Act and the Baggage You Carry 59

4. The Environment You Bring Your Child Into 62

5. The Plan for Nurturing 65

II: Plant the Child in Good Moral Soil 69

1. Pray First 69

2. Strive for the Best, Employing Right Conduct 71

3. Cleanliness Is Next to Godliness 72

4. Good Manners 77

5. Actions Speak Louder 80

6. Puberty 81

III: Bend the Tree with Love and Discipline 87

1. Early Support and Direction 87

2. The Terrible Twos 88

3. Getting Directions and Making Decisions 91

4. Balancing the Forces 92

5. Open Ears, Open Eyes and Open Heart 94

6. When Buffeted by the Forces of Life 95

IV: Be in Charge of Your Child, Not the Other Way Around 97

1. You Must Dictate 98

2. Who Is in Charge? 107

3. All Social Systems Dictate 113

4. The Systems of Life 115

  5. Schooling 116

  6. The Military 121

  7. If You Break the Law 124

  8. The Work World 125

  9. A Good Child 126

10. Society Is Global 127

V: Be There—Really Be There **129**

  1. What Does Being There Mean? 129

  2. From the Cradle 135

  3. Preschool and the First Babysitter 137

  4. Grade School 141

  5. High School 148

  6. College 160

  7. Post-College and Marriage 170

VI: Get Involved in Every Aspect **175**

  1. It's Our Responsibility 175

  2. The Clothes and Things 177

  3. Where Things Come From 181

  4. Things Consumed by Body and Mind 183

  5. Where They Live and Who They Marry 187

VII: Be Unified for the Sake of the Child **191**

  1. Demonstrating Respect for the Other Parent ... 191

  2. You Picked Your Child's Other Parent 193

  3. Old-fashioned Parenting Worked 195

  4. Tough Love 197

  5. Agree to Agree in Spite of 199

  6. Your Child Can Learn From the Way You Do It 202

VIII: If You Separate from Your Spouse, Don't Separate from Your Child **205**

  1. You Can Get Along With Your Child 205

  2. Your Child's Future Without You 209

  3. Why Punish Your Child? 211

  4. It's All About Your Child's Life 213

IX: Be an Example for Them, and You Can Demand More of Them 219

1. Who Are Their Role Models 219
2. Bad Parental Examples Not to Follow 222
3. You Can Set Positive Examples 229

X: Surviving as an Independent 237

1. I'll Stay, as Long as I Can Have My Way 237
2. The Transition is Taking Too Long 240
3. I'll Be Glad When I Get Grown 242
4. Her Parents Parted Ways 245
5. She Was Alone and in Charge of Her Studies 248
6. She Had Responsible Summer Work 251
7. When the Going Got Tough 253
8. Leaving Childhood and Entering Adulthood 257

XI: Is It for the Child or for You? 265

1. Your Dreams and Goals 265
2. Through the Years 271
3. Do You Want to Do It for Your Parents? 275
4. Let the Child Do It 277

XII: Be Strong, but Also Be Human 283

1. Your Child Thinks You Are a Rock 283
2. Do Children Really Care? 286
3. Being Strong Is Our Role 289
4. Parents Also Have Needs 292

XIII: Buy Them the Right Toys for Life's Conditioning 295

1. What Is a Toy? 295
2. Let the Toys Show 298
3. Don't Accept the Guilt Trip 299
4. But Why So Much? 301
5. It Isn't in the Sizzle 303
6. Balanced Toys, Balanced Life 304

**XIV: Don't Interfere in Their Life, but Always Condemn
Wrong Behavior** **313**
1. Throwing Them to the Wolves 313
2. They're Still Crying Out for Discipline 318
3. Character and Life Destroyers 321

**XV: Don't Hold Your Child Forever in Your Arms, but Keep
Your Arms Forever Open** **329**
1. Breaking Up and Letting Go 329
2. Your Child's Safety and Well Being 331
3. Mother, Butt Out! 343
4. If You Must, the Door Is Open 344

Glossary of Slang Words and Phrases 347

MY SURVEY

Recently I conducted a survey to see just how today's parents go about the task of raising their children. The survey population consisted of a cross-section of professional and nonprofessional parents that cut across all racial lines, religious lines, educational backgrounds, professions, job titles, salary ranges and family sizes up to five children. I was interested in knowing what they did in their parenting style, the type of parenting style employed and the results achieved based on the way the task was approached.

Since today's society seems to be fostering so many children inclined toward radically different behavior, as compared to those children who came of adult age in the late 1950s, I was interested in knowing how today's parenting methods differ from those of yesterday. I can say that the conclusions garnered from the survey didn't seem to differ from the conclusions I had come to expect as the reason why the children of today (for the most part) are either headed for an off-track adulthood or are already in an off-track childhood. The survey confirmed a sense of leniency existing in today's parenting that guides children toward unstable behavior.

The results of the survey are as follows:

1. At least 90% of the parents surveyed believed in the parenting style referred to as indulgent permissive (lenient).
2. A wide variety of disciplinary methods were employed, including talking, grounding, time-outs, no toys, no TV, no special trips and no special snacks.
3. Only 25% believed in any form of corporal punishment and only for the under-five-year-old age group.
4. Roughly 38% of the parents employed the same parenting style as their parents, and 62% admitted that they were more lenient.
5. Roughly 38% raised their children as single parents.
6. On a scale of 1-10, 80% of the parents rated their parenting satisfaction 8 or above.

7. An equal number of children were raised in an urban setting.
8. On the question of what advice would you offer to other parents, the following mirror these parents' opinions:

    A. 26% said Just love them.
    B. 12% said Set an example.
    C. 12% said Wait until you get old enough to be a parent.
    D. 14% said Spend time with them.
    E. 28% said Listen to your children.
    F. 8% said Strive to get at least a basic education to help you in your child-raising process.

Roughly 150 surveys were distributed; about 67% were in the age group under forty years of age, and approximately 33% constituted an age group of those whose children were born in the 1950s and 60s.

Roughly 90% of those whose children were born in the 1950s and 60s expressed the need to give love and to discipline your children, and roughly 75% of this 33% believed in corporal punishment.

In addition to the written survey conducted, a verbal survey was conducted over a time span of approximately thirty years, beginning at the time I first began to witness behavior that perplexed me and behavior I found to be alien to that of those individuals in my age group and older. I began asking questions of parents and peers, and the answers I got, most of the time, were, "I'm not going to raise my children like my parents raised me. They were too strict." After conversing with roughly 100 individuals on this matter, I concluded that here lies the problem: The answer to "not being too strict" meant being too lenient. Being too strict meant too much discipline, but being too lenient meant not enough discipline. That's where the problems began. The 10% of the parents in the verbal survey category who didn't stress love and discipline seem to have lost many of their children to the street, as did also a large percentage of the 25% who abandoned corporal punishment. This is an indication that modern-day discipline methods don't work as well. Evidence of the same can be seen in the survey results.

The primary reason for my conducting the written survey was to convince myself that:

1. There was substance in my observation and conclusions concerning what's wrong with the children of the most recent three generations and,
2. To validate and substantiate my former beliefs and observations.

Neither the written survey nor the verbal survey takes claim to being scientific, but both make the point concerning what I concluded as being some of the problems with today's children. We all know, without a doubt, there is something wrong. Psychologists haven't been able to tell us what's wrong, sociologists haven't been able to tell us what's wrong, educators have no answer, and the modern-day parent seems to have no clue. Well, this book is telling society what's wrong by telling it what worked in generations prior to the 1960s, what problems need fixing and what needs to be done to fix the problems.

I challenge anyone to give a better solution than can be found in the pages of this book. I believe if someone had a better solution it would be in place by now and the society of children would be getting progressively better, rather than getting progressively worse.

RESEARCH SURVEY
PARENTING STYLES AND PHILOSOPHY

I. How would you describe your parenting style?
    ☐ Authoritative *(command absolute obedience)*   ☐ Indulgent/Permissive *(lenient)*
    ☐ Democratic *(accepting & encouraging)*

II. Name two of your disciplinary methods.
    1.
    2.

III. Did/Do you employ corporal punishment as part of your disciplinary methods?
    ☐ yes   ☐ no

IV. Does/Did your parenting styles differ from your parent(s)/guardian? (yes) (no)
    If yes explain:

V. Describe your child(ren).

Child	1	2	3	4	5	6	7	8	9	10
Age										
Compliant										
Strong-willed										
Highest level of education *HS AAS BA MA/MS PG* *[use one]*										
Most Challenging Years										

VI. Name one thing that you are most proud of about your child(ren).

VII. Name one thing that you regret during your active parenting years.

VIII. On a scale of 1-10, how pleased are you with the result of your parenting?
    (   )

IX. What advice would you offer today for parents?

Additional data:
1. Two- or one-parent family? (   )
2. Residential community where child(ren) were raised: a. urban   b. suburban   c. rural

The Survey Form I Used

PREFACE

My daughter's name is Celeste. She was born in the 1960s, graduated from Rochester Institute of Technology and is a packaging engineer for a Fortune 500 company. She was married in 1995, to David, who was also born in the 1960s.

David also graduated from Rochester Institute of Technology, as a computer-engineering major, and was employed as a team leader for one of the major information systems companies. They were both bright, focused individuals.

Celeste was attractive, and David was handsome. Celeste wore a traditional mainstream hairstyle, and David wore a traditional mainstream hair cut. They both interacted well with people of all races, religions and ethnic backgrounds. Each possessed traditional mainstream Christian values. Both of them played by the rules, and neither of them were ever in trouble with the law. Neither was addicted to gambling, alcohol or drugs. Their marriage to each other was the first marriage for each of them, and neither had any children prior to this union.

The wedding was one of the noticeable social events of the season and shared an announcement with other such eventful weddings in the *New York Times* of Sunday, October 1, 1995. The wedding was performed by a New York congressman, who is also an Episcopal Minister. It had plenty of everything needed to satisfy the loftiness of the occasion and to make for a very pleasant event.

David and Celeste left their wedding and went off on a honeymoon, consisting of an organized safari in Africa. Some four or fives days after returning, they moved into their own four-bedroom home in suburbia, and they spent most of their free time doing things together. I believe Celeste really loved David, and I also believe David really loved Celeste. He was a true and dedicated husband, and when their child came, he was a true and dedicated father.

David has since transitioned into eternity, but he left behind a sterling legacy that indicated that successful parenting had impacted his life. Celeste is my daughter, and David had become my son, and I am deeply proud of what they both had become. But I am not giving their profiles here as an opportunity to brag. So then why am I giving their profiles? I am giving their profiles to demonstrate the results obtained when children are raised successfully.

The early schooling of both David and Celeste, their college education, their profession, their wedding, honeymoon and all of the other pertinent events speak to the efforts they put forth in exhibiting a positive path of accomplishment. This positive path speaks to results obtained when children are parented successfully. To get the connection, contrast the above example with a child who drops out of school, has no viable profession, has a child outside of marriage, has no meaningful employment, lives together in an unmarried relationship and has no godly principles. Would you wish for your child the first scenario or the second? Or does it really matter? I believe any well-meaning parent would be proud to have a child who transitioned into adulthood in the form of this first scenario.

That example speaks to the results of successful parenting. However, this success is meant for the present. One is not able to look into the future and see where children will be or what they will be doing five years, ten years or fifteen years from now. The elements contained in a successful child's profile, once he or she transitions into adulthood (as well as others that are not contained therein) are all characteristics embodied in the life of a child who has been properly raised and is considered to be a success. Having said this, I must think that the nurturing parents (in cooperation with God) did many things correctly.

There may have been parental, intellectual prowess on both sides of the marriage, but that wasn't what mattered the most. Intellect is not a primary, or basic, requirement for successful child-raising, nor is the lack thereof a primary, or basic, element in raising an unsuccessful child. The basic and most important requirements are enumerated in the chapters contained in this book, and they can all be rolled up into two measured elements: love and discipline.

The above conclusion, along with information obtained from surveys and extended interviews with parents, observations of successful as well as failed parenting styles, make up my autobiographical account of how we employed the elements in our parenting style in raising Celeste. If they mean anything to you, and you believe them, use them if you can, and you may also achieve success in shaping your child for his or her future.

This is my story. Some of the connecting information supporting the premise may be generalized, but in most instances I am speaking directly to my personal experiences in raising my daughter. I am not a child psychologist, nor a guidance counselor, nor an elementary school teacher. Neither were my parents, nor my parents' parents. Neither were a host of other parents from bygone days or today. And yet, my, how well they could raise children! They were not prepared for the child-raising task by any special qualifications that could be found in a textbook. As a matter of fact, one of the most noted textbook authorities of that period on the subject of raising children was Dr. Benjamin Spock, and it has been noted again and again that his methods were a failure, even a near disaster, when applied in many cases. There is no noted authority or scientific deduction that can be applied in its pure form to the effort of child-raising that will guarantee the positive results of bringing a child to adulthood, as a normal, rational person in the way she or he integrates into mainstream society.

From this perspective, I would conclude that a properly raised child is one who listens and accepts the positive guidance of the parent or guardian, respects the institution of authority, steers free of trouble with the law, strives to keep conversations and actions on a higher moral plane, stays in the educational environment long enough to satisfy herself or himself that she or he is properly equipped by reason of education, to earn a satisfactory living relative to her or his own desire and one who has learned, from interacting with others, how to fairly treat her or his fellow man.

So we all have the potential for raising this type of child, and that potential does not come from a book on scientific matters, but will more likely come from a book on common sense matters. This type of book may or may not have already been written, but the leaning is on the side of it not having been written—because each generation seems to be putting children out into society less and less equipped to be solid contributors to the good of that society. However, the fact that it has not been written does not prevent any parent—average or above average, white, black or other, rich or poor, Protestant or Catholic, Christian, Jew or other—from sending a properly raised child out into society.

Some of the most successful child-raisers of times past were of no particular ethnic persuasion and were individuals with no formal education, some of whom could neither read nor write. I can recall many examples of this, but one in particular comes to mind. It is that of an individual land owner and tobacco farmer who amassed several hundred acres of land, a considerable sum of money and other assets. He could neither read nor write. He signed his name with an "X." He, in his turn, raised a child who had very little formal education. This offspring raised four other children, three of which could be considered properly raised based on the parameters set forth above.

There are certain basic tenets that every parent must adhere to, if the parent wishes to successfully raise the child. Other rules or ideas of positive worth that can enhance the basics may be added, but any parent who does not adhere to the basics will probably not produce a successfully raised child. The more basics a parent adheres to the more success qualities will be evident in the life of the child.

These basics (for the most part) must be adhered to within a defined timeframe. For instance, you cannot begin bending and shaping the child's direction after she or he reaches the age of ten; neither can you wait until the child reaches fifteen before you begin asserting your authority as a parent, by letting the child know who is in charge. Many parents make this mistake and pay dearly in later years. In successfully raising a child, you will need to bring to bear all of your natural instincts and intuitions.

The tenets set forth in these chapters do not propose to cover every thoughtful aspect and requirement for successfully raising children. I am certain there are other unmentioned aspects which could be quite necessary and helpful. Child raising is not a science. It is a procedure which requires constant adjustments to compensate for the changes in the nurturing environment, both inside and outside of the home. The procedure also requires adjustments to compensate for age and hormonal changes, which are both a part of the aspect of growing up and reaching adulthood.

The changes in the nurturing environment inside the home can be controlled by you, the parent or guardian. The changes in the environment outside the home are changes you cannot control. However, if you are in control of the child, you can steer her or him around the negative effects of the outside environmental changes. As the Bible speaks of being in the world and not of the world, your child can exist in the environment and not become a part of its negative influences. You can set the correct discipline path and moral tone for your child's behavior.

I know you can do this because I did it. There was nothing unique about my child as a child, and there was nothing unique about myself and her mother as parents. She, as a child didn't come from Mars, and neither did her parents. We just decided what rules our child would play by and required her to play by them, because they were for her good. This can be done, in spite of what may be going on in the environment around the child. It requires the help of God, tenacity, patience, determination and that ever-necessary duo called "love and discipline."

I grew up in the generation just prior to the age of Dr. Spock and prior to the rebellious 1960s, the age wherein young adults suddenly wanted to reinvent the wheel of discipline. Some wanted to oppose anything and everything that stood for positive moral values and discipline. One of those positive moral persuasions was opposed to sex before marriage. This does not mean that everyone adhered to it, but that moral persuasion did act as somewhat of a breaking mechanism, to help prevent out-of-control sexual behavior, which (in turn) acted to prevent the proliferation of single-family households, as well as many other social ills.

It was the generation of the 1960s that ushered in the idea of sex at any time, married or not, and with anyone you pleased, be it a person of the opposite sex or of the same sex. This was all a part of the "new thing." It was not only the age of a new moral persuasion, it was also the age of new technology in the form of vast new products and services. Plastics had come into its own, and so had computers, nonstop intercontinental jet travel, open advertisement of escort services (another term for high-class prostitution on-demand) and the open display of formerly private products—such as bras, panties, sanitary napkins and condoms.

I remember the time when a man would rarely ever go to purchase sanitary napkins for a lady—even in an emergency. If a man went into a drugstore to purchase condoms, he would whisper into the pharmacist's ear what he wanted. The 1960s ushered in a time when a lady would freely purchase condoms to give to her potential sex partners. I remember the time when a lady's sacred bargaining chip was her virginity, but with the 1960s, women were suddenly asking men to take it.

The 1960s also ushered in an era of new and very potent designer drugs, which could alter a person's mind to such an extent that the person experimenting with them could not function as a normal, rational human being under their use. Individuals sometimes hallucinated and envisioned themselves as birds with the ability to fly, jumped out of windows and off of balconies, often killing themselves in the process. This was the age when

LSD, cocaine and heroin openly-proliferated and were used with abandon. This was all the runoff of loosening the reins on proper parenting.

This was the age when the American flag no longer stood as a symbol of freedom, liberty and respect of country, but was seen as just another rag to be trampled on and burned. And it happened in America by Americans. The desecration of the flag symbolized rebellion against authority, not just freedom of expression. This rebellious attitude came out of the home, from loose parenting styles.

This was the age when government buildings and institutions were no longer sacrosanct; the fear of tampering with government property no longer existed. Such buildings shared equal billing with any other public building or institution. The idea of robbing post offices was no longer crackpot, but became a living reality. Before this, people had often robbed banks, as did Jesse James, but the idea of robbing a government entity required a bit more guts.

This was the age in which churches were no longer looked upon in a spirit of reverence, with respect for God's dwelling place, but came to be subjected to service interruptions, stickups and burnings. The rebellious spirit was also against the parent, and in many families the fear of God or parent was now scoffed at. This was the age where, in many neighborhoods you could leave home in the morning going to work and come back in the evening to find your home completely turned upside down–desk drawers, dresser drawers and all.

In the 1960s we moved into a home that had only a chain lock on the back door. Before we moved out, we had installed deadbolt locks on both exterior doors, and still the home had been robbed twice. It was all blamed on drugs, but bad parenting should share equal blame. I raised my child during this period, and I doubt if she ever did drugs, and I know she never broke into anyone's home.

This period ushered in the age when homosexuality no longer existed "in the closet" or had to be clandestinely practiced. It became okay for one to admit that he or she was gay or lesbian, and even go on national television to announce one's life-style, by waving to the whole world and saying, "Hi Mom, I'm gay!" or "Hi Mom, I'm lesbian!" There was once a time when a parent was ashamed to have a homosexual child, but now a child can bring his "partner" home to meet his parents, and the parents accept the relationship—as if it were a normal heterosexual relationship.

The movement had begun for acceptable same-sex relationships in the form of recognizing same-sex couples living together in what was once known in the heterosexual community as common law marriages. Some governmental entities came to allow the relationships as representing a family unit. The push for legalization of same-sex marriage was soon to follow. When I was a young adult, I never envisioned in my wildest dreams that I would see the time when a high court would be arguing the position of whether two people of the same sex could be legally joined in matrimony. Society has made a mockery of God's union, intended only for a man and woman. If you believe the Bible, the cities of Sodom and Gomorrah were destroyed for this same behavior. Could this become an element of America's demise?

America reached this point only after parents stopped demanding that children stand for something. As the saying goes, "If you don't stand for something, you'll fall for anything." During this period, parents began to compromise on the expected behavior of their darling children. Parents came to see the wrong in their children as right, and the bad as acceptable. They went to the jail cell where their child was being held and proclaimed: "My son is a good boy," even after the child had been rightfully convicted of first-degree murder. Parents mortgaged their homes to put up bail for children, who then sometimes fled (because they were guilty), causing the loss of the parents' property. The child knew she or he was guilty, but the parent could not bring themselves to believe that their child could have committed such an act.

This was the age that ushered in the desire for a "marriage contract," or prenuptial agreement, on a broad scale, and as a result, the institution of marriage will be forever altered. For some, there is no longer a belief in the vows that state "till death do us part." We would need to add to those the words, "as long as you stick to the contract." And the words "in sickness and in health, for better or for worse" seem to have little meaning in many marriages today, because when the situation gets worse, one spouse or the other often picks up and leaves.

This was the age when (because of some complaining parents) it was decided that some aspects of military training and discipline were too tough and needed to be made a bit less challenging. This demand grew out of a situation where trainees were mistakenly marched through a swamp, and some drowned. The rigorous training of the drill sergeants came to be labeled as abusive, just as did the spanking of children. Suddenly any parent who spanked their child was an abusive parent.

Some sergeants may have been abusive, and some parents may have been abusive as well, but the dramatic change came to be similar to "throwing the baby out with the bath water." As a result, many soldiers found themselves lacking in their ability to cope with the rigors of combat as well as their predecessors had, and some parents found themselves unable to cope with the rigors of parenthood. Quite possibly, due to the relaxation of preparedness issues, some soldiers went off to the rigors of combat and lost their lives or got hooked on drugs. Older soldiers seem to have been much better equipped for duty, both physically and mentally. We only need to listen to or read some of the accounts of the soldiers of the great world wars to see how well they coped in comparison. And some parents lost their children to the streets, due to undisciplined parenting and the relaxation of firm disciplinary measures.

The era of the 1960s ushered in a different kind of war, the likes of Vietnam, and thus, required a different kind of fighting man. Due to the social changes of the time, some of the soldiers were not quite up to the task. They had been exposed to the mores of a different society and didn't have the guts to refuse to accept unacceptable behavior. They went off to combat, and many of those who returned did so as useless specimens, unable to function with or in society. Of course, this excludes those who were under the prior rigorous training methods and those who may have been unwittingly exposed to the debilitating chemicals used in modern warfare.

Many of today's homeless, mentally unbalanced, drug dependent, crack babies, unwed mothers, welfare dependents, abandoned children, jail inmates, functional illiterates, "ADHD" children and other physically and mentally maladjusted individuals are evidence of the fallout of the 1960s generation and the aftermath that followed—the age of the new thing. This was not true of everyone who came of age in the 1960s. There were others who raised their children in the fear and admonition of God, with strong moral values and principles, strict family discipline and with love and positive nurturing.

My generation, which reached adulthood around the end of the 1950s grew up (for the most part) under a set of strict rules of parental direction. Our parents exercised love and discipline in measured proportions, giving adequate amounts of both to produce children equipped to integrate into society as positive, contributing adults. Some of the parents growing out of this generation took this type of discipline, under which they had grown up, as an affront to their individuality and independence and decided that they would not subject their offspring to this same "harshness." They preferred to be pals and buddies to their children, and not parents or overseers. They wanted to be "regular," hanging out and partying with their children. They concluded that this was the manner in which a parent should relate to a child, not as an authoritative figure. As a result, the child began to view her parents as equals. She no longer feared their wrath if she chose to exercise out-of-control behavior. But there was a price to pay.

The bottom line is: "What you fear, you respect." That is, you fear what can or cannot happen to you, if you go up against, or oppose, the forces of a person or thing. It is this healthy fear that causes you to learn respect for that person or entity.

I can recall a remark made by a person of my generation. She said, "When I was growing up, you could pass through the neighborhood on Sunday morning, and the sounds heard coming from the radios as you passed, were the likes of 'Wings over Jordan.' Now, when you pass, you hear the likes of pop rock and rap on Sunday mornings." That change speaks of the change in parental views and the discipline exercised in the households in which these generations are raised. That's the result of the decision of some of the parents of my generation, who chose not to raise their children under the same set of rigid disciplinary standards as their parents had raised them. As a result of this decision, many of my generation lost their children to the streets. I have seen it happen over and over, and those parents are still wondering what went wrong or, more precisely, where did *they* go wrong? Still, they refuse to take responsibility for what their children became.

I remember an acquaintance of mine who had three children. She determined early that she would not raise her children like her parents had raised her and her siblings; they were too strict, she considered. Well, she raised her children with not-so-strict a hand, and two of them turned out to be not-so-good. In essence, we have much to say concerning the direction our children take in life and about what they become or don't become. We have much to do with how well they pass over the stage of life upon which they must walk.

I made a decision early that I would raise my child with the same type of firm discipline, love and positive moral values I grew up with. They hadn't made me perfect, and they didn't make Celeste perfect either, but they did keep me out of jail, off the streets and off of drugs. They gave me a strong sense of well-being, a positive attitude about who I was and where I was going. In addition to that, they gave me the kind of stick-to-it attitude that kept me going when the thought was to quit.

Parenting is intuitive; it's instinctive; it's second guessing; it's discernment; it's psychology; it's philosophy; it's rationalization; it's realization and also a myriad of other things. As a parent, you must be involved before the beginning and in the beginning. You must plant the child (so to speak) in the right moral soil and bend the tree (child) early using the pressures of love and discipline. You must be there for them, I mean really be there with your presence. You must be able to recognize that some of the things you do as a parent aren't really for the child, but for you. You must sweeten your authority by not being so quick to say things with the "I" pronoun. Say, "Dad wants this," or "Mother wants that."

Get involved in every aspect of your developing child's life. Let your child know that you are strong, because strength is one of the most positive virtues a child can acquire. However, you must also let her know that you are human and also vulnerable to the winds of life and that will make her more sensitive to your needs and shortcomings.

Be in charge of your child; don't let your child be in charge of you. As parents, where there are two of you, don't be divided on instructions given to the child, but be unified for the good of the child and yourselves.

Teach children how to care about you and others. You should not make excuses—especially fathers—for not supporting your child, because of separation or divorce. Buy them the proper toys for life's conditioning and teach them the things they will need to know to survive in life as independents, because, as parents, we do not know how long we will be around to hold their hand. They should know how to walk alone when necessary, because at some time in their life they may find it necessary to go it alone. Set a good example by the way you live, and in so doing, you can demand more good behavior out of them.

Never consider them to be too old for you to tell them what is right—if it is for their benefit. Don't depend on them so much that you may be inclined to compromise on matters of fairness and righteousness. Don't interfere in the lives and living of your adult children, when they are going about it in a positive manner, but also don't hesitate to condemn wrong behavior. Don't keep your child forever locked in your arms, but keep your arms forever open to her. Give the child a measured amount of love and discipline. That's the recipe for raising a proper child.

Based on the above tenets, I consider myself as having successfully raised Celeste. I decided, even before she entered the world, what rules I would play by in raising her. I and her mother utilized rules that appealed to a child's basic instincts and behavior, given the circumstance and climate at any given time. These rules were not unique, and you will witness them at work as you go through the chapters of this book.

My parents used the same basic type of rules, and the next-door neighbors, who successfully raised their child or children, also used the same basic type of rules. There is no specific set of rules that need be applied to Black children, as opposed to Caucasian children, Native American children, Asian children or Spanish children, etc. All children must come into the world with a basic personality structure because, based on the survey taken, all parents taken from a cross-section of ethnic backgrounds indicated similar needs, instincts and responses in their children.

The basic personality structure is identified by the word "child." The environment and conditions imposed on a child after birth have everything to do with the child-raising success. And what you're able to tolerate as a parent, from a child's behavior, will determine how you will direct the behavior. For instance, I was unable to tolerate Celeste talking back to me in disputation, so I established a rule early on that this would not be the mode of her behavior. I also concluded early on that talking to and reasoning with Celeste after she exercised unacceptable behavior was not sufficient to prevent a future occurrence of that type of infraction. Children at certain ages lack a mature sense of reason about certain things. That's why they're labeled "children," and that's why society gives parents the responsibility of taking care of them. Children from any ethnic background can possibly be directed by the use of alternate forms of discipline—when the situation demands it. Some children require more and stiffer punishment than others. It should be exercised on a case-by-case basis.

So what you may do in a particular case is instinctive and must be applied in conjunction with the basic rules of raising a child. In the chapters that follow, I will set forth some of the basics I used in raising Celeste, which brought about a successful parenting experience. They were borrowed from the rules my parents used in raising us, and the essence of all of them is embodied in love and discipline—balanced love and balanced discipline. The more of them you use the more success you may have in your parenting experience.

Some parents didn't use any of these basics, much to their later regret. By the time a parent is able to see the outcome of negative parenting, it is usually too late. For instance, when you look around you and see a three-year-old screaming at the top of his lungs and the nearby parent unable to quiet him, you should know that the parent didn't apply the basic rule that says, "Bend the tree early with love and disciplined pressure." When you observe a five-year-old hitting the parent back, you are witnessing a parent that didn't apply the basics that suggest "You be in charge of your child, and not allow your child to be in charge of you." When you see a belligerent, rebellious seventeen-year-old who is always in trouble with the law and who refuses to obey the instructions of his parents, you're probably looking at parents who utilized very few (if any) of the basic child-raising procedures.

For those parents who are perplexed at what the child came to be and are sincerely seeking answers to what they may have done wrong or what they may not have done right, this book can surely give some insight. Those parents may be able to look at some of the basics contained herein and get suggestions in terms of what may have been done differently to achieve more positive results.

Parents often ask themselves, "Where did I go wrong?" Maybe they should be asking themselves; "Where did I go right?" If you desire to raise a proper child, you must get down to the basics. Apply basic child-raising principles and what-ever other positive, intuitive, instinctive methods that come to mind, and you will look at your child years from now and say, "Thank God, this child is on target; my efforts were successful." It isn't by accident that children turn out proper or don't turn out proper. Child-raising isn't a guessing game, nor is successful parenting a trial-and-error process—if you apply the basics (love and discipline).

Even today, those who know Celeste cannot put into words what we may have done to guide her toward becoming what she became or being whoever she came to be, but I wasn't surprised. I know what we put into parenting her. I know for a fact that I exercised the basics that I am setting forth here, and those basics helped to shape Celeste. Therefore, my reply to those who wonder is always the same: "Between me and God and her mother, she became the child that she is."

A Literary Agent's Comments and My Rebuttal

It is quite obvious that few of our modern professional "child-raising experts" have been able to put forth something that works. So many articles and books have been written on the subject of parenting, and yet children reaching adulthood have grown to be progressively worse, when it comes to behavior. The reason, I believe, is that recent generations have rejected the very values I espouse in this book—love and discipline. It is easy to see that most parents have not been taking this path, because the great majority of the past three generations of children have been obviously off-track in values, morals and ethics.

The percentage of individuals populating our correctional institutions today and those who have had various negative encounters with the law can attest to the above statement: Most of the parents of the prior three generations have pursued the wrong path of proper parenting. Why is this so hard for many to see? Can so many of today's parents be in denial? It is apparent to all of us that our society is in shambles, but is only a mere handful of individuals recognizing this fact? How could the challenges of daily life be any more properly addressed for today's young parents than to offer them a better course of direction? Such a course is cited in detail in this writing.

For today's young parents, it is important that the parenting methods being employed change, and for those who have not as yet become parents, it is important that they begin their parenting journey on the "right footing." The proper methods are all set forth in this book.

How could anyone say that these methods will not work today, when they have worked so well in our yesterdays? Sure, the structure of family life is different today, the culture is different, and the problems faced by parents today are different than they were when I was growing up. But it is precisely the parenting methods utilized over the past three generations that have brought our society to where it is and brought to bear most of the problems we now face. To correct this, we must get back to the basics—love and discipline.

We're experiencing a similar parallel in the educational system, where we are turning out a generation of children who cannot read, write, spell or count. Teachers are now required to teach to a testing system that is mainly geared toward getting children through the school system, not preparing them to think and function successfully in a modern world. This required teaching method brought about the No Child Left Behind program.

I recently tutored children of the seventh and eighth grades who are still counting on their fingers. When they need to know what 4 X 4 equals, they pull out a calculator. None of them knows their multiplication tables. I and my siblings knew ours before we even entered first grade. In education, just as in parenting, we need to get back to the basics—reading, writing and arithmetic—and when we begin teaching these, the children will be able to pass any educational progress test.

In parenting, we need also to get back to the basics and when we do that, we'll begin to eliminate the problems of family structure, such as single-family households, and we will begin to eliminate the problem of cultural differences (which should not be a problem in the first place). Good morals, good values and good parenting techniques transcend all cultural boundaries. Three generations ago, America was as much or more of a cultural melting pot than it is today, and yet America flourished. America built an industrial base that was unequaled by any nation. Its educational direction and literacy base had few rivals. Today, studies have shown that we are fast losing our edge in both these areas, as well as in others—such as technology and exporting.

If we get back to the basics in parenting, we can then begin to eliminate the problems prevalent in today's society—such as unwed motherhood, drug abuse, law breaking and weak or deteriorating family structures. This will allow us to use some of our time and resources to make America great again.

We raised our child through the time when the above types of problems were accelerating at a rapid pace, and so did many other good parents, and none of our children became wards of today's bad parenting examples. Our children were no exception; our parenting style was the exception. We used good basic parenting techniques–love and discipline.

A literary agent referred to some of my parenting suggestions as being "anachronistic"—meaning dated, outdated, out of fashion or old-fashioned. She may very well be correct in her assessment, but if these old-fashioned concepts worked yesterday, and all of our new-fashioned ideas are not working, then which should we choose? These old-fashioned parenting techniques employed the basics—love and discipline—while the new-fashioned techniques employ time-outs, expensive toys, not enough love and very little discipline. And the result is a disaster.

Let's take a long, hard look at the children of today's society and see how well the current parenting techniques are working. We have much more than outside terrorists at work destroying our society. Our own parents and children are contributing greatly to the effort. The need for good parenting is universal, and the positive rewards can be evidenced in children of any culture or any society. The parenting techniques described in the pages of this book can serve the not-so-well-educated, as well as the better educated, and good parenting is never solely dependent upon good education. Better educated, thoughtful parents are not the only ones who can benefit from this book. There is so much to be gleaned from this book that any one chapter is worth the price of the entire book. Even one thought from this book can change the life of a child and the hope of a family.

Rather than wait for the good graces of a mainstream publisher (which may never surface) I decided early on to self-publish this manuscript. As a first-time author and a non-famous individual (merely a college-educated tax accountant who had successfully helped to parent a child to adulthood), I knew I would be unable to break into the mainstream publishing arena. Still, I remained open to the possibilities and had the manuscript examined by a publishing agent. I was not surprised when she told me how difficult it would be to get my book published. This did not surprise me.

Others of her comments were very helpful, in that they allowed me to answer what represented the viewpoint of the skeptics of our day. Most of these responses are scattered throughout the book, but I have reserved a few for reference here, at the very beginning, so that you can see what she said and my answer to it.

1. This is an ambitious manuscript, with lots of good common sense. (**Note:** She started off with kind words.)
2. The organization and writing are mostly good.
3. Large trade publishers look for an author with great credentials and a platform or national recognition—someone who appears regularly on national television or radio or in newspapers or magazines. (**Note:** Obviously, not me.)

4. Mr. Gandy's credentials and experience are supported by a survey which I didn't find convincing. (**Note:** She failed to recognize that an introduction, a preface and various other chapters also support my credibility and experience. The survey does not stand alone. It is, however, self-explanatory.)

5. Mr. Gandy didn't cite a lot of outside experts, except that he illustrated what does not work. (**Note:** It is quite obvious that few if any experts in this field have surfaced in the past three generations with convincing information demonstrating what *does* work, because the behavior of children for the past three generations has grown progressively worse. I did cite what does not work, and I also cited what does work, because it worked in prior generations and still is working today when applied. [See the inside cover, the preface and the introduction.])

6. There is obviously a lot of wisdom in the material. Mr. Gandy needs to better address life as it is now for young mothers with children. (**Note:** Poor parenting and poorly directed children can be put on a more positive course using parenting methods found in the pages of this book, and these methods are for the "now" and can be successfully applied by parents of any age. The basic premise is love and discipline, and that works for any parent in any situation.)

7. The structure of family life and culture and problems are very different from the time when the author was growing up and raising children. (**Note:** Yes, the structure of family life today is different from yesterday, precisely because of the introduction of negative parenting techniques starting with the parents of my generation. Some of my generation and subsequent generations chose to stick to the old-fashioned, while others chose the new-fashioned. The old-fashioned worked, and the new thing did not. I raised my daughter in the era beginning in the late 1960s, employing the so-called "old-fashioned" parenting style, and she came to be a product of positive parenting. [See the preface and the introduction.] She is also an on-track adult, fitting the definition of a successful child.)

8. The manuscript seems too long and dense to draw in the less well-educated parent and always-busy moms. (**Note:** There are many areas in this book which are very basic and simplistic, and the main theme of successful parenting in this book is love and discipline.

Does one need a Ph.D. to know how to exhibit love and apply discipline? Our fore-parents had no formal education, in most instances, but were parenting successes. [See the preface and the introduction.] The less well-educated and always-busy moms seem to find adequate time for various social activities that don't positively impact the parenting experience. Parents of prior generations devoted more time to parenting and less to social activities. There is also the option of using these well-grounded parenting principles to teach the less well-educated parent how to do it better.)

9. The manuscript will work best for the thoughtful parent looking for confirmation that she or he is on the right track. (**Note:** Since we have a better educated segment in our society, the above type parent constitutes a segment large enough to positively impact and change the negative direction of parenting for future generations.)

10. I suggest a religious or regional publisher or self publishing. (**Note:** I am self publishing this writing and exposing it to all available markets.)

11. There are lots of people writing these days and many worthwhile manuscripts do not get published by the mainstream presses because they are beholden to the investors and not to editorial integrity. (**Note:** That is why a mainstream publisher published comments and a possible fictional analysis of a convicted murderer [in a civil case] whose comments appear to offer no positive value toward the betterment of social values. However, this material appears to be worth $3 million + to the publisher—if the news reports are correct. If the mainstream publisher gets enough readers to purchase this junk and generate the above amount, plus a profit, that can be a stark indication that our society is more sickly than any of us ever imagined, and this book is therefore needed more than even I imagined. I am fully aware of the editorial integrity problem of mainstream publishers, and that is why I now present this book to you, the reader, self-published by me, Donald L. Gandy, the writer. Read it, explore the ideas contained in it, and then make your own decision as to its worth to you and others.)

INTRODUCTION

I don't pretend that this book will be a cure-all for all bad parenting and all misguided children in our society or those that will be born into our society tomorrow. As a matter of fact, it may not speak at all to those parenting situations and out-of-control child behavior patterns that are too far gone. This means the child has reached an age at which he or she can't be rescued and turned around. For the younger, out-of-control child, if the parent can take charge and institute a dictatorial style to bring the child back into line, there can be hope. This dictatorial style (as harsh as the word sounds) is a parenting style that says to the child, "I'm in control now, and you will do what I instruct you to do. Before you reached this point, you were going your own way. But now you must go the way I instruct you to. My guidance and direction must take center stage." If you establish that position and stick to it, you may be able to recapture the child and become a parenting success. Success in parenting means a properly-raised child.

This book will speak to many parents who think they did everything right in their parenting experience and are still perplexed as to why the child turned out as he did. I have often heard the expression, "I don't know what I did wrong; I did everything I knew how." Maybe you didn't know what to do or maybe what you knew was not enough or the wrong thing to do. This book will speak to every aspect of your parenting life—except minute details of certain aspects of development—with hardly any stone left unturned. This book can greatly benefit those who have just become parents and those who are expecting to one day become parents.

The book was born out of a melding of personal experience, personal observation and interaction with other parents over a period of approximately forty-five years and a survey conducted on a cross-section of a parenting population spanning various races, cultures, age groups, educational levels, professionals and nonprofessionals alike. Conclusions were drawn from personal experience in helping to raise my own child, observation of how other parents raised their child or children and the survey conducted. The most dynamic conclusion drawn out of the above is that the dictatorial type of parenting (exercised as the norm) in the generation that came to adulthood in the late 1950s and before worked best in bringing children to adulthood. These children were assessed as "properly raised." That same parenting style, exercised as the exception rather than the norm, still works in terms of children being the object of successful parenting.

The dictatorial style (as I have come to label it) is what modern-day psychologists refer to as "authoritative." There is much less of that style being exercised today, which is why I refer to it as being the exception rather than the norm. That style demanded absolute obedience and tolerated little or no exceptions. The parent/s called the shots, told the child what was expected and what would be accepted and what would not be accepted, and that was how it was. The parenting styles being used in our present-day society are (as a rule): (1.) The indulgent permissive, and (2) The democratic.

The indulgent permissive is a lenient parenting style which seldom (if ever) administers corporal punishment and finds a majority of the child's behavioral habits acceptable or not worthy of reprimand. In this arena, a child is not disciplined from an early age, when the first signs of negative behavior surface. The parent operates on the assumption that the behavior is related to the age of the child, and the child will learn better or grow out of the bad habits. When the child reaches two years of age and says "No" to the parent, it's okay because he'll learn better at three. So when the child reaches three years of age and throws himself down on the floor in public places and refuses to get up at the parent's instruction, that's the result of a lenient or indulgent parenting style that is construed as normal—although it may, at times, be a bit embarrassing to parents.

The parent feels the child will have grown out of that habit by the age of four, and maybe that particular habit will be gone. But another, less acceptable, habit will have replaced it, and this process continues until the child is uncontrollable. At four years of age, the child tells you "No," stretches out on the floor, and if you hit him, he hits you back.

You feel that at the age of five he'll be preparing for preschool and will have adjusted and rid himself of these bad habits. However, at five he hits the teacher, fails to remain in his seat and tells the teacher "No." You think that by the time he turns six and goes into regular school he will be very well adjusted and free of those prior bad behavior patterns, but at six you take him to school, and as soon as you leave him, he begins throwing things around the room, hitting other children, running out of the classroom and refusing to follow any of the teacher's instructions.

At ten he sucks his teeth and talks back to you. At twelve, you discover, through a teacher's report, that the child has hardly attended any of his classes. At fourteen he's hanging out with the wrong crowd, and at fifteen he's in trouble with the law. Through all of this, he's still a good child, and you love him dearly.

At sixteen, he takes the family car without permission, wrecks it and slaps you when you reprimand him. However, he's a good child, only getting through the uncertain teens. But at seventeen he's on drugs, needs money to support his habit, kills both of you and flees with the credit cards and whatever money he can find around the house.

This may be an exceptional example, but similar patterns have emerged in children in the past, as well as various patterns falling in between these extremes. All of these result from the particular parenting style that is exercised. That same parenting style pushes the child toward an off-track adulthood and the parent toward a parenting failure.

The democratic style of parenting is what we refer to as accepting and encouraging. It accepts the child's course of behavior with little redirection and permits the child's decision on what he wants or does not want. This style actually embraces the indulgent style and takes it to the extreme, by allowing the child to tell you what he will or will not do.

We can conclude that neither is good, because when we look at our society today and contrast it to generations coming of age prior to the 1960s, we can see a stark difference in the moral condition of today's society, as compared to that of yesterday. The two main ingredients embodied in the dictatorial parenting style of times past were love and discipline. You knew your parents loved you, and they proved it by disciplining you. The discipline in the dictatorial parenting style often included the use of the rod or a similar instrument of correction.

Proverbs 13:24 states: *"He who spares his rod hates his son, but he who loves him disciplines him promptly."* Proverbs 15:10 says, *"Harsh discipline is for him who forsakes the way, and he who hates correction will die"* (NKJ). I know the modern-day parent ignores these biblical proverbs, just as he does many other biblical concepts. But discipline exacted with a rod of correction creates fear in a child and generates a healthy respect for proper behavior, as a way to avoid the rod of discipline in the future.

I was reading an article written by John E. Bonfadini, Ed.D., Professor Emeritus of George Mason University, and it concluded by saying: "In my opinion parents are sanctioning more and doing less to promote good discipline. The bumper sticker that reads 'Have you hugged your child today?' should be rephrased to say, 'Have you hugged and disciplined your child today?' " In the past, discipline with a rod of correction, more often than not, directed the formation of good habits and acceptable behavior. Children came to understand what it meant to respect God, parents, their seniors and institutions that merited respect. The village could help raise the child, and quite often did. There were more eyes looking on to assess out-of-line behavior, and that also helped to keep a child on track.

I began my first observations with the parents I finished high school with and those from my neighborhood where I grew up. I immediately noticed that the attitude among most of them was that they resented having grown up in an environment where the dictatorial parenting style reigned. This resentment was deep seated, and those who had it vowed they would never raise their children in such a way. I came to see this as the beginning of unsuccessful parenting, and out of it we are witnessing the results in the behavior of the children in today's society.

The first set of children born in that altered parenting cycle is now in its forties and fifties, and a large segment of that age group was lost due to failures resulting from unsuccessful parenting. Those who survived the indulgent and democratic parenting styles saw nothing wrong with themselves, and many repeated the process in their own parenting style, raising children we are observing today who have no fear of God or parents, no moral boundaries, no respect for elders, a poor work ethic, values centered around the love of money (because their chosen life-styles require and demand the use of money), no compunction as to how one comes about the money and no fear of the consequence of the behavior. These generations live mostly in the now in everything except for money, and in that arena they want more for today and even more for tomorrow—making theirs a world of extreme greed.

This is evident in corporate greed and the lack of a desire on the part of many to render honorable service without the attachment of excessive financial rewards and demands. Very few desire to serve in the public arena or even in the service of God, without the guarantee of hefty monetary rewards. This shoe certainly may not fit everyone but will indeed fit some.

Parenting styles brought about these actions, and as a result of these parenting patterns, we not only see rampant greed and selfish behavior, but others such as teenagers working in escort services, young adults freezing to death after being disoriented while under the influence of designer drugs, disgruntled citizens blowing up public buildings, students returning to high school classrooms and killing teachers and students, teenagers bludgeoning housewives to death and teenagers meeting dates on the Internet for sex and other immoral purposes. These values are all represented in today's society. Things look bleak don't they? They *are* bleak and will get worse unless parents begin parenting again, abandoning those liberal parenting styles and opting for control over the behavior of their children.

There have been quite a few books written on parenting over the past few generations, but few of them seem to have made a dent in putting a halt to turning out problematic children into society. It seems that children are getting worse as each generation emerges. The truth is: there are two opposing forces operating in the universe. There are the forces of good and the forces of evil. The forces of good are those sanctioned of God, and those of evil are sanctioned by Satan. Children are choosing sides, and they're choosing based on how they have been parented.

Society could greatly improve the behavior patterns of children by instituting one simple act, and that is "taking your child to the right church and teaching him the fear of God." A child who fears God will usually respect parents, and children who respect their parents will usually obey them. The rest is upon the parent, in terms of what to teach. But what you should teach them is embodied in the pages of this book.

This book didn't emerge from the mind of a child psychologist, a mental therapist, a guidance counselor or a pediatrician. Those various disciplines have already written books, and the children of our society aren't getting any better. It is therefore obvious that another slant is needed, and that slant is the one that worked three generations ago and before. That slant utilized old-fashioned parenting methods that instilled fear and garnered respect. No one respects that which he does not fear. You must either fear the entity or that which emerges from the entity. In generations past, parents instilled fear by not sparing the rod. The saying is: "Spare the rod and spoil the child." Utilizing such a rod of correction is called corporal punishment. Some parents don't believe in it and say they will never use it. Those who don't want to, don't have to, but sometimes it can be to the child's own detriment not to.

If a parent can teach a child to fear God and his parents without the use of corporal punishment, that would be good. However, it appears that it has not often been successful. In our witness of children involved in ritualistic murders, sex from the Internet, the obsession for money through any means at one's disposal, parent murders, school slayings, bombing of public buildings and children molesting children, we must conclude that children have drifted so far away that it becomes obvious they had no fear of God or parent.

When I was growing up, I feared my parents' wrath, and because of that I turned away from many acts of misguided behavior. I also feared the wrath of God, because my parents would teach us examples from time to time of how God punished certain acts of bad behavior. I can recall, for instance, my mother telling us the story of some children who were poking fun at an elderly man, and God sent three she bears from the woods, and they devoured the children. That taught me to be mindful of not poking fun at elderly people. It wasn't until recently that I was going through my reading of the Old Testament and came across the very story which my mother related to us so long ago. There were also many others, and I took them all to heart.

I will relate here two other examples of children who were brought up under strict rules of discipline, where corporal punishment was the rule rather than the exception. Both children went on to raise their offspring in like manner, and the offspring became products of successful parenting. One of these individuals was a classmate of mine, and the other was a church sister. Let's just call the classmate Joe, and I will relate the story as he related it to me.

He was one of seven siblings, reared in a Christian home with much love and very strict disciplinary measures. These seven children were the product of a father with only an eighth-grade education and a mother who finished high school and, in addition, obtained several certificates in areas of vocational training. These two parents were also brought up in households embodying love and strict discipline. The seven children of these two parents grew up in a household that adhered to diverse, but strict, Christian values, one parent being Presbyterian and the other Seventh Day Adventist. In this home, a formal education was first and foremost, and along with this also came a requirement to obey and respect established authority.

The mother of these children was home most of the time and provided the day-to-day guidance, as well as most of the discipline. She never flinched from wielding a strong rod of discipline whenever she felt it to be needed. When she spoke, you moved with deliberate speed. Now and then she would repeat herself, but never did she have the need to tell you a third time. Love came along with the discipline and was understood and accepted by the children.

The father's disciplinary style was more fearful, and to them, he appeared to be mean and lacking in love and understanding. I think that most fathers with strong disciplinary rules sometimes appear that way to their children. I saw my own father in a similar light. However, in the reality of the sacrifices made for the children, even by the father, you realized that he loved you as much as your mother.

When the father of these children spoke, you responded in a hurry. He very seldom repeated himself, and if he did it was usually with a razor strap of discipline. He never spared the rod. If the mother ever had to say to a child, "I'm going to tell your father," you had better begin counting your good earthly blessings, because it may be the last chance you had to do anything like that again. The father often reminded you that he brought you into the world and would also take you out if need be.

Neighbors and teachers were also aware of the exercise of strict discipline, including corporal punishment whenever necessary. In this home, as well as in most others, corporal punishment was associated with fear. Fear aided in the discipline process and created an environment conducive to good behavior, respect and learning. While corporal punishment may not have worked with all children, it prevented a great deal of misbehaving by many. Today's society is grossly lacking in that area.

The seven children of these two parents apparently learned their lessons well, although they all agreed that corporal punishment seemed quite often to be too harsh. However, each child developed character of good rapport. Their parents' demands required them to finish secondary school and high school, and for those who cared to, their parents strived to provide them with education beyond high school. Six out of the seven attended college, with four receiving college degrees.

Each of these children established respectable careers in his or her own right, and none brought shame or disrespect to the family heritage. They were taught and shown by example how to live and adjust in society, and each claims the utmost respect in the various communities where they reside. Those who had children will tell you they learned from and employed much of the strict disciplinary style used by their parents and teachers in raising their children—even though they exercised a greater sense of reasoning than that used by their parents. Joe's offspring is a successful music director on one of the well-known cruise lines.

Even considering the vast changes in today's society, the third generation of this family is still raising its children with basically the same values. It can be reasonably concluded that love and strict discipline with necessary corporal punishment was not without merit. It didn't kill the child, and society was better as a result.

The second family I followed which enumerated the results of its family parenting techniques was (in the later years of the children's development) parented by a mother only, and I also relate this as it was told to me: The father of these children was a noted surgeon, and the mother chalked up many "firsts" on her own account. The mother was a product of a family of eighteen siblings emerging from a small town in the state of Mississippi. I'll just refer to her as Rose. Her parents also exercised very strict disciplinary parenting techniques and fervently believed that it was almost criminal to spare the rod. They believed that God required the exercise of the rod of discipline to keep a child in line. The father was a devout minister, and for him, discipline problems were akin to failing God Almighty. So the eighteen grew up in good form and pretty much walked the straight and narrow path under the discipline of completely involved parents.

Among these eighteen siblings was the parent Rose, who also believed fervently in not sparing the rod, because she also believed that God deemed it appropriate and necessary in addressing some disciplinary problems. Rose, her spouse and the three children comprised the family unit. The father was a physician, and Rose was a nurse-educator. Both of these parents were parented by parents who were guided by biblical principles, specifically Christian principles. These principles were applied in Rose's nurturing, as well as that of her spouse. They included recognition of the fact that God was the heavenly Father who created all and that His commands were to govern our homes, for they were rules for basic living.

As Rose and her husband saw it, love was the profound characteristic. They felt that one must love the ways of goodness, truth, mutual respect, honest hard work, obedience, reverence and righteousness. Each parent demonstrated these values in order to be an example for the children. They recognized, very early in the parenting process, that each child "reads" his parents almost perfectly, and they tend to learn exactly what they see in the older models.

As unity was developed in Rose's family, the parents recognized that guidelines had to be set and adhered to. They tuned into the basic general needs of the individual, as physical, psychological, sociological, educational and economical. The children were taught how to be responsible members of the family unit. The welfare of the five comprising the family unit had to be the goal of each member within the family. Each child was treated as an individual, with the right to be him- or herself under the authority of the parents. The parents recognized that they were under the authority of God to act properly by the children He had given them, as He stipulated in His Word. The biblical concept of training up a child *"in the way he should go"* was understood by Rose and her spouse as meaning they should seek God for guidance to carefully assess each child and watch prayerfully to see God Himself aiding in the child's development process. They knew that God was at work in each child, because each child belonged to Him, but was entrusted to the parents to be His loving guides.

Careful teaching and adherence was absolute, and patience was imperative. An attitude of giving and taking and stepping back when the situation warranted it was necessary and fruitful, but the role of the authority figure was never and should never be relinquished. It was established up front that obedience and respect were not to be violated by the children. The rules in this family were explained, adjusted and reset. Thoughts were solicited from the children, but in proper perspective, giving due consideration to the matter at hand and the age and maturity of the child at the level in which the input was solicited. Even in a dictatorial parenting style, input from a child isn't out of the question, however the input has to be relevant and cannot put the child in a position to make a decision that is too mature for him to make or one that would best be made by the parent. Also, the input from the child should fall within the boundaries of the parent's ability to act on the input and the positive benefits to be derived from the child's input.

Positive benefits and negative repercussions were considered on an individual basis as related to that particular child. Positive results were always acknowledged and rewards were given accordingly. Corrective action was also administered because the children had to learn that acceptable behavior was required to get along with others in going through the life cycle. Rules in this household were to be respected and followed, and when they were not, consequences came speedily. The extent of the consequences was relative to the extent of the violation. When there was an infraction, the child was carefully questioned to be certain that he or she understood that a rule had been violated, and the consequences had been duly earned.

In this home they tried to create an atmosphere of love, responsibility and good character. They taught their children that God had made them to be the very best, to work hard, to become independent, competent and caring individuals, in order to stand and occupy their God-given place, respecting self and caring for others in the grace and mercy of God.

In the few lines that follow, Rose spoke candidly about other aspects of their parenting experiences. "In the direction toward proper behavior, discipline was administered in many forms. When the child was very young and insisted on unacceptable behavior, appropriate and reasonable physical spanking was definitely administered (in the proper manner), never abusive and with much self control. When the child grew older and could be dealt with in other ways, we explored the benefits and results of discipline other than spanking. We employed a sense of reasoning and attempted to encourage the children into acceptable behavior. We never neglected to pray for understanding in dealing with each child. We knew that God was at work and surely had the answers we were seeking."

Rose intimated that later in her life God allowed her to hear some remarks from their children concerning the parenting experience. Her son is a college-graduated, professional animation artist of note. In a telephone conversation with his mother, he told her of a debate going on between him and various other individuals in a group of professional associates. He said, "My mother spanked my 'butt,' and I am so glad she did. She also taught me and my siblings everything she knew would benefit us, and it paid off well."

Her daughters, one a teacher/actress/singer and the other an attorney, said to her recently before a packed church audience (where she was being honored for thirty years of voluntary community service, "Mother, we want you to know that as you taught and taught, you probably thought we were not listening, but have no doubt that we heard you. We were and are listening, and we love and appreciate you."

Rose expressed that there is something very wonderful about seeking God's help along the parenting journey. It is that God is a *"present help"*!

Rose and her spouse always tried to be an example of doing the right thing, but the children knew the parents were not perfect. When either of the parents made a mistake, the child received an apology and was asked to forgive the mistake. It would have been difficult to seek an apology from the child when he had done wrong if the parent could not offer an apology to the child for a mistake he or she had made. And from Rose's perspective, much of their parenting meant being a good example. Children are more apt to see what you do rather than hear what you say. In the old parenting style, it was good to have so many others of like values helping in the parenting process. No parent can do it alone.

Rose expresses her thankfulness to God for how He orchestrated their walk. She consistently planned activities and involvement in various activities and needed succinct answers as to who, what, when, why and how. Strict consistent attention and loving constructive actions led to positive outcomes by the love, grace, goodness and mercy of God, and Rose can proclaim that due to this parenting style and the outcome of the children, she is truly blessed. This is the outcome, but it didn't start there. This was the transition phase into adulthood for Rose and Joe (the other parent chronicled in the prior passage), but the journey really began prior to conception.

The journey from conception to adulthood is a long one, and applying the basic rules is necessary, as the following chapters will indicate. However, that, in itself, is often not sufficient. The professionals with backgrounds related to the aspect of parenting have a strong desire to critique the results and give a socio-scientific slant to what did or did not come out well. Like following a recipe, you put in the required ingredients—baking soda, salt, baking powder, sugar, cinnamon, etc. and the dish turns out well. All of the ingredients perform as expected. However, the cooking professional could explain that the soda and baking powder help it to rise, the sugar sweetens it, the salt enhances the sugar's ability to sweeten, and the cinnamon spices it up. Cooking borders on the scientific, and one is able to state before the dish is prepared that if you put in this ingredient and that ingredient, you will achieve a dish with this or that quality.

Sometimes there is a definite point at which you should add the ingredients, as some recipes suggest. And if you don't add them at the suggested point, it may cause the dish to fail. In cooking, you're dealing with a consistent dish, requiring the same ingredients each time in order to produce what is expected. If the ingredients are the same in quality and quantity, as called for, the outcome will always be the same.

In parenting, one is applying the same basic elements to differing child personalities, so one is unable to determine how to apply the basics to Joe or Rose or Celeste or Don prior to the time they need to be parented. After they come before you as children, you should be able to assess how the parenting elements should be applied. In the parenting process, if you don't apply love and discipline in the required proportions, you're likely to turn out an unsuccessful child, just as in making yeast rolls. If you don't put in the yeast, your rolls will fail to rise.

Therefore, disciplines such as Psychology, Early Childhood Education and Counseling have the ability to critique and substantiate the "why" in successful parenting. The writing of this book was critiqued by my spouse, who is an Early Childhood Educator and has a graduate degree in the same. It was also critiqued by a friend of ours who worked as a professional counselor and has a graduate degree in the same. Any passage that may sound authoritative was probably critiqued by one or both of these individuals. In their own professional way, they endeavored to give credence to why my parenting style yielded success in my parenting journey. It embraced the parenting methods used when children exhibited the results of successful parenting, before the modern-day parenting styles took hold. As for our daughter, Celeste, we just thank God that these methods worked, and I am confident that the methods put forth in this book can also work to make you a successful parent.

Imagine receiving an instructional manual, while in the hospital, after giving birth to your precious little one? In reality, that would be too late! You should receive such a book at the office of your doctor during prenatal care. And, in addition to going to prenatal care, you would also be required to attend prenatal classes. How many of you would have done this?

Your classroom text would have fifteen chapters—the same number of chapters as are found in this book, and the manual given would include all of the information that you are about to read in the following chapters. You would be required to read the first nine chapters during your gestation period, one chapter each month. By the time you entered the hospital to be delivered, you would know how to prepare yourself for your baby and how to prepare your baby for the world. The parenting role is too vital for us not to have any proper preparation.

A large number of parents may feel they don't need to read a book or go to a class in order to be good parents. But through observing and conversing with parents today, we can surely agree that something needs to be done. If not, we must continue to deal with the results of ineffective parenting. I was discussing this issue with a colleague of mine recently, and she seems to think that we are still bearing children, but have stopped being parents.

Parenthood has the potential to bring both joy and heartache into your life, but you have the potential to be a successful parent, able to deal with both ends of the spectrum. Parenting can also be the most gratifying experience you will ever have. Preparing a child to function effectively in this world is a huge responsibility and requires a serious personal commitment. Many of you are already aware of the fact that the role of a parent does not end with providing the physical needs of a child, such as room and board and designer clothes. You are also responsible for strengthening the child's emotional and spiritual well-being. The child's first lesson in social consciousness, moral principles and his or her place in the world need to come from the parents. It has become evident that the responsibility of parenting, to a great degree, has been relegated to educators and, to some extent, to the children themselves.

The questions that are sometimes raised are these: What do I owe my children? Or what do my children owe me? A place was provided in the womb by God that was safe and protective in which the child could grow until every part of its body systems had developed enough for it to safely enter the world. You, as the mother, are responsible for keeping your body safe and uncontaminated until the birth. After the birth, you owe your child another safe, loving and nurturing environment until full development of mind and body has taken place.

Yes, father of the child, you also must be just as involved as you were in the beginning. Nurturing the child means providing all the things necessary to promote emotional, educational, physical, psychological and spiritual growth. During this process, the child owes something to herself or himself also. The child owes to herself or himself acceptance of those positive things given by loving parents or guardians to ensure growth and positive development.

You might parent your child successfully, as well as you know how, and yet your child may or may not be what society considers "successful." Nevertheless, after every measure of care has been given, the rest is in the hands of God and the child. The parent ensures safety, love, nurturing and education. These are the things which are humanly possible. That's all they can do.

The chapters that follow contain information grounded in the application of love and discipline. Love is powerful and can be overpowering. Someone said that you cannot love a child too much. I believe you can—if it clouds your judgment, and it precludes you from adding proper discipline. While our little one is so tiny and helpless, our heart is full of love and awe at this miracle that belongs to us. As the infant grows, we sometimes forget to add the other ingredient that will lend direction to the child's developmental life. I once read an article in the *Ladies Home Journal:* "Raising children is like baking bread; it has to be a slow process, or you end up with an overdone crust and an underdone interior."

This book was born out of a passionate desire to let every parent-to-be know that he or she has the ability and potential to be a successful parent and send well behaved productive children into society. Now, let's take a journey from conception to the time you "let go," interspersed with actions and principles used by a proud parent who has chronicled every step of his parenting experience in his daughter's life and who gave parenthood the dedication he gave his profession. It is refreshing to see, and it is time to highlight and reemphasize the significance of the role of the father in the life of a child—especially a female. However, the recipe found in this book is not just for playing a successful parenting role to raise daughters; it was inspired by one father and a mother using this method with their daughter, but it is meant for all children. These simple, practical, no-nonsense, loving, discipline methods of leading your child into this universe will allow you to be guilt-free, as you will have done everything within your power and knowledge to send an emotionally and spiritually equipped person out into the world.

An author in a New York Times editorial stated "Forget about getting an MBA to become a manager; maybe all you need is to become a parent". He went on to say that "to be an effective manager, make the rules clear, don't overreact to mistakes, know when to let go and to stay calm when something goes wrong." One difference between managing and parenting is this: in management, you are working with "big" people, and in parenting you are working with "little" people. Additionally, the "love" component will probably not be a factor in the business arena.

This book focuses on preparing your child for the world, but in actuality, the first step for the parent-to-be should be to prepare oneself for the child. The parent is the child's first teacher. It would suffice to emphasize how important it is to get a good education while you are young, because it will come in handy when you need to help your children with the homework. However, the absence of the same will not preclude you from raising a successful child. On the other hand, if aspects of your life are miserable, you will certainly cause misery in your child and, possibly, everyone else in your household.

Consistency is also essential, so as not to confuse your child. If a parent begins to suffer from mood swings—exhilarated one day and depressed the next—the child is sure to bear the brunt of that personality disorder.

Chapter III walks you through that phase of shaping your child. The shaping should start prior to toddler-hood. Each chapter is considered a foundation that builds from one to the next, based on love and discipline. Each one (love and discipline) must be weighed carefully, and the parent should know which one should tilt the scale and when. None of the ensuing principles should be omitted—just because you may consider them to be too time consuming.

I am reminded of a story of a mother talking to an acquaintance and telling her that she had eleven children. The acquaintance exclaimed with awe, "How in the world do you have time for eleven children?" The mother replied, "When I had only one, it took all of my time, and I figured the others wouldn't take more than that."

Being a parent means being "in charge" because you are responsible for what happens to that child during the developing years. Staying calm during those times when your child is sure to try your patience means that you need to be emotionally mature and have resolved the inner frustrations and conflicts about your own life. Prior to becoming a policeman, part of the training process requires going through some psychological testing. The same is true for counselors, social workers, psychologists and psychiatrists. Being a parent involves a bit of every one of the responsibilities of these professions, and yet no formal training in these professions is necessary or required—only the desire to be a successful parent, and sometimes that desire relates only to the process that can cause you to become a parent.

Going through a testing process to determine if you qualify to be a parent would most likely reveal issues that could indicate a lack of the ability in this arena. These unresolved issues would tend to have a negative effect and could corrupt the best parenting skills. However, many issues have the potential of being resolved positively during the parenting process, which spans many years.

Testing might render many of us incapable of being a parenting success. The negatives and positives embodied in one's personality are not the determining factors. The determining factors are whether a parent is able to pull the emotional and psychological resources together in such a fashion as to dispense a measured amount of love and discipline. All roads lead to these two factors. They constitute the recipe for successfully raising a child.

It would be helpful if every parent knew something about the stages of growth, knowing what happens in each stage of development. The stage from infancy to crawling or walking is a crucial period, when your interaction and temperament in dealing with the baby has a profound effect on the child's ability to trust or distrust others and their feelings. Two of the most challenging phases are toddler-hood and adolescence. In toddler-hood, the child is exploring his or her environment, and the natural propensity is to experiment with testing his/her will and trying your patience. Patience is a necessary virtue in breaking the will of a child, while trying to not break the child's spirit.

Preschool ages (three to five) mark the stage when the child is responding to intellectual stimulation and growing in confidence and self-assurance. Being overly critical during this stage can cripple the child for life. Those critical phrases you utter "without malice or forethought" can define the child for life, since he or she is in the learning stage. My associate said she had counseled individuals who, as adults, are still playing the tapes of negativity flung at them by their parents when they were children. This caveat extends forward to the other stages of development as well.

In middle childhood (age six to eleven) the child's world is rapidly expanding but still needs parental support and nurturing. This is a time when many parents let go, citing the old proverbial phrase: "He is big enough to take care of himself now." Encouraging independence by giving appropriate responsibility is recommended, but too much self-reliance can border on the child being a victim of neglect. He still needs love and discipline. This is not the time to let go.

At adolescence, the child is plagued with inner turmoil, confusion and disorganization, while struggling to build an identity. This is also the stage when the child may think he knows more than the parent. You may hear the phrase: "What do you know about being a teenager?" After all, children think their parents were born old. This might be a good time to share the family photo album. "Being there" is never more important than at this stage. Throwing your hands up in despair sends a message to your child that you do not know what to do and are contemplating giving up on him, but this is not recommended. The message "I don't know what to do with you" gives the child a license to do whatever he wants to.

This book reminds parents that parenthood should be their primary role, even though it is sometimes necessary to multitask and have dual roles, due to economic circumstances. Conditions have indicated that the true role of parenthood, in some aspects, has been abdicated, and the hierarchy in the family has become blurred and even extinct in some instances. As I stated earlier, the parent is the person in charge, and children can detect when the parent is not exercising a leadership role.

Just as the educational system has seen the need to return to the basics, we want to emphasize the need to get back to the basics in the parenting process. The result of the lack of successful parenting and the effect it has had and is having on society is evident in the streets, the schools and the home. Whenever a child commits an infraction or gets into trouble with the justice system, there is a tendency of the one reporting the incident to look at the family and the parental background—especially if the child is still in the developing years.

Upon observing the behavior and conduct of children ranging in age from preschoolers to adolescence, it is easy to see when a child is neglected, when he has not been shown adequate love, when he or she has been rewarded for inappropriate behavior, and when he has not been taught basic appropriate behavior. Sessions with children in many instances have revealed gross neglect and the absence of exhibited love. The child doesn't know how to tell the parent what the parent has failed to give him. Children rely on their parents to be role models, so be careful what you display; you may see it again in your child. I am reminded of a phrase I heard: "children see better than they hear."

One should thoroughly absorb the chapter that talks about "being there" for your child. From discussions with other educators and counselors in various fields, there is cause for great concern. The African adage, "It takes a village to raise a child" has been used by many and, in particular, by politicians to pepper their speeches, and has become somewhat of a cliché. If more people really believed in this adage, we could make great strides toward improving our society by better parenting. I know parents who have cried out openly in anguish when a child has thrown a temper tantrum in the middle of a store or gotten on the wrong side of the law. The parent threw up their hands in despair, exclaiming, "I just don't know what to do with him. He won't listen to me." At that point, it is a bit late. It is important to get a child's attention in the early stages of development.

Each generation of parents primarily teaches by example, or what they learned from their parents. Some of what was exhibited from a previous generation should not be inherited by a future generation. Isaac Goldberg states, "We spend half of our lives unlearning the follies transmitted to us by our parents and the other half transmitting our own follies to our offspring."

Some of the information in this book will be familiar to some and will be recognized as steps you took to successfully raise your child. Those of you who subscribe to the methods mentioned will probably say it is not impossible—if you just use your hearing, heart and common sense.

Children expect to be loved unconditionally by their parents. Surprisingly, I have reason to believe that a great majority of parents today have failed to recognize the meaning of "unconditional." A vast number of parents only show love to their child if the child is doing well in school, is well behaved and obedient. I am not suggesting that you reward inappropriate or unacceptable behavior, but even through the disciplining process, the child needs to know that the discipline is borne out of the love that still exist for them.

For those absentee parents—including those of you who are still in the home but are absent emotionally—reconnect with your child. You don't know them, and they probably don't know you either. Those of you who abandoned your child and are geographically disconnected have missed some precious moments in your child's life that can never be recaptured. Those of you who have never seen your child and yet have not given up all parental rights can still contribute something to the life of the child. Sometimes a child just wants to know who the parent is or what the parent is like. I caution you to consider the child's age and consider getting professional advice prior to making contact with the child.

Even if the child has grown to adulthood, there may be a great hole in his or her heart where your love and discipline should have been. The child may have become successful and tried to fill that hole with drugs or alcohol. That child who became successful may have been blessed enough to have been given love by a qualified caregiver but still goes through life harboring many unanswered questions. If you get the opportunity, you should endeavor to answer those questions. Children have a huge desire to please their parents, a desire to be validated. There is the need to hear the words, "You're okay, and I love you and am proud of you."

I recently read a story of a star athlete who is in his late thirties and remembers that his father never uttered the words "I love you." He vowed to do things differently with his children. Another adult who became a successful actor revealed in an interview that he regrets that his father did not live to witness his success. Your children want you to be proud of them, but you should also want to be a parent they can be proud of. A child is always in need of a parent—even in adulthood. Be the kind of parent your child won't hesitate to return to for advice and wisdom.

Just as the robin waits until its baby is strong enough to flap its wings and to gather its own food before it is allowed to leave the nest, you want your child to be strong in all the necessary areas before it is let go. Hopefully, when your nest is empty, you will have no regrets as to whether you have fulfilled your responsibilities as a parent, and, hopefully, you will have had moments when you actually enjoyed the parenting experience. Just remember; the tape of the parenthood experience cannot be rewound—so enjoy the journey while you can.

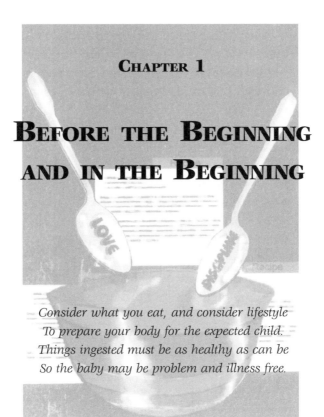

CHAPTER 1

BEFORE THE BEGINNING AND IN THE BEGINNING

Consider what you eat, and consider lifestyle
To prepare your body for the expected child.
Things ingested must be as healthy as can be
So the baby may be problem and illness free.

1. THINGS YOU EAT, DRINK AND INGEST

Do you want children? Have you ever thought about the possibility of having children you do not want? Do you think you will love the child you want or the one you do not want? All of these questions involve very serious thought and consideration. Those who want children have (in most cases) the desire to love and nurture the child or children, when and if they do have them. Those who may not want children also have (in most instances) the desire to love them—even if they did not want them. However, in the first instance, it is more likely that the parent to be who wants children would spend more time and effort preparing for the possibility of being a parent than the latter. And so, those would-be parents should give much thought to the possibility of parenting a child or children—wanted or un-wanted.

A TABLESPOON OF LOVE, A TABLESPOON OF DISCIPLINE

This is another reason to give serious consideration to the things taken into the body, as well as to the behavior exhibited during the course of going about life. You should not want to put anything into your system that would have a lasting, harmful effect on the life of the offspring you may have a part in bringing into the world. And, on the other hand, your social behavior should not be such that the child you help bring into the world would be ashamed or embarrassed by your past. You should be mindful of the negative behavior you pick up, because it could become baggage for your child or children to carry.

This book doesn't, in any way, mean to suggest or attach scientific significance to the discussion put forth. These thoughts grew out of the ashes of observation, trial and error, and, thus, has built a platform upon which to rest the conclusions. These considerations were a part of thought and discussion in our consideration of parenthood. We gave thought to the timing of when the parenting process should take place and to body and mind preparation for the parenting role. When we decided to prepare for having the child, we had no idea what sex it would be or that it would be a female named Celeste. However, we prepared our body, mind and finances for whatever the child would be, and in due time Celeste entered the world.

In the process of raising her and observing the behavior of other children growing up before and after her, I came to ask many questions mentally, which were relative to the actions and behavior of other children, as compared to the actions and behavior of Celeste. Some of the questions took a form such as: Why is her attention span so short? Why is she so nervous? Why does she keep such a disorganized environment? Why is she inclined toward alcohol abuse? Why is he inclined toward drug abuse or why is his behavior so "off the wall"? When any of these types of questions are asked in one's mind, the next questions that tend to follow are: "Where did he or she come from? Who are the parents? And where does he or she live?"

Contemplating the answer to these questions, one endeavors to look further, and in the process of looking further, we do often find some social baggage carried by the parent or parents. Some had a history of child abuse; some had a history of spousal abuse; some were products of dysfunctional families, and some abused alcohol or drugs. Any of the above could possibly weigh heavily on the behavior and direction of the child. Some of the above experiences of the parent may have been unavoidable, and some may not have been. Some were beyond the parent's ability to correct, and others could have been corrected through sheer discipline and determination to rise above the prior hurt.

Some of the above antisocial behavior taken on by the parent was a matter of choice, and those bad choices often led to the child of this parent having social and sometimes physical shortcomings born of the parent's prior behavior. This is quite unfortunate, and because of it, potential parents-to-be must be aware of and considerate of possible consequences of what is done to the body and to the mind before the beginning and in the beginning.

Parents-to-be should avoid (at all cost) any form of drug or alcohol abuse, or any other habit (including eating disorders) that may clearly alter, in a negative way, the mental and physical makeup in a way such as could be passed along in some form to the offspring. So what one does as a future parent prior to conceiving the offspring is very important.

Scientific studies have had much to say about the effects, both positive and negative, concerning the foods and other things taken into the body of a pregnant mother. From the positive health side, much advice and discussion is being put forth concerning the positive benefits to the unborn child of certain vitamins and foodstuffs consumed by the carrying mother. On the other hand, the negative aspects of other harmful things such as drugs, alcohol, nicotine residue and negative foodstuffs—such as fats, sweets and preservatives—are being stated loud and clear. So the careful monitoring of those things ingested by the mother during and prior to pregnancy, and also things ingested by the impregnating father can have profound effects on the child that will be born out of their union.

It is not of little importance that mothers and fathers give very serious consideration to the child yet to be born. Since this book is based on firsthand experience of our mind and body preparation in all of the above areas, I wish to point out those things we experienced that may or may not have had an effect on the successful raising of Celeste.

It has been indicated by health professionals that the unborn child eats what the mother eats, drinks what the mother drinks and ingests what the mother ingests. So also may it be said that any other substance taken into the mother's system through any other means and reaching the bloodstream of the mother can also reach the bloodstream of the unborn infant. Warnings are clearly displayed on prescription drugs and on other herbal products that can cause known and unknown harm to the unborn child.

All of those who are old enough must surely remember the devastating birth defects caused to unborn children of mothers who took the drug thalidomide. We are also very much aware of the warnings and harm done to the unborn children of alcohol and drug addicted mothers. The ingestion of any negative substance by a mother can vastly alter the parameters and necessary conditioning required in getting a child raised successfully to reach adulthood and beyond.

As parents, in successfully raising a child, you will be dealing with shaping and directing the child through and around the challenges encountered in the process of growing up and in handling these challenges in such a way as to make them work for the child's benefit or to prevent them from working in such a way as to get the child off of life's main course. The child needs to be completely in control of all of her or his faculties. It is, therefore, imperative that the would-be parent does nothing or takes nothing into her or his system that could in any way alter the faculties of the child to be born.

2. Get Ready, Your Child Is Coming

I can recall a period in my childhood when I found so much joy in having my mother around the house. I didn't have quite the same feeling about having my father around, because when he was around, we had to be so well behaved until there seemed to always be a lot of tension. However, there was always one or both of the parents you so loved and enjoyed that you wished for her or him to always be around. Somehow, you would feel very unhappy when that parent had to leave, even to go to work.

I know my feelings were the rule, rather than the exception, because I've seen many children cry when their parent or parents had to leave them, or they had to leave the parent. The crying happened when the parent had to part from the child—even after they had become adults. That is why it is vitally important that parents be there for their child or children through all of the everyday routines, through the challenges of growing up, through the parent-teacher reviews, the school functions, the graduations, the awards ceremonies, the first day of college, and through all of the other in-between times, when a child falls down and bruises her or his lip, skins the knee or bumps the head, or has to be given vaccinations or goes to periodic doctor visits—and on and on and on.

BEFORE THE BEGINNING AND IN THE BEGINNING

Celeste's coming was planned for, even before her arrival, which was not unusual, except for the fact that I had to be a "take-charge" type of father, had to take the initiative to seek out the things needed for her arrival, and had to find the source to acquire them. I would seek the needed items and the source from which to purchase them and then come back to tell her mother what I had found. We would then go back together to examine my discovery, and if my wife approved, we would buy those things. I even planned for the name the baby would be given. I got the dictionary and looked through the section containing the names of boys and girls and picked out several as possible choices to be used when the child was born.

Celeste's birth was quite eventful, due to the fact that the delivery wasn't as would be expected. It was a difficult delivery, and for a while it seemed as if neither the mother nor the child would survive the birth. I distinctly remember it being a Sunday evening when my wife began experiencing labor pains. We called her doctor for advice as to what should be done in this circumstance. He advised us to bring the mother-to-be to the hospital, and he would meet us there.

We got ourselves prepared and went to the hospital. The doctor was there to meet us when we arrived. He was on staff at Mercy Hospital on Long Island. When we arrived, he immediately rushed my wife up to the delivery room, and shortly thereafter came back downstairs to inform me that the delivery would need to take place immediately and must be by caesarean section. It was an emergency.

I waited and paced the floor, while the procedure was taking place. Then I waited and paced the floor some more. Finally, after what seemed to be an eternity, the doctor came back downstairs, soaked with perspiration, and uttered (even as he breathed a sigh of relief), "We made it; we just made it. The mother and daughter are doing fine." I also breathed a sigh of relief, thanked God and the doctor, and left for home.

Since my wife was incapacitated for a while, due to the nature of Celeste's birth, I had to take charge of getting the crib home and set up and purchasing the necessary bed clothes, bumpers etc. I also acquired the necessary utensils for baby formula, bottles, diapers, baby oil, baby powder and all of the other necessary items to be used for the proper care of a newborn. I was very familiar with all of the necessary requirements and what to buy, because I had eleven sisters and brothers, and six of them were younger than I.

A TABLESPOON OF LOVE, A TABLESPOON OF DISCIPLINE

I was familiar with the wash basin and also remembered that my mother always wanted to use only Johnson baby oil, powder and Q-Tips. I was also aware that diapers needed diaper pins. In those days, the use of disposable diapers with Velcro strips wasn't yet widespread. In addition, I was determined to keep most, if not all of the old-fashioned techniques my parents raised us by, for they seemed to have worked so very well in getting us to adulthood intact.

When I went back to the hospital the following day to visit my wife and the baby, my wife wanted to know what we would be naming the baby. I gave her one of the names I had picked out of the dictionary. The name was Celeste Yvonne.

Celeste Yvonne was born that Sunday evening, January 21, 1968, and I was there to get the news. I was not at my wife's bedside because, in those days, we weren't able to watch or participate in a caesarean section. I was in the waiting room, pacing back and forth, anxiously awaiting news from the doctor. Thank God everything came out all right.

I was not only there for that ordeal; even before that, I wasn't out of town, working or out with the boys, drinking at a bar or at a football game, or any of the other places modern fathers-to-be often find themselves, when their child is making his or her debut into the world. During this time, some fathers are often noticeably and inexcusably absent. Some reasons for absenteeism at that moment are excusable, but others make one sigh with disgust.

I've heard far too many tales of circumstances involving a delivering mother, where the husband or the father of the expected child was nowhere to be found or accounted for. I've heard other tales of fathers-to-be being out with a girlfriend, at the bar getting drunk or at any other place—except there with his child's mother and his child. The list goes on and on.

This should not be. Father, you should be there for your child—really be there. Your absence at the time of birth may be setting a pattern that could continue throughout the developing years of the child, and the child could very well grow up feeling the void. If the absence was due to questionable circumstances, the child may hear the mother repeat the reason over and over again in anger. The birth of your child should be one of the most important events in your life, and you should not want to miss it.

Of course, you can't always pinpoint the day, because there are such things as false alarms. Also, it is not always easy for the father to be there at the exact time of the delivery, because deliveries come at unexpected times. But even then, if it is possible, the father should be reachable, and should come to the side of the mother of his child and the child at the earliest possible moment—dropping all other things of lesser importance.

The birth of your child is important enough for you to take off from work or to take leave from a girlfriend (not suggesting that you should have one), to come home from abroad, or to take leave from any other less important event. Most other events should take a back seat to the birth of your child.

The mother is always physically there for the birth, if she has carried the child (not giving discussion to surrogate mothers). Birth is the act of a long drama, and getting off on the right foot is important because the journey will be long.

3. THE WAY YOU ACT AND THE BAGGAGE YOU CARRY

Life is a race, and a competitive one. Your child must participate in this race, along with all the other children of her or his society and the world. The most important segment of this race is the transition from birth to adulthood. For the transition to be successful, the child must be given the opportunity to compete on a level playing field with all the other children who will also be running the race of life. The condition of the playing field has less to do with the child making a successful transition than does the equipment the child has to aid her in competitively running the race.

To run the race well, the child needs to be as light as possible, carrying a minimum of baggage. The baggage a child is made to carry can become a heavy weight, and a race cannot be run successfully if the runner is weighed down with negative baggage. Often, such a race cannot be successfully completed because carrying heavy baggage tires anyone out. You (the parent) are responsible for getting your child started in the race of life.

The starting shot is fired, and the race begins even before the seed of conception is planted. Then, once your child comes into this world, she must get into the race; she has no choice. The child must run the race of life or be dragged along by its current. A child who is running the race of life may complete it successfully, may complete it less than successfully, or may not complete it at all. A child who is dragged along through the race of life will have less of a chance of completing it successfully, because at the very least, she will be bloodied and bruised in the process. At the worst, she could be killed as a result of the trauma experienced in this process. So no child can sit and watch the race of life go by; she or he must get into the race.

Every child born upon the face of the earth must participate in the race of life; that is a given. The child cannot choose whether or not she wants to participate; she has to take part. A child cannot be an uninterested by-stander, an unconcerned onlooker or even a concerned onlooker. When the child breathes the first breath of life, she or he is in the race—like it or not.

You have given your child, by reason of your behavior, the baggage she will carry through life. The amount and weight of the baggage has to do with how well or how poorly you, as a parent, have behaved in the past. The way you've behaved references the way you've treated your body, your mind and your social activity. The negative things which you have done in these areas will impact your child's life, as negative weight, and increase the burden of life's load on your child. The positive things you have done in life in these areas will impact your child's life as positive weight and will decrease the burden of life's load.

If you want your child to have the best chance of successfully competing in the race of life and making a successful transition into adulthood, don't do things, as a parent, that will create negative baggage that must be borne by your child. Just as parents would desire the child to represent them proudly in the eyes of mankind, a parent has a like obligation to represent the child proudly in the eyes of mankind. The types of behavior that can impact your child's life as negative baggage includes antisocial behavior, such as illegal activity, criminal behavior, off-center beliefs and philosophy, substance abuse, alcohol abuse, sexual abuse and deviant sexual behavior. Included in these would be such things as illegal gambling, theft, illegal drug selling, racketeering, contraband smuggling, illegal gang activity, drug and/or alcohol addiction, being a child abuser, being a career welfare recipient, being a white collar criminal, having and exhibiting extreme racial views, having extreme views against a legitimately-established government, or any other legitimately-established institution, having extreme views contrary to those of the society in which you live (such as being a communist in a democratic society or being a democrat in a communist society), having extreme religious views (such as atheism in a Christian society), having extreme social views contrary to those of the society in which you live (such as exercising nudity in a clothed society), or exercising extreme family values (such as exercising bigamy in a monogamous society or exercising the belief in same-sex marriage in a society whose family values are built of male-female relationships). Any of the above that you may have practiced before your child was born or were still practicing after your child was born can gain you a reputation as an individual passing along negative baggage, and this can become weight for your child to contend with along the path of life.

Children quite often find out about the parent of their friends or associates whose past may have included a bout with drugs or alcohol or an infraction with the legal system. Your past tends to follow you, and, unfortunately, it often follows your child also. The burden can and often does alter the destiny of your child's or your children's future. The world has become very small. No matter what country, what state, what city, what village or what town one may settle in, he or she often encounters someone who knows her or his past. When this is discovered, the word starts to get around, and if the information is other than admirable or positive, the word gets around even faster. When the individual's past is discussed, his child is often privy to the information divulged in the discussion. Subsequently, children use this information to tease or get back at the child whose parent was the product of a negative past. This hurts and shames your child, often leading to confrontations and fights. It can wear negatively on this child and even lead to the child developing low self-esteem, developing a hostile attitude and even a position of lawlessness. Any of these encounters could put the child off-track and cause the child to fall short of required goals.

Some children gather the strength to carry the weight of the parent's baggage, and with challenges and sometimes difficult struggles, can run the race successfully; many cannot. As a parent, don't create baggage for your child to carry, because the odds are against her or him being able to carry the baggage and still successfully complete the race. One of the most negative forms of baggage not mentioned above (and one taken lightly by today's society) is birthing a child into a family where there is no legitimate family structure—such as a mother and father by marriage. Society does not scream loud enough about children born out of wedlock, but this cannot be a happy position for any child born to this type of relationship.

If you were the product of such a relationship, you know how much it hurts when the other children inquire about your illegitimate father. In some instances, the father is an absentee father, and the child doesn't even know who his/her father is. If you think the child doesn't care, you're wrong. When you, as a mother, bring a child into the world without her having a legitimate father, you're only thinking of yourself and are stigmatizing the child. What makes you think it is okay with the child? I'm sure if you asked the child and the child could answer, she would probably say, "No, mother, I'd rather not—because the other children may tease me and say I'm an illegitimate child." Never mind how popular the practice has become; it is still not the right thing to do, and it is definitely not pleasing to God. Should this not matter? There are many negative moral practices accepted in today's society, but that does not mean they should be acceptable.

You can be the greatest influence in determining the potential success of your child in her or his transition from birth to successful adulthood. Don't say it is all up to the child; it's not. It is a partnership between the parent or parents and the child, with the parent playing the primary role. Children can overcome many things, but most of them cannot overcome the impossible. Even some adults are unable to overcome difficulty, and they are better equipped to negotiate the challenges of life than are children. Don't put your child in a position in which she would be required to overcome extraordinary odds in order to make the successful transition into adulthood.

My daughter was the product of a legitimate family. In my generation, we still believed in the importance of this—even though not everyone practiced it. The it-doesn't-really-matter attitude came along later. Thank God, my child did not have to carry that baggage. Children must carry enough of their own life's baggage, without being weighed down with that of their parents. Your child does not deserve to have to carry the baggage you created. If your parents handed down baggage for you to carry, break the cycle and decide you will not continue the pattern in the life of your child. Lighten her or his load and give her a fast, smooth start in the race of life. If you love her, you will do all you can to assure her success. Love is one of the most important ingredients in the recipe for successfully raising a child.

4. The Environment You Bring Your Child Into

The environment you bring your child into is very important to the potential success of the child. Success is first nurtured in dreams, and dreams are nurtured in the mind. They are the products of inner thoughts and aspirations, but are built upon the foundation of what the dreamer thinks is possible. When a child reaches the age at which she is able to assimilate thoughts and ideas, she is able to form pictures of the things she thinks will make her happy (to the extent she understands what happiness is). She looks at people, pictures and other things around her and how these things affect the lives of others, and then she decides in her mind, that is who she wants to be like or what she wants to have or do. She begins to build dreams, based on what her mind tells her is possible.

A child doesn't seem to nurture dreams that extend beyond the realm of possibilities formulated in the nurturing environment. I am reminded of a program I was watching which was produced from the housing projects on the Southside of Chicago. The interviewer asked a child what he wanted to be when he grew up, and the answer was, "I don't know. I just want to grow up." This child was nine or ten years old and had no dreams of growing up to be a doctor, lawyer or Native American chief. His dream was merely to come out of his environment alive.

On the other hand, I've witnessed a child from a neighborhood at the other end of the spectrum, and when asked what he wanted to be when he grew up, his immediate reply was something positive, such as a scientist, doctor or lawyer. He obviously had nurtured that in his dreams and deemed it within the realm of possibility. The environment within which he was being nurtured gave him dreams completely different to those of the child from the Southside Chicago projects. The environment you bring your child up in has much to do with the dreams she or he will nurture and the success he or she may achieve.

We brought Celeste up in a home and an environment within which she could nurture bright dreams. She attended small private schools during her entire school career. Her high school graduating class had thirty-two students, and thirty-one of the students opted for college. We decorated our home around dreams. We educated ourselves around dreams, and sought employment that, at the least, gave us a visionary perspective. Success is nurtured in dreams, because, as the Bible states, *as [a man] thinketh in his heart, so is he"* (Proverbs 23:7). Rene Descartes said, "I think, therefore I am."

On this note, a thought comes to mind. I heard it, and I don't know its original source, but it goes like this, "Think a thought and reap an action; think an action and reap a habit; think a habit and reap a destiny." So much can be said about thoughts which nurture dreams and dreams which reap destinies. Therefore, be mindful of the environment in which you bring your child up; it could weigh heavily on her success in life, especially if the parental love and discipline patterns are weak. Bad environments can prove to be distracting to a child who lacks other firm discipline values, and the distractions can quite often get a child off track.

In prior years, subsequent to the turn of the twentieth century, where a family settled had more to do with cultural similarities than with economic position. People wanted to be around others with which they had common ways and customs. Neighbors were divided more on the basis of origin similarities than on race or ethnic background, and it wasn't always economic. In today's society, people are more likely to be grouped by race and economic similarities, and the economics usually define a class of people rather than a race of people.

Economically deprived neighborhoods often mean crime-ridden, drug-infested environments because, along with economic depression, goes illegal activity, as a way of survival and a way of life. At least, that is the excuse often cited for the level of crime in depressed neighborhoods.

In times past, some of our most successful and outstanding citizens came out of neighborhoods in economically depressed areas. Immigrants came to this country and settled in areas where there were others who had origins similar to theirs. The European Jews settled in common areas. The Polish settled in common areas, the Russian Jews settled in common areas, and the Italians settled in common areas, etc. In those days, to be poor didn't mean to be disadvantaged. Parents were poor in money, but their children were rich in dreams. Such seems not to be the case today. People usually reside in depressed areas because that is all they can afford, and parents who raise their child in this type of environment often stifle that child's dreams.

Give your child the opportunity to dream, and give her dreams a chance to come to fruition. Strive to bring your child up in an environment where dreams can be born and nurtured. Dreams are sometimes born out of the ashes, but most often they are not. The slums represent a poor environment in which to build a child's dreams. Where their dreams are nurtured is partly up to you. Don't bring your child into a world where dreams can be stifled. If you love your child, you won't bring her into a world of poverty. Society recognizes that there will always be poor among us, but you need not choose it for yourself. Society also recognizes that we all have choices. There is no redeeming value in birthing children into an environment that virtually dooms them before they even get started. They need not be counted as having lost the race even before they begin it.

5. The Plan for Nurturing

How do you plan to support and sustain the development of the child or children you will potentially bring into the world? Have you thought about it? Do you care how you will go about it? If you have neither thought about it, nor care about it, the sexual activity you may be engaging in must be for your own enjoyment and gratification or that of your partner. Unprotected sex under ideal conditions (if there is any such thing as ideal) never yields all positive benefits. The only positive benefit to be derived (if you want to call it a positive benefit), if you are not engaging in sex to procreate, is the pleasure (if it is, indeed, pleasurable) derived from the act itself?

I'm not even certain that the sexual activity one engages in is always pleasurable. I've heard women say their first sexual encounter, out of which a child was conceived, wasn't even enjoyed. I've heard other women say that with certain partners they don't enjoy the activity. If this is true, what else is there to be derived from the activity that can be considered a positive benefit? Not only are there no positive benefits sometimes; sometimes there are a host of negatives, including transmitted diseases—some of which can kill.

On the other hand, the act of conception can yield a wanted or un-wanted child, and this child can be burdened forever, due to the lack of preparation for his or her coming into the world. Just think about this: the child had no choice in the matter. The activity was all done out of an act of selfishness on your part—the conceiving mother and the impregnating fa-ther. No two individuals have a right to do this to a child. The Bible says, *"Be fruitful and multiply,"* but this was speaking to functional families with a mother and father. When conceived, God meant that the parents should do whatever was legitimately necessary to properly raise and nurture the child conceived. It wasn't speaking to a new, unmarried generation of parents who bore children out of the sheer pleasure of the sexual act, having no intentions or means for supporting them.

Countless numbers of men have cohabited with countless numbers of women, bore children, and then walked away—with no intention of supporting the child or children. If your parents did that to you, were you happy about it? I'm sure you were not, because I've heard too many stories about children who didn't know who their father was, where their father was or hated the father they didn't even know. If that describes you and, as a child, the hurt was so bad, why would you want to bring that same type of hurt upon another child?

Even if that wasn't the case in your life, don't make it the case in your child's life. Children don't ask for it, nor do they deserve it. I've known men who had children all over the country and other countries and were not taking care of any of them. Some of the men thought this to be proof of their manhood, to have various children by different women. That is a very poor way for a man to prove his manhood. What it does prove is that he is selfish and ignorant. Most wild animals are more responsible than to father children and immediately go off and leave them to fend for themselves. Most wild animals nurture and care for their young better than some men who go about fathering children, and this is true—whether the man is married or not.

I was once watching a television segment in which wild animals would go hunt and fend for food to bring back to their young to make sure they were properly nourished. They also watched over them with protective eyes to make sure no danger or harm came to them. They taught them the skills of survival and made them capable of being independent—before putting them out on their own. God expects us, as parents, to do all that and more. Animals may not fully comprehend the consequences of their behavior, as we understand (or should understand), but do a much better job of seeing after their young than do some humans who supposedly have the ability to think, rationalize, make decisions and understand the possible results of their actions or inactions. Maybe we should learn from the animals and stop bringing children into the world whom we are not fully committed to nurturing and supporting.

Common sense, if one indeed possesses common sense, should indicate the number of children one might be capable of supporting. If you have no visible means of income (welfare doesn't count), common sense should indicate that you cannot afford to support or nurture any children at all. Under those conditions you can hardly support yourself. The time should be long past when parents conceive children and say, "God will take care of them." God expects *you* to take care of them.

BEFORE THE BEGINNING AND IN THE BEGINNING

In societies of days past, when parents had a whole brood of children without visible and concrete means of support, it was recognized as foolish behavior. Parents who conceive children as a recreational pastime would be better off going out to church or engaging in some other positive pastime, rather than engaging in sex, because the sexual activity may yield a house full of children they are incapable of supporting. Many parents grow weary of the effort required to support these children and walk away from the family. Children should always be conceived out of an act of love, not just desire for the person you're having sex with, but also love for the child that may result from the activity.

There is a distinct difference between "love" and "making love" or between "love" and "sexual activity." It's impossible to truly love a child you may bring into the world, if you have no visible means of supporting her. Having a part in conceiving children you cannot or will not support isn't child love; it's parent fun. You, the perspective parent, should go and engage yourself in some other pastime that will be better for the child you may otherwise conceive. Don't make a child or children the product of your selfish pleasure, when you know you cannot afford to parent. Don't tell anyone you love your child, if you bring the child into the world under hardship conditions. That isn't love; it's child punishment.

Children never asked to come into this world. You chose to bring them here, and you should not have made that choice unless you were committed to doing whatever was legally necessary to provide a safe environment conducive to properly raising and caring for the child.

Raising a child in an impoverished environment, without basic necessities, without time to teach and direct them, and without a plan for furthering their education in order to equip them for life's survival isn't doing whatever it takes. You must have a plan in mind—even before conception. Don't just get together with a partner and decide you want to have some sexual pleasure, out of which a child may be conceived, when, all the while, you have no plan for her proper nurturing. Have a plan for nurturing or don't have a child. A poorly parented child is likely to be an unsuccessful child and a parenting failure.

Chapter II

Plant the Child
in Good Moral Soil

Like planting the tree, so it will grow,
You plant your child, so she will go
In a right direction to survive life best.
And God will direct her and do the rest.

1. Pray First

There is something wonderfully mystical about the power of prayer, something we can't quite explain in terms of how it works and why it works, but those of us who have had an encounter with God in the form of a prayer request and witnessed that awesome joy of receiving a positive answer to our request are living testimonies to the fact that prayer does work. As the old spiritual attests, "Prayer changes things." And it can also work for you, as you start your child out in life with the blessings of God upon her or his life.

The ceremony commonly called a Christening and the prayer the minister or priest or whatever title the individual invoking the prayer be called by can be one of the best moral directions toward which you can point your child. When the prayer is prayed, invoking God's blessings, protection, nurturing success, care and direction upon your child's life, you can be setting the stage for giving your child the best possibility for survival and positive growth. I sincerely believe that our having had Celeste offered up to God in that Christening prayer was the foundation, moral soil, which kept her safe and on track and allowed her to grow up, surmount the hurdles of her childhood, reach the adult age and be looked upon as a child who was raised successfully.

God hears and answers prayers, and that very ceremonial prayer admonishes the parents to raise the child in the fear and admonition of the Almighty. It implies that in this godly process, the discipline will invoke positive moral behavior and direction, because godly values embody the highest standards of moral uprightness.

And what does the word "moral" imply? It implies that conduct will be in accordance with principles of right and good, hence, ethical behavior. And when one exercises ethical behavior, the behavior is moral, principled, proper, right, righteous and right-minded. So if parents plant their child in good moral soil, they will be mindful of raising the child to be all of the above, as well as other things that have not been mentioned among the above descriptive adjectives.

Right conduct refers to the values or behavior peculiar to those in a given society who aspire to higher standards, to godly behavior. That requires one to be honest, truthful and highly principled (which means avoiding any temptation to compromise good values) and proper (which means conforming to established standards of behavior or manners that are correct and fitting).

As Celeste grew in age and understanding, she was taught to exercise that form of proper behavior that was fitting for that stage of her development. She was also taught things that would become permanent parts of her pattern of behavior throughout the course of her life. Some of the things you teach a child will be held by the child and will be ingrained in the child's behavior for as long as she lives. These things will shape the child's conduct, and this will lead to the development of a successfully-raised child.

A child planted in good moral soil, who obeys the teachings of the parent or parents, who fears God and who is not swayed by the negative elements in her environment, will ultimately have a good chance of being a success in life.

What keeps a child on track? Prayer is one thing that keeps a child on track. The prayer offered for the child at birth, at the time of Christening and the constant invoking of God's presence and guidance throughout the child's life can serve to help keep the child on track. That Christening prayer at the stage of innocence and immaturity can have a most profound effect on the direction of a child's life. God will hear and answer the prayers of the righteous, even on behalf of the unrighteous. He's just the kind of God who shows mercy on behalf of those who love Him—and even for those who do not love Him.

How often have we heard the expression "My mother's or my father's prayers have kept me alive?" Or "My grandmother is always praying for me," or "Her priest [or minister] prays for me for her." The Bible says, *"The effectual fervent prayer of righteous man availeth much"* (James 5:16). So it behooves us to start our child off in life with a prayer for her or his right direction and protection.

As a part of this first requirement, we should pray constantly for the child. Is your child's future important enough to you for you to change your pattern of thinking if need be? I know that prayer may not come easily for some of us, but if we could adopt a prayer stance from time to time, we would reap positive benefits and big dividends in our child or children's life, as well as in our own.

How do you pray? You can start by thanking God for what He does for your child, whatever that happens to be. Then you can ask God for what you want Him to do. That's just how simple prayer is. Among the prayers you pray should be a prayer to put you in a right relationship with God, because His Word implies that He has an obligation to look after His children, and we are not all God's children; we are all God's creation.

Pray, and as often as you can muster the desire to, take your child to a house of God. You should make a concerted effort to do this. I can recall tutoring a group of younger students and noticed the difference in the mode of conversation and the attitude of the students. One of them, who had such a friendly refreshing personality, said, "I go to church." I mused to myself, "Aha! That made all the difference."

2. STRIVE FOR THE BEST, EMPLOYING RIGHT CONDUCT

The second thing that will be instrumental in keeping your child on track is the constant reinforcement of the values embodied in proper behavior. Very early on in Celeste's development she was admonished to tell the truth. Telling the truth builds honesty in character. Honesty creates strength in character, because it takes strength to tell the truth in the face of possible discomfort or punishment, when telling a lie may allow one to be free of the burden one may have created for herself. My daughter grew up thinking or knowing that the punishment or aftermath of not telling the truth far outweighed the benefits of telling a lie. And from this, she learned that she got more respect from her parents, teachers and others who may have had a role in shaping the direction of her life.

A while later, we began to instill in her the desire to do her best at whatever she attempted. When the goal of what she was attempting was difficult to achieve, she was admonished to keep trying and not give up until she had either mastered the endeavor or concluded that success at that endeavor was beyond her capacity to effect. Striving for her best and continuing in the task until it was mastered was character strength, because to be determined means being focused on winning. You can only win if you don't quit. As the saying goes, "Quitters never win, and winners never quit."

In some instances, it is not important how quickly you master the task; it is only important that you master it. As it is with some races: it is not important how fast you run the race, but whether or not you finish it. There is a saying which can fittingly be applied to challenges, and it says, *"The race is not to the swift, nor the battle to the strong"* (Ecclesiastes 9:11). The race goes to those who endure to the end. Some of life's races need only to be completed for one to be considered successful.

The idea of instilling in your child the incentive of determination can be introduced very early in the child's development, even at such time as when the child is only able to perform simple tasks, such as tying her shoes or putting away her toys. Direct the child in continuing with the effort until the shoes are tied or all of the toys are off the floor and in their proper place.

3. CLEANLINESS IS NEXT TO GODLINESS

At the next stage, we began to teach Celeste about cleanliness, cleanliness in her environment and personal cleanliness. Most of what we taught at this stage was done by demonstration, as opposed to hands-on participation, because she was too young. She was probably about the age of four when we began calling her attention to cleanliness aspects. Prior to that age, we merely performed the necessary cleanliness chores, except for those such as picking up her toys.

PLANT THE CHILD IN GOOD MORAL SOIL

Her shoes were polished daily. I would sit on the top step of the stairs leading up to the second floor, put down a covering and there I would polish the shoes. Most often, this was done the night before and often she was invited to sit beside me and watch. This gave her a sense of camaraderie with her dad, and it also gave her a mental fixation about the importance of having clean, polished shoes. Today, at the age of thirty-nine, she still polishes her shoes. We sowed a thought and reaped a habit in our child.

That brings to mind an incident told by her mother concerning the polishing of shoes. One day her mother was about to send her off to school with unpolished shoes. She promptly remarked to her mother, "Mommy, I can't wear these shoes; you didn't polish them." Her mother replied, "They don't need polishing." "She said, "No Mommy, my Daddy polished my shoes every day." So the habit of having her shoes polished every day stuck in her mind. Good direction and habits, as well as bad direction and habits, can be implanted in the psyche of children and remain there throughout their lives.

After this came the teaching of things such as brushing her teeth as least twice a day, getting a bath every day and sometimes twice a day, getting her little face scrubbed and, for good measure, washing behind her ears. There must be something magical about the idea of teaching a child to wash behind their ears. All parents bent on cleanliness teach children to scrub behind the ears as an unforgettable ritual. Is that where all of the body dirt hides? Washing behind the ears seems to be a ritual that a child never forgets. I certainly remember it from my mother.

And don't forget to teach them to clean up and organize their surroundings, whether it is their individual room or a space shared with another. Remember, one day they may be going off to college or the military or camp or any number of other places or events, and they will probably share quarters with someone else. For us and Celeste, cleanliness and neatness in her environment was important. This got her accustomed to organizing her space and keeping it clean.

Cleanliness is very important, and will epitomize one of the most endearing qualities in a child's development, as well as in her life as an adult. It is also important to keep a child's clothes clean and neat, without holes and with all of the required buttons attached. A child need not have a hundred changes; it is only necessary that her clothes be clean. All children don't have equal access to abundant supply, but all can have access to the supply of clean clothes in good repair, because soap and water and needles and thread are relatively inexpensive.

One thing that really upset me then and still does today is to see a person wearing a garment with missing buttons. I hated that almost as much as seeing an individual wearing an unclean garment. Even to this day, I am against wearing any garment with a missing button—if I'm aware that the button is missing. I feel equally strong about garments with holes in them, especially undergarments. When a hole has worn into the garment, it is time to discard it and retire it to the rag pile. As a boy, I was reminded over and over again about the possibility of having an emergency requiring hospitalization or something similar, and if it happened to you, it should be your hope that your underwear will not embarrass you if emergency personnel need to see it.

There is great redeeming value in being certain that a child's clothes are always clean and neat. The thought of putting clean, fresh-smelling clothes on a child will create a memorable quality in a child that she will carry throughout her life, and she will be likely to repeat the habit in her own child. You must also teach them how to properly care for their clothing, to avoid sloppy behavior, such as throwing their clothes down rather than hanging them up. Children should be encouraged to be playful and to play as hard as they care to, but they should be taught to avoid unnecessary soiling with drinks and foodstuffs. This is good direction toward establishing positive eating habits, properly handling their food with the utensils they use.

And don't forget the washing of hands. That's one of a child's most important habits relative to good hygiene. There are many germs all around us on everything. You want to avoid, as much as possible, your child getting these germs into her body from dirty hands that may be carrying one or more of any number of viruses or other germs transferred to a surface your child may touch. How often have you seen adults sit down to eat without even the thought of washing their hands? How often have you been driving along the highway and stopped in a rest area and observed the other individuals in the restroom? Too often they finish using the restroom and then walk out without washing their hands, even going directly to a food counter, ordering food and sitting down to eat it?

Sometimes there is a door handle that must be touched when exiting a restroom, and those who go out with unwashed hands contaminate this door handle. Everyone has different standards in this regard, and each one considers his hands, and other body parts, to be clean enough. Well, they may be clean enough for them, but they may not be clean enough for some other person—especially a child.

Adults who refuse to eat with dirty hands were probably taught as children to always wash their hands before eating. It is also a good habit to require children to wash their hands when coming into the house from outside. This can help to keep outside germs outside. There are some mean viruses and infections in our world today. Proper and frequent washing can help prevent taking these germs into the body.

As a child, I can recall the times when my mother would take me to a medical facility, and she would always admonish me not to put my hands on the benches where others sat. I couldn't quite understand (at that time) why she kept telling me not to put my hands on the seats. After I got to be an adult, I came to realize that the cleanest part of a not-so-clean individual is usually not the part that sits on the seat where I (as a child) might have then placed my hands.

If you live in a big city with a large homeless population, it is especially important to teach your child these hand placement and hand washing habits, because some of the homeless individuals may not have ready access to washing facilities, and germs are often allowed to accumulate on their bodies. Many of these germs are transferred to public facilities and may be transferred to those individuals with inadequate hand-washing habits. As children travel with their parents, there may not be frequent exposure to these germs, but when the children become adults and begin traveling on their own, they will need to have these habits in place.

I spent the better part of my life in a big city, where public transportation was the popular and necessary means of getting around, for most people. While riding the public transportation, I often witnessed individuals sneezing or coughing into their hands, picking at their noses or even scratching their backsides. There may have been germs in any one of these cavities. Then this individual would hold onto the rail, strap or pole we were likely to hold onto as well, and if it was not them, then some other individual had already come along before us and done it.

Hand washing, body washing, scrubbing the neck, washing behind the ears and frequent hair washing are all a part of basic good hygiene habits that should be taught and practiced by all. I remember a teacher in grade school who said, "Wash everything possible, and then wash possible." Good personal cleanliness habits should extend to the frequency of bathing, washing the hair, caring for the feet, nails, etc. We taught these things to our child at an early age and let her be mindful of our practicing the same. If you'll do it, it will sink in and become a routine part of the child's habits as she matures.

Cleanliness is one of the most important aspects of good moral behavior and will, no doubt, find a lodging place in virtually every aspect of a person's life, because the desire to be clean in one area of the body will spread to other areas of the body. The desire to be clean in one area of the environment will lead to the desire to be clean in other areas of the environment. A child who is taught to wear clean shoes will probably want to wear clean socks, and that will probably extend to the desire to wear clean undergarments, and then to clean outer garments.

The cleanliness process tends to work from the inside out, rather than from the outside in. An individual who wears clean outer garments will not necessarily clean the things you can't see, but a person who will clean the things you cannot see will be likely to clean the things you can see. Teach your child to be clean from the inside out. Polished shoes, clean fingernails and clean hair are good signs of how well an individual practices habits of cleanliness. Rusty shoes, dirty fingernails and dirty hair are probably indications of one who does not practice good hygiene. Teach the basic cleanliness habits to your child, and those will extend to other cleanliness habits.

Basic cleaning habits in a child's environment begin with teaching a child to clean and tidy the living space. Once these habits are adopted, they will likely extend outward. If your child is taught to clean her room, by picking up things from the floor and placing them in the proper place in an orderly fashion, it will become a part of a child's routine habits and desires. Demonstrate to a child the method of keeping a clean bed by putting on clean linen and bedcovers. One need not have a hundred blankets and sheets to change a child's bed frequently. Just keep the ones that you have clean. If you don't have a washing machine or access to a washing machine, you can wash things in the tub if need be. Do whatever it takes. However, for those without washing machines, laundromats are readily available almost everywhere you might live.

You must have the desire to be clean, and then pass this desire on to your child by starting her off with the practice of clean habits. It is not something that is enjoyed exclusively by those who can afford it, nor is uncleanness relegated to those who cannot afford to be clean. Cleanliness is cheap; everyone can afford it. It only has to be introduced to be desired. The desire to be clean and orderly in the home will lead to the desire to be clean and orderly in the school room or the college dorm. This will ultimately lead to the desire to be clean and orderly in the office or the military barracks.

By this time, the child will be growing into adulthood and will probably be aspiring to own his or her own space. Having learned the basic habits from childhood, a child will likely desire cleanliness in her own environment. If she has children, she will more likely teach cleanliness habits to them, and the cycle will continue. I have witnessed this in Celeste and seen how she has passed cleanliness habits on to our grandchild.

It was often thought to be a "given" that ladies represented the more tidy set. This is only because, as a practice, cleanliness was stressed more in the life of a young lady. Ladies, by nature, are expected to be cleaner than men. However, society has been reminded time and time again that this is not necessarily true. I have heard remarks such as, "If you think men are dirty, you should see the ladies' room." This is an indication of the proliferation of ladies who do not practice cleanliness habits. Obviously some of these ladies had not been taught the proper hands-on method of cleanliness. They have been allowed (as children) to gravitate toward unclean habits and sloppy behavior. This results in the type of uncleanness spoken of in the ladies' room or other environments where ladies congregate in a group.

Some are comfortable in this type of atmosphere. Others, who have been taught cleanliness and practice it, will not be comfortable. Clean individuals will not want to be around individuals who exercise poor cleanliness habits. Cleanliness will be a major plus along your child's success path.

4. Good Manners

Another aspect of good moral behavior, one which should be taught early in a child's development, is good manners. This encompasses saying "please" and "thank you," eating properly, sitting properly, walking erect, chewing gum discretely (if it is to be chewed at all), covering your mouth when you cough, sneeze or yawn, not picking or digging in your body cavities in public and putting refuse in the proper receptacle, rather than improperly throwing it down somewhere. This does not propose to cover all of the basic behavior manners, but it does speak to the most basic and necessary manners required of your child, if she is to get minimal recognition from her peers as being the type of individual they would feel comfortable with in a private or public social setting.

On this note, I am reminded of an incident that occurred during my dating days. I met a young lady on a job site in the area where I was employed at the time. When I first saw her, I thought she was one of the most attractive, neatest, well-groomed ladies around. I considered it a "must" to invite her out to lunch. Being the dapper guy I thought I was and being articulate with a "gift of gab," I knew I wouldn't be refused. I thought I would not want to pass up the opportunity to lunch with a lady of her appearance. I considered her a lady after my own heart. So I invited her out to lunch and she accepted.

I took this lady to the type of restaurant I deemed fitting for the style she exuded. We went through the usual "get acquainted" conversation and, after such, we ordered the food we were going to eat. It came, and we both dined sufficiently. Afterwards she took the napkin, folded it a few times in a triangular fashion, then took the peaked end of it and began cleaning the residue from between her teeth. I didn't say anything, but I was so disappointed with her poor manners that every good feeling I had for her virtually vanished. All of the stylish apparel, beauty and grooming went right out of the window. It was obvious that she had not been taught proper manners.

I will not go into detail on proper etiquette; that can better be left to the many books written on the subject. However, there are some basic things that a child needs to know, and those things that go beyond the basics will be acquired by the child as the need to know arises. Society will direct her toward the other worthwhile and necessary lessons.

First and foremost, when a child is asking someone to do something for her, she should always say "please," and if someone has done something for her which she is glad about, she should always say "thank you." The words *please* and *thank you* should be two of the first things one is taught to say in learning any language.

Children should be taught to eat properly, because a child's eating etiquette will speak loudly to those she may be around, and poor eating habits can make a child the butt of jokes and teasing. This could lead to altercations with other children, who have been instructed in proper eating techniques. So teach your child about napkin placement, eating utensil use, how to pace herself when she eats, proper eating posture, how to cut and separate her food, about not trying to talk with food in her mouth, about keeping her elbows off the table, about not picking her teeth in public and about improper burping in American company. In some cultures, burping (I'm told) is an indication that the food was good, but in American culture, burping in public is considered ill-mannered. You can teach your child to indicate the goodness of the food by eating it and by telling the provider of the food that it was good—if such is the case. Also your child should be taught not to leave the company of the table without first properly excusing herself.

Early in life a child should be taught the proper sitting, standing and walking posture. I've read various accounts where individuals were required to walk around with an object on the head in order to develop erect walking posture. There is nothing wrong with this gesture.

Teach your child to sit erect, with back against the chair back, to stand erect, without slouching, and to walk erect with head held high. When you see a child walking in this manner, it is an indication that the child is going somewhere. Upright walking posture also gives a child a sense of well-being and self-assurance. Teach the child to walk with her head in the clouds; it makes her reach. If she walks with her head toward the ground, that's as low as her spirits can descend.

A tree growing straight and stately certainly looks more appealing than one bent over. Even a weeping willow has a straight trunk, even though the branches bend. In general, weeping willows denote an unhappy thought. Weeping comes mostly through unhappiness, rather than from joy. (There are exceptions.)

Good posture is not confined to standing and walking. Your daughter must certainly be taught good sitting posture. She should be taught to sit with her knees together, her legs closed. She should either close her legs or cross her legs. One of the telltale signs of a girl's proper or improper upbringing is how she sits. It is not a foolproof sign, but it says a great deal about the quality of her parenting. So you're probably wondering what posture has to do with a child's success. It's all a part of being raised properly. Success and improper posture are in conflict; success and proper posture are in agreement.

5. Actions Speak Louder

One of the most visible red flags indicating an improperly raised child, and one that probably lacks the basic elements of right upbringing, is any behavior that attracts attention to a child in a negative or non-positive way. Noisy gum chewing or gum popping can certainly do this. Any child or adult who chews gum in this manner and deems it to be "cool" or "cute" is quite off base. Chewing gum in an indiscreet manner is a dead giveaway concerning the quality of an individual. Blowing bubbles in public and popping gum is obnoxious and ignorant. Any individual with that type behavior should be corrected. Don't permit your child to engage in this type of display. It's neither cute nor funny, and is not acceptable behavior in proper company.

If your child has this habit, quality people will shun her as she grows older. As a parent, don't make ignorant assumptions concerning what is cute and acceptable. If you're unsure, get a book or seek information from a quality source. Don't permit your child to take on negative habits. They will not serve her well in later years and may lead her to feelings of low self-esteem.

Have you ever noticed an individual sitting across from you who yawned or sneezed with uncovered mouth? That individual may also not have the most beautiful set of teeth to display. And what about the individual who digs for gold in his or her nostrils? If you witnessed this and you would not exercise this type of behavior, what would be the first thing you thought about that individual? You would probably say to yourself, "What a pig," or you would make some other similar negative remark. Sad as it is, this might be a fitting description for that individual.

Good company would probably not want a "pig" at the dinner table. It doesn't matter how well dressed that individual may have been; she or he lacked proper training and upbringing. That same type of individual will probably not reach the point whereby he or she can be labeled a successfully-raised child. The child may make lots of money, may be financially able to reside in an upper-class neighborhood and may even obtain a college degree, but success in relative terms may still elude her. This is because success is not represented by any of those things—individually or in conjunction. Those things represent only a part of the success formula.

Some of society's worst "slobs" have money, live in multimillion-dollar neighborhoods, belong to exclusive country clubs, may play golf or tennis or both and still may miss the success mark. Success is about having a proper upbringing, which directs a child toward required goals of achievement. That means having balance in every aspect of the maturing process, as described earlier in this writing. If you love and discipline your child as she is developing, you will not allow her to be lax in areas that can embarrass her, ostracize her, degrade her, deny her or stop her from achieving her full potential.

Another important aspect of a child's existence is her name. What you name your child could make a more significant difference in her life than you could ever imagine. Names have meaning, and children should be given meaningful names. Don't give your child a silly name that has no meaning or no relationship to anything in particular. Don't give a child a name that is not only meaningless but difficult, for you as well as others, to pronounce or spell. Often children attempt to act out or live like what their name implies, which may be far different than what you expect for them or of them. So be very careful and give a great deal of attention and thought to what you name your child. If you are at a loss for a proper name, go to the dictionary. Any good dictionary will have a listing of meaningful names to select from.

If you want your child to lead a "mainstream" life, start her off in life with a mainstream name. There is nothing wrong with giving your child a much used name, as long as it is a proper name. Sometimes, in an effort to find a name that's "different," a parent completely misses the mark, and the child ends up with a name that is completely "off," one that she will be likely to carry for the balance of her life. Quite often a child is embarrassed by her name, because the name sometimes becomes an indication of a parent's ignorance.

Children often wonder: "Why did my parents name me this?" So when you're in the process of naming, you should think more about the child and what he or she may be happy with and less about yourself and what you would be happy with. Names make a difference, so let the name you give your child make a positive difference in her life. Give her a name with meaning and power, and she may be projected to higher goals in life.

6. PUBERTY

As your child begins to approach the age of puberty, you must begin to guide her in the ways of the proper use of her body. At this point in her life, hormones start to go crazy, and unless she is properly nurtured and instructed, she could begin to act crazy too. She may not even know and understand what's happening to her. All she knows is that her body feels different. If you have properly prepared her for this period in her life, she will enter it and pass through it, as if it were a normal process of life, as it is.

Too many parents have decided early that they want their daughter to be sexy, beautiful and desired, plus all of the other things they think will bring her happiness. Some wish the daughter to become what they may not have become, and others seem not to care if their daughter walks in their own negative footsteps. Don't wish either of these paths for your daughter. Immoral behavior is improper behavior and will more likely than not deny your daughter her full success potential. Don't endeavor to prepare your daughter for her sexual maturity by exposing her to experiences that will neither serve her well nor advance her maturity.

Neither should a father attempt to prepare his son for sexual maturity by introducing him to a strip act or a prostitution experience. If it is going to be done, the child will choose the time soon enough to undertake the experience. Don't be guilty of shepherding a child toward experiences that both you and they may later regret.

I've witnessed parents who executed strange interactions with their children, such as mouth kissing and more. A child should not be kissed in the mouth, and no reasonably-thinking parent should ever put his or her tongue in a child's mouth. Whether you think so or not, that behavior is "off the wall" and serves no worthwhile purpose. The child will learn that aspect of intimacy soon enough on her own—if desired. Hopefully that will be at the proper time and with the proper individual. It is a gesture of intimacy reserved for a specific proper relationship.

There is a cutoff age at which a father should not be bathing his daughter, and likewise, a mother her son, and that point is early in life. A good reference point may be at five or six years of age. A father should not be parading around nude in front of his daughter at any age, and likewise a mother her son. That may not be the valid way to teach a child the difference between the sexes. The father should teach this to his son, and let the mother teach the facts of life to her daughter. The teaching will become reinforced soon enough at school and/or from their peers and associates. Your child should be taught the proper use of her body, and the proper place to begin this teaching is in the home. If she is properly taught, she may avoid the pain and inconvenience of premarital pregnancy.

PLANT THE CHILD IN GOOD MORAL SOIL

Make no mistake about it, there is nothing honorable about bringing a child into the world void of a proper family structure into which to place them. It is being done on a daily basis, but that doesn't make it honorable or proper. The moral decay of our society has many of its roots in this social dilemma. If your daughter does this, she will be (in most cases) scarred for life. It doesn't always prevent marriage, or completing college, or obtaining success, but it is a definite scar. If the child's desire is to marry, this scar will (more often than not) limit the choices among the best pursuers. In this way, she gives up the opportunity to pick from the better quality group of male prospects, who may be seeking a proper mate. Every man isn't accepting of a ready-made family.

There is something strange about men; they like to feel (even if it is not true) that they are getting a lady who has been untouched by other men. Men don't seem to relish the thought of marrying what they consider "damaged goods." One who undergoes premarital pregnancy isn't necessarily any worse than one who doesn't, but the pregnancy certainly lessens the chances for success and indicates an area of failure by the parents. Something had to be misdirected or misunderstood for a young lady to engage in adult-type activity, while still a child.

I said to Celeste, "You shouldn't engage in sex with boys, because they are merely having fun and trying to enjoy themselves at your expense. Boys have little to lose from your getting pregnant; the girl is always the big loser. What's more, boys will be responsible for spoiling your career—if you allow them to do so. Then they will go about their business, as if nothing had happened. And you will be left holding the baby."

When a young lady yields to the wishes of a man rather than the wishes of the parent, it is fair to say that the parent failed somewhere in getting the message across, or in giving the child another avenue for expressing her emotions. Maybe the parent wasn't really there. As a parent, you must let your child know early that certain behavior will hurt you, disappoint you, or will show a lack of gratitude for the effort put forth in trying to make her a quality person.

I told Celeste that there were certain things I could not accept, tolerate, sympathize with or understand. I said to her, "I'm not a very sympathetic father. I wish I was, but I am not, so if you get pregnant before marriage, don't expect me to be sympathetic and understanding, because I probably will not be. I'm just not made that way." I can't say that message alone caused her to avoid a premarital pregnancy, but I can say that I endeavored to send the right message.

Maybe Celeste wasn't even inclined toward adult activity as a child. Maybe her thoughts were on her school work, and God, which is where they should have been. Some parents send the wrong message. They make the daughter think that if she makes a mistake (which she shouldn't be allowed to make in the first place) they will forgive her and understand it was a mistake. However, the mistake isn't the premarital pregnancy; the mistake is engaging in adult activity before it is time. Young ladies doing this are engaging in risky behavior. The parents have already implied that if she makes a mistake they will understand. Inviting risks sometimes brings dire consequences, and those consequences can remain for a lifetime.

Some parents send no message at all, and that is also bad. A parent should at least discuss the subject. Don't be "out to lunch" on the matter. You need not harp on it day in and day out, because doing this is like promising the child a due punishment that you never get around to executing. You should say what you mean and mean what you say. You should demand, not settle.

You must also supply the right direction and support, so that your daughter will not be prone to exercise negative behavior against your wishes. You must raise your daughter in such a manner that her mind will be dealing with things in perspective. A child's mind should be on school things at school age, on grown-up things when she reaches the grown-up age and on family things when she has a family of her own. That's the path the developing and growing-up process should take.

I told Celeste she should have the experience of partaking of anything good and right, but always at the proper time. I also told her that I would be the first to tell her about anything I thought would enhance her life or bring her joy and happiness. I said, "I don't want you to miss out on anything that is good for you." I began to call off some things, and I said, "Don't smoke. I did that and found it to be nothing worthwhile to engage in. Drinking a sociable glass of wine is okay, as long as you don't overdo it. Don't do drugs under any circumstance. I never tried them and had no desire to try them, because I had read too much, heard too much and seen too much concerning the harmful effects of drug use. After witnessing all the drug addicts in our society, I believed drugs could do to you what the experts said they could do. Sex is wonderful and something to be enjoyed when the time comes, and that time should preferably be in a relationship after marriage."

PLANT THE CHILD IN GOOD MORAL SOIL

If your child believes you when you tell her these things, she may listen to you and act accordingly. Celeste obviously believed me, because she doesn't smoke. As far as I can discern, she doesn't do drugs. I think she has an occasional glass of wine, and I hope she has enjoyable sex in marriage, which is the proper setting for enjoyable sexual activity.

Celeste married and lived happily with her husband and their daughter, who came along when they were both well into their thirties. She is well past the age of needing my help to transition her from childhood to adulthood. She made that successful transition not long after reaching the age of twenty-one. We planted her in good moral soil, directed her, nurtured her and supported her through all of those times when she could have and would have gotten off track.

We did all of this and (I'm sure) more that I didn't think to mention, but the balance of her life is hers to live as she sees fit, and in her living we hope that the direction given and the nurturing seeds planted will keep her rudder steered in a positive direction. I'm not responsible for keeping her on track as an adult. She has to be allowed to take charge of her own life as she sees fit. My job and her mother's job as parents is complete, and the fruits of parenting should be evident now in her adult posture.

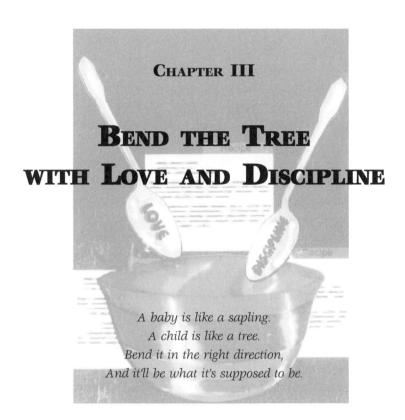

CHAPTER III

BEND THE TREE
WITH LOVE AND DISCIPLINE

A baby is like a sapling.
A child is like a tree.
Bend it in the right direction,
And it'll be what it's supposed to be.

1. EARLY SUPPORT AND DIRECTION

Early after a tree is planted or in conjunction with the planting process, support stakes are placed on either side of it, and it is anchored to these support stakes. The reasons for this are: (1.) To keep the tree from falling down, (2.) To shape the direction of the growth, and (3.) To keep the elements in its environment from knocking it down. Once the tree's growth is established (and that can take a few years), the supports can be removed, because the growth direction has been completed and it is moving toward that expected direction. From time to time, outside intervention may need to be undertaken, because there is always the possibility for the forces in its environment to attack it and, without help, it could be overcome and destroyed.

The process of supporting and directing the growth of the tree must be undertaken early on, because it is unlikely it will reach maturity—unless it is supported and directed. If the support is strong enough and directs it to grow straight, it will grow straight. If the support is weak and permits it to lean or fall over, it will fall over. The support has to be firm, and the direction has to be conclusive.

There are very few trees, if any, whose natural direction is toward the ground. A tree is usually directed to grow upright, but not always straight. Once it nears the stage of complete maturity, if it is inclined toward another posture, natural and peculiar to its inborn characteristics, and such posture will not prevent its continual existence, then it will naturally incline itself in that direction.

As it is with a tree, so it is also with a child. The analogy is perfectly fitting and parallel. You must bend or steer the child in the direction of desired growth, and the support pressure is to be love on the one side and discipline on the other, with the child in the middle, being kept on a straight path by those two pressure forces. With a child, as with a tree, you must begin the bending process very early. A newborn baby is similar in its growth to a tree sapling. At this stage, there is very little harm that can be done by the newborn or the sapling on its own to self-destruct. The most important requirement at this stage is to protect it from the forces in its environment that could harm it or prevent it from reaching the stage at which it is able to respond to the directive or shaping pressures. When the sapling reaches the stage whereby it and its root structure can be dug up, encased in its usual burlap or similar wrap, it can be placed in permanent soil and called a tree, as opposed to a sapling. At this point it is time to begin the process of directing its growth.

In like manner, when the newborn reaches the stage whereby it begins to respond to and understand natural stimuli, such as smiles, frowns, voice pitch, words like *yes* or *no*, pain, likes and dislikes, it is then referred to as a child, rather than as a newborn, and it is time to begin the process of establishing the direction of the child's growth. This can start to occur around an approximate age of twelve to eighteen months, because once a child reaches the twenty-four month age, it has some behavior patterns pretty well determined.

2. THE TERRIBLE TWOS

If there has not been parental intervention prior to the age of two years, and a direction has not been established concerning what will and what will not be permitted, the child will be well rooted and grounded in her or his own pattern of acting out what she or he feels will get the desired attention or response from the parent or caregiver. The acting-out process of behavior includes things like unnecessary crying, when it has been established and obvious that nothing is wrong, laying down on the floor and kicking and screaming, saying *no* to the instructions of a caregiver, spitting out food or just spitting at the parent or caregiver, throwing objects, hitting the parent back, refusal to go to sleep when placed in the sleeping environment and/or failure to go to sleep in his or her own bed, and any other of many acts of undisciplined behavior.

Because of this, the age of two is often referred to as "the terrible twos," because this is the age when children who have had no directive pressure up to that point seem to be acting "off the wall," in ways that are obviously displeasing to the parent, and in ways that are completely unnecessary. So if a parent waits until this stage to start applying the two important directive pressures (love and discipline), it will be necessary to first unlearn bad behavior patterns, which the undirected child has established on his or her own.

Some of these may come from what the child sees other children doing or from instinctive bad behavior, which, if left unchecked, the child will come to think of as cute or even correct. If your child comes into this stage of "the terrible twos" with behavior habits that are very undesirable or "off the wall," don't throw up your hands and quit. You haven't lost the child nor the battle of successful parenting. You've only made your shaping and bending process a bit more difficult. You must now backtrack to "Point A," erase all of the bad behavior patterns and begin again by introducing the proper mode of behavior. You've learned a hard lesson, and if you learned the lesson well, now take corrective action and reverse the negative behavior established. In this way, your future and that of your child will be better served.

My child never went through this "terrible twos" stage, because we didn't adhere to that pattern of direction in her behavior. Her behavior wasn't allowed to be terrible at any stage. She was properly directed. We, the parents, were in charge—not our child. Developing children know nothing except what they learn from the parent or parents and their immediate environment, or from others in their extended environment. This is why it is extremely important for a temporary caregiver, such as the nanny or babysitter, to exercise habits and values similar to your own or such others as would be acceptable to you and you would be pleased with.

Habits and values acquired outside of the home or espoused by others inside of the home are just as easily adopted. How often can you recall your child bringing home habits or attitudes that you found to be utterly foreign and displeasing? They were picked up from the environment or behavior of the caregiver, if they were habits alien to your teachings or liking. In these instances, you must unlearn and reteach your child daily and let the child know, in no uncertain terms, that the pattern of behavior will be the one taught and adopted in your household, or the behavior has to be such as you would be pleased with.

You should accept no compromise. When your young child comes home and begins jumping up and down on the bed or climbing all over the upholstered furniture with dirty shoes, spitting on others or any such similar behavior, you must stop it right then and there. Chastise the child firmly and make her aware that the next such infraction will be met with even more serious discipline. Spank the child, if needed, and let her know in such other ways as she understands that those acts do not and will not constitute an acceptable mode of behavior in your home.

You should have no concern about the fallacy that hitting a child will damage her self-esteem. If you don't discipline her at an early age, she will later damage her own self-esteem and yours, as well.

Both of the directive pressures must be in place—love pressure and discipline pressure. If you omit either, use too much pressure of one or too little of the other, one result will be an imbalance in the direction of the child's behavior. Just like a tree with counterbalancing staves on either side, if one pulls it too strongly in the one particular direction, the tree will tend to lean toward the stronger pulling force. There must be equal counterbalancing forces in play. The formula isn't scientific, but it is measured, and if either of the ingredients is applied in a significantly unbalanced fashion, the results may be an unsuccessfully-raised child. A child raised without enough love or discipline, or with too much of either of the two, is a child who will be likely to go off track at some point in life. The story of too much discipline is often repeated, just as the story of not enough love—justifiably or not.

Everybody needs and wants love, especially a child. Every child needs and often cries out for discipline in her life, because discipline is direction.

By the time a child reaches adulthood, she should have her direction, so the discipline required in the life of an adult is different to that required in the life of a child. Children need discipline to get on track, but adults need discipline to stay on track.

A child wants discipline and needs discipline, and a child without discipline is a child without direction. If one doesn't know where to go, she certainly will not know how to get there. What is the direction to "I don't know where?"

3. GETTING DIRECTIONS AND MAKING DECISIONS

We should never assume or give a child undue credit concerning her ability to make important decisions in life or concerning her ability to properly analyze circumstances relative to life and living. Most children cannot and will not be capable of making adult decisions through the mental facility of their childlike mind. If we, as parents, having traveled much distance down the road of life, can't always make the best decisions, what can we expect from a child who has barely gotten onto the road of life? The child has been under the parent or guardian's care and guidance since birth, so why should we assume that, at some point in her pre-teens or teens, she will (all of a sudden) get a stroke of genius concerning life and be able to know what it is all about—especially not having lived it yet?

Since this is the case, we must direct teenagers, as we have done with them as children, until they have learned the basic "ins and outs" of coping with life based on the decisions and directions we have given them. Day by day and circumstance by circumstance, we aid them in evaluating the condition, or we evaluate the condition for them.

Most of the conditions of life which they will be facing are those which we, as parents, have already faced. Some of the new social ills introduced into society from time to time and faced by a child may be new to a parent. For instance, when drug use became prevalent in society and out in the open, beginning in the late 1950s and early 60s, it was new to many parents, because they had not previously been exposed to such a thing. Some parents knew little or nothing concerning the reason individuals used drugs, who they were or the ultimate consequence of drug use. However, they were smart enough to know that anything which forced one to steal, kill, become dysfunctional, disinterested, diseased or die prematurely was something a child should not partake of.

Many children were not smart enough to know that. Others did not believe their parents, when the parents told them about the consequences resulting from the use of illegal drugs. Many parents knew from reading about them or from observing other individuals who had gotten involved with them. Many children partook of them anyway and became all of the above and more. They evidently thought they knew more than their parents.

Many children didn't believe their parents, when their parents warned them concerning the ills of promiscuous sexual behavior, and subsequently they brought children into society who became members of dysfunctional families and single-parent households. This behavior often created generation after generation existing in an unbreakable cycle of misdirection and failure. Many of the parents directing the children had not been there, but they were wise enough, concerning the path of life, to know that a child born into an unstructured family had less of a chance at success. I feel certain that many of these parents told their children the reasons for not doing these things and the consequences of doing them. Then, it was up to the children.

When a child lacks discipline, she lacks direction, and if she has no direction, she will either not reach her goal or be delayed in reaching it.

4. BALANCING THE FORCES

Life is a journey that takes a child somewhere, and that "somewhere" is a goal. If a child is seriously delayed in reaching her goal, it is due to the child getting off track, because parents often misdirected the child, failed to follow direction, or God intervened because He had something else in mind. However, God doesn't create misbehavior or wrongdoing. That is caused by Satan in the parent or Satan in the child or both, which puts a child off-track. The parents' hopes and prayers are that the child will achieve a successful transition from childhood to adulthood in normal time. This is the goal. Normal time could be considered to be by age twenty-one or sooner—as the child's learning progress permits.

Some children never reach the goal, because they never make the successful transition. More likely than not, the accusing finger should be pointed toward the guardian. Whether the guardian wants to admit it or not, if the child failed to reach her goal, there was something wrong in measuring out the key ingredients—love and discipline. The parent/s didn't balance the two elements properly, and therefore the tree (child) didn't grow straight.

In some instances, there could have been mentally compromised circumstances that may have precluded the successful parenting endeavor. That is usually the exception rather than the rule. The forces of love must be just as strong as the forces of discipline, and neither should overpower the other. They must be measured. If you give the child too much discipline and not enough love, the child will likely not succeed, because too much discipline borders on cruelty and lacks love. If you give the child too much love, the child will likely not succeed, because too much love borders on the inability of the parent to make the difficult decisions which may be right for the child's proper development.

Too much love often leads to not enough discipline. When a parent loves a child too much, he doesn't want to hurt the child or make the child uncomfortable in any way. However, in raising a child, we must sometimes execute "tough love" for their benefit. Tough love often hurts, but it must be done for the positive benefit of the child, further down life's road. Exercising tough love hurts the parent as well as the child (at the particular moment), but the positive fruits of the outcome more than offset the temporary pain of exercising the tough love. You will know this all too well, if you are a parent who has hung in, disciplined when necessary, loved your child as necessary, been there when necessary and executed tough love when the occasion called for right behavior that may have been contrary to the child's desires. I did all of the above, and today, when I witness my daughter's movement along the path of life, I am so thankful to God that He gave me the wisdom to hang in there as I did.

Celeste and I all but fell out with each other on several occasions, when, in my personal judgment, I deemed it necessary to speak against her desired direction in several aspects of her life. Fall out if you must; exercise tough love if you must.

Someone once said to me that you cannot love an individual too much. But you can, and too much love destroys both the giver and the receiver. What greater love can one have than to lay down his life for a friend? Jesus did this. What greater love can one have than to give his life to save another's life? Jesus did this. Through all of this evidence of boundless love, God exercised tough love in our lives when we got off track, and if tough love didn't work, He sometimes suffered us to meet total destruction at the hands of Satan.

Some parents may be a bit confused as to what really constitutes tough love. Love is many things, and there are many other things love is not. Love is not giving your child every material want and not being there; love is not working two jobs to have money to buy expensive, unnecessary apparel and toys for the child; love is not helping your child grow up too fast by letting her exercise adult-like behavior while she is still a child; love is not being a pal to a child, as opposed to being a parent; love is not being overprotective at the expense of your child's independence; love is not believing your child can do no wrong; love is not believing no one can correct your child but you; love is not thinking your child is too cute or smart for you to see her or his bad behavior; love is not permitting your child to speak to you in a disrespectful manner; love is not jeopardizing your own well-being to provide unnecessary comforts for your child, and love is not the failure to stand up for right behavior for fear of displeasing your child. In addition to these, there are lots of other things that love is not, but if you exercise any of the above types of behavior under the guise of showing love, you may be setting the stage for your child to have a disastrous future life.

In essence, you don't love your child if you prepare her for a life of failure. Love doesn't cover up; it opens up. It doesn't prop up wrong at the expense of allowing right to fall down. Love condemns wrong; love rewards; love is friendly; love is forgiving; love is understanding, considerate and attentive. It listens, helps, cares, supports and encourages. It is always there; it inconveniences itself. It is giving; it is sharing. These and more represent ways you exhibit love and these, in addition to others, combined with a right measure of discipline, should result in producing a properly-raised child.

5. Open Ears, Open Eyes and Open Heart

Condemning your child's wrong behavior sends the message to the child that wrong behavior will not be tolerated. Rewarding right behavior with praise and words of encouragement and appreciation gives the child the incentive to strive for the best behavior, as well as accomplishment.

Parent-child relationships should be friendly, without compromising your role as a parent or sending a wrong signal to the child. Be a friend to your child, but not at the expense of being a parent. Friends can confide in each other, and that is good. When your child tells you things, you can get a sense of her thoughts, and it will help you to keep her steered on course. Be forgiving of honest mistakes but not of habitual bad behavior. Listen, try to understand, and be considerate of your child's weak points, and don't expect the impossible. Your child may not be able to do what you think she or he can do.

Watch for and be attentive to your child's habits and moods; you may be able to pick up some off-track behavior brewing. Listen to your child, even when she may be telling that long, uninteresting story. This opens her up to sharing her frustrations and triumphs and makes her feel she has a person to confide in. Don't be too busy to help your child in the little things; it makes her feel she can depend on you for the difficult things. Show her that you care. Take the time to go and support her in those (not-so-important) school performances. While they may not seem important to you, they may be very important to her.

A child will lean on the person she feels is there for her. It is better for her to lean on her parent than to lean on the outsider who offers her cigarettes or drugs. You're one of the supports; that's part of the love. I remember once asking a person why he did drugs in the first place or hung out with those who did. He said to me, "Those people are my friends. They understand me, and I can talk to them."

6. When Buffeted by the Forces of Life

Try to understand your child by listening attentively; she may be saying something she is not able to express in words. Watch your child's behavior; she may be showing you something you're not seeing. Some parents are looking, but they are not seeing. Watch the change in the hairstyle, in the type of clothing, in the sleeping habits, in the exit time and return time, in money spent and money needed, in friends and associates, in school grades or anything else which may indicate something is taking place that needs parental attention. It may require love and/or discipline.

When you exercise the necessary discipline, along with the proper amount of love, your child will certainly be apprehensive concerning the possible consequences of wrong behavior. As my child said to me some months ago, long after she had reached adulthood, "I wasn't afraid of you, but I believed you meant what you said." When you create that type of belief, you, in essence, are creating respect. What a child doesn't fear, she doesn't respect. I can recall a teacher telling us at one of the PTA meetings we attended that she never really had a discipline problem with Celeste. She described her as pleasant, well mannered and a very helpful child. She then went on to describe various things Celeste did to help the teachers, things such as watering the plants. She said if Celeste did anything she thought was wrong, she would say to her, "Please don't tell my father." That was her way of describing the possible wrath (or what she thought the possible wrath) would be.

In spite of the respect born out of the belief that her father meant what he said, Celeste knew that her parents loved her, and that made all the difference in her life. A child's knowing that she has parents who love her can make a world of difference in her behavior and her accomplishments.

I often reflect on my daughter's early childhood, when I might have had cause to spank her, and there were times when I did, because she wasn't a perfect child. No child is perfect. She was a good child, but not a perfect child. I would spank her, and as the tears would be running down her cheeks, because her little feelings would be hurt, I would admonish her to come and hug me. I wanted her to know that even if I had hurt her feelings and maybe her bottom, I still loved her, and she had to continue to love me, because I was her parent and had the responsibility of taking care of her. You must continue giving love, while stressing the point that bad behavior will be punished. That's what the combination is all about—love and discipline—the two pressures to be exerted in a child's life to bend her or him in the required direction.

That direction is straight toward the goal of a successful transition from childhood to adulthood. When a child grows straight, she stays on track and subsequently reaches the expected goal of positive fulfillment, evidenced by a successful transition from childhood to adulthood.

CHAPTER IV

BE IN CHARGE OF YOUR CHILD, NOT THE OTHER WAY AROUND

*Can children really know what to do
or make a better decision than you?
I don't think so; that's why you're there,
to guide them through their every snare.*

Is it better for you to tell a child what to do or for that child to tell you what to do or what she or he is going to do—even if it is against your wishes or better judgment? If a child tells you what to do or what she or he is going to do, you (at the very least) should feel very insulted and helpless. You should also feel that you have lost control. That is not what parents or guardians are supposed to feel. The term *parent* or *guardian* denotes a position as overseer. An overseer usually guides, or oversees, a situation for the purpose of giving direction.

In the role of guardian, a parent must virtually be a dictator, especially in the early stages of a child's growing up—if she or he is to keep control of the parenting situation. It is difficult for two people to talk at the same time, and when you have two opinions on the table, someone must have the final say concerning which opinion is the best opinion or the one that should govern. Should the accepted opinion be the one put forth by your child, rather than the one put forth by you? I don't think so. Opinions and decisions are both a part of the process of raising a child, and it can only be your decision or opinion or the child's decision or opinion. A child's input can be considered, but the ultimate decision must be that of the parent.

Can there be any middle ground? Yes, there can be. But where is the middle ground? Is it that point where the parent and the child argue with each other and scream at each other, or where the child decides sometimes and the parent decides sometimes? That's a "no-man's land." And, as a parent, you never want to go there.

Running a family and directing a child is like a dictator coming into power in a country for the first time—except on a smaller, family, scale. You can't be democratic until you first establish order. Children want to have their way; that's human nature. However, it should be your way, because you are presumed to be in charge and to have the better judgment. So what will it be: the child's way? Your way? Or both? Both spells conflict and confusion.

1. YOU MUST DICTATE

When systems are begun anew, the person taking charge of the new system must be in charge and totally in control. This happens when an old system is overturned by force, either through bloodshed or bloodless means. In such a case, the first order established is usually dictatorial. This dictatorial power is usually wielded by one person. When this initially happens, there is no room for dissent, democratic ideas or idealism. If the person taking control has good intentions and is taking over to affect a better status for the people, she or he will eventually relinquish control to others, in addition to her or him, and will gradually reach a final stage of control by the people for all of those concerned.

At the initial stage of a child's development, a parent must take charge of the child or children, in a manner such as this, so as to be able to control the child and direct the process of development. A parent or parents must be something akin to what we may call a "benevolent dictator."

A dictator is an individual who exercises absolute power, one who assumes absolute control. It is an individual who authoritatively prescribes conduct. A person fitting these characteristics and having a godly manner and intentions should be able to take charge of a child's life and direct it for the greater benefit and good of the child. All parents' or guardians' desire in raising a child should be for the benefit and good of the child. Since children, as children, don't usually know what's good for them or bad for them, parents must take charge in a dictatorial manner. They must be in control of the child and not let the child be in control of them.

There are only three possible scenarios that can take place in the child-raising process: (1.) You tell the child what to do, (2.) The child tells you what she or he will or will not do, or (3.) You both are in dispute or disagreement over what is to be done. In parenting, these are the only choices; there are no more. As a parent, which one would you choose? If you don't choose one, one of the other choices will be thrust upon you by force. You don't need a Ph.D. to realize that a child or children will not choose to let you be in charge, simply because you are the parent.

Some parents are aware of this fact, and they never finished grade school. Some knew this a hundred years ago, and yet they had no formal schooling. Parents should realize that it is within the makeup of one's human nature to want to have her or his way. As adults, we want to have our way also. The difference is: we pay the cost to be the boss.

When it comes to children, it seems that the more educated one gets, the least she or he is able to understand the fact that it is within one's nature to choose one's own way—unless channeled in another direction. The old-fashioned parenting style was a take charge, dictatorial type of parenting that worked and worked very well. If you don't believe it, look at the honesty, respectability and integrity to be found in individuals of generations past. That isn't to say that everyone was honest, respectable and had integrity, but it was true more so of those of prior generations than it is today.

The modern-day parent-child sharing is one, where the parent feels the child should have her input until the possibility of it not working is established. Sometimes that's too late. This doesn't work nearly as well as the old-fashioned method. The procedure that allows too much input from the child in the nurturing process has proven to be a dismal failure, because a child has no knowledge or hands-on experience about life and raising a child. That's one of the reasons "children raising children" is shown to be such a disaster. When you allow your child to decide what the nurturing rules will be, you are letting your child raise her- or himself. And what does a child know about raising herself? Not very much.

This same procedure allows a child too much control in the decisions relative to his or her well-being. If you doubt the fact that this increased child-control in the nurturing of the child has been and continues to be detrimental, look around at the society of today and the social ills that exist, and then compare it to your fore-parents' generation. In comparing, you must be able to admit that something in the child-raising process has changed for the worse. The evident change depicts children out of control, and parents *not* in control. Parents have lost the ability to direct the behavior of their children. They seem unable to direct what children do, what they say, what they wear, who they associate with, what type of entertainment they partake of and on and on and on.

One day I tuned in to a program featuring, "Concerts in the Park." Various artists are featured on the programs, and this one wasn't lacking in the popularity of the featured artist. The featured artist was acceptable as an artist for those who like his brand of entertainment, but that did not include me. However, the accompanying sideshow was very puzzling to me. The gyrations and the movements of the performers were such that in times past they would have been looked on as the epitome of vulgarity. Some of the performers were grossly overweight, and part of their act was to turn their behind to the audience and shake it and move it in a most disgusting and vulgar manner. Needless to say, the audience found this to be entertaining, and it was also broadcast on national TV.

Those performers were somebody's children, and they were improperly raised. They were a part of the behavior of this society that has taken "sex" to its limit. This is the same society that has taken child pornography to its limit. The elements fueling and supporting this behavior were raised by someone. I'm a reasonably intelligent individual, with normal values and morals, but the behavior witnessed today is far beyond the pale in terms of proper behavior. This behavior is the action of improperly-raised children coming from improper parenting.

Too many children are falling short in making a successful transition from childhood into adulthood, and many of those who make the successful transition are unable to sustain a positive footing and remain on track. This is often the result of the weakness in the value system that is being used by modern-day parents in raising their children. Some parents have allowed the child too much input in choosing the right or wrong of life's processes. In many of these cases, children made the wrong choices, and their wrong choices proved destructive—either before adulthood or after reaching adulthood. They didn't ride out of life on track; they fell out of life off track.

BE IN CHARGE OF YOUR CHILD, NOT THE OTHER WAY AROUND

A change is in order. Such a change is probably too late for those parents with children who have already reached an uncontrollable state. Parents have not been able to rehabilitate these children, and neither have the correctional system and penal authorities done such a great job.

Rehabilitation is a word that seems to be on everybody's lips, when it comes to referencing out-of-control individuals. Many of these individuals are scooped up and put in the penal or correctional system, as a means of protecting the functional elements of society from their disruptive behavior. But every time the question comes up: "How are we doing?" we seem to get the same answer: "It doesn't seem to be working." Our society has raised the level of punishment and adopted a modern means for putting criminals to death in the form of lethal injection. We've created "three-strikes-and-you're-out," and we are allocating more and more money for prisons. Still, the resounding cry is: "It's not working!" We have more individuals on death row than ever before, and they are waging lengthy battles to stay their executions, costing the taxpayers hundreds of millions of dollars to keep them away from society, and the resounding cry is still: "It's not working!"

Society is spending larger and larger amounts of money in an effort to rehabilitate off-track individuals, and yet when many of those individuals are thrust back into society, they end up committing the same or worse crimes than before the rehabilitation process was administered. They entered the criminal justice system in the first instance due to bad parental guidance, and in the system they got pointers on how to better perpetrate their criminal behavior, because they exchanged notes with other criminals. The overall tone of our society is so off key that crime types have surfaced that were virtually unheard of in generations past. Today's society is the society of murderous pedophiles, letter bombers, date rapists and serial killers (who kill and eat the victim's organs), child kidnappers on a grand scale and carjackers who often murder. This term *carjackers* had to be invented for today's society; it didn't exist before.

Today's society is a society where individuals take out their anger against the government (and rightfully so), because in today's society the people aren't governed by all elected officials who strive to exhibit honesty and integrity. It's no longer a government of the people, by the people and for the people. Many of our elected officials are pursuing their own agenda and entering into pacts with lobbyists and other elected officials in behavior such as "you scratch my back, and I scratch yours." Politicians are elected, in part, due to the size of their political "war chest." So they are swayed by the desires of the individuals or groups who financially help them get elected. Because of this, honesty and integrity is often removed from the agenda.

These politicians were raised by someone, and I'm afraid that someone so loved their darling son or daughter, until laxity of parenting set in and changed the "proper child" direction. Some of these parents went "south" and soft. So a faction of the citizenry came not to like the government and resorted to blowing up government property. One such incident claimed the lives of one hundred and sixty-eight innocent people in Oklahoma City. The principle perpetrator sat through the trial, hardly showing one glimmer of remorse. Somebody "tried" to raise that child, and I must think that something went terribly wrong in the values and direction given him, in order to generate a level of anger, such that he could seek the destruction of so many individuals who were unrelated to the cause of his frustrations.

We can kill the rest of those men, and maybe they deserve to die, but I'm not so sure it will dramatically change the direction toward which generations of children are headed. One thing is certain, if those individuals are put to death, they will no longer be around to commit a similar act in the future. However, the possibility exists that other such children are in the making, because other bad parenting styles are still being used. Children are out of control, and parents are no longer in control.

It isn't at all surprising that not many parents seem able to rescue out-of-control children once they reach this stage. The punishment and corrective procedures required to be executed by the parents to possibly bring a child back in line would, no doubt, be construed by the law as "child abuse." Some of these children have been out of control since seven or eight years of age, and all that may be required is a good strapping, or a curtailing of the activities that bring the child some of her enjoyment, or taking away some of the benefits that are befitting the child.

I was watching an account on television about a student who was grounded from playing football by his parents, because of his grades and attitude. The child would sneak out the window and go to practice football anyway. That tells you two things: (1.) The parents were not in control, and (2.) The parents had no idea what the child was doing. I guess whatever the parents may have wanted to do would have been considered child abuse. Maybe the parents should have killed him then, because the law enforcement system is likely to kill him later.

BE IN CHARGE OF YOUR CHILD, NOT THE OTHER WAY AROUND

Lawmakers have passed laws restricting parents and guardians from executing punishment that the courts consider cruel and abusive, but when the child is out of control and runs afoul of the law, policemen often execute punishment that is ten times more cruel and abusive than what most parents would have administered. Policemen often kick children in the backside with heavy boots, virtually destroy children's brains by beating them about the head with a heavy instrument called a "billy-club" or "nightstick," put their foot on children's necks, put chokeholds on children and snuff out their life and shoot them in the back, face or side to end their life. Would you, as a parent, do this to your child? Most parents would not. Would it not be better for you to start early and take charge of your child, before she or he gets off-track and ends up in the hands of law enforcement?

When some children misbehave, parents sometime restrict them from attending their favorite social pastime and ground them from going out, except to do necessary chores and school. They often even feel bad about that and eventually lift the restriction early. When a child is restricted, it is presumed that he or she has exercised off-track behavior and deserves the restriction. The child may not think she or he deserves it, but who cares what the child thinks? You should be calling the shots and making the judgment decisions.

When a child gets far enough out of control, a judge will sentence him to jail, where the repercussions are much more far-reaching, and the environment is much harsher than that encountered in the home. In jail, your child may be subjected to beatings much harsher than you might have meted out. Jail inmates are often victims of rape by other, stronger prisoners. The child will be completely separated from his friends and family, because they are not likely to be there. The jailhouse food may not always be good. Freedom of movement is severely restricted, and your child (depending on the severity of the crime) may never return to society again. Your child may even die in jail, either from lesser causes, or from homicide.

As a parent, you need to envision this possibility when you're sparing the rod and spoiling your child. You need to envision this possibility when you're allowing your child to take control, rather than you exercising control. The main purpose for your taking charge is to direct the child in the formation of positive behavior patterns and values.

This doesn't, in any way, advocate child abuse. Some of the things considered child abuse today were mild punishment in years past, and the law had no thought of interfering. Parental discipline was much harsher in those days. Was it wrong? In most cases it was not. It was difficult for the child, and it, in most cases, worked to redirect the child away from a life of future trouble. Some children didn't adhere to the discipline and ended up in trouble with the law or dead. In those days, there were also some parents who were lax in upholding their parental responsibility. There is no reason to assume that all parents were on target in those days, and all parents of today's society are not.

In those days, not only would the law not interfere in the disciplining process, but few if any parents would have permitted any outsider to tell them how to discipline their children. None would have dared to try to tell my father not to whip his child—if he saw fit to do it. And if the police had told me not to hit my child, I probably would have completely ignored any such police instructions. If she had called the police on me or threatened to, she probably would have wished she'd never done that. One thing I know: if you don't discipline your child properly today, the police will improperly do it some other day. Then she or he may wish she had accepted your discipline, but it will be too late. Many belligerent children have been shot down by the police or spent their life in jail or been legally executed by the State or Federal government.

Most parents' intentions in disciplining the child aren't to abuse the child. The desire is to administer punishment befitting the bad behavior. Many of the child abuse cases being perpetrated today are at the hands of mentally unbalanced or drug-affected parents. No normal parent would require a child to drink a fatal concoction, as a disciplinary procedure, and no normal parent would put a child in a hot oven as a disciplinary procedure. Neither would a normal parent burn a child's hand on a hot stove, just to teach the child a lesson.

I do remember cases of parents who washed their child's mouth out with soap for speaking in unacceptable language, but soap didn't kill children. It wouldn't have been my method, but that may not have been the worst type of punishment a parent could administer. I remember parents (including my own) who gave children caster oil if they sounded like they were about to come down with a cold. That was like executing child abuse, but it purged a child's system from the onslaught of germs—which may have made her ill.

Today's society needs to begin getting to the real problem of child abuse, which may not be about normal parents disciplining their child. It may be about abnormal individuals who have been thrust into the role of parenting. It was not expected nor intended that these individuals would ever function normally or be mentally stable enough to procreate and properly nurture a child. Many individuals such as these don't have the capacity to properly take care of themselves, let alone take care of a child. But we can't restrict these individuals from engaging in the activity that sometimes brings children into the world, so we pass legislation that impacts the normal parent and the abnormal parent alike in their ability to discipline their children. The law applies, in a similar fashion, to the drug-affected parent, and also to the parent operating as a normal individual.

The professional elements of our society know this all too well. Studies have clearly documented the effects that drugs have had on an individual's ability to function within the normal realm of expectation. These individuals also bear children sometimes. However, child abuse cannot be legislated away. Child abuse is an abnormal, out-of-control form of behavior. I shudder to think that legislators are telling us that most of our society is either abnormal or out of control, therefore we must have laws to deal with their abnormality.

Passing laws doesn't always restrict or prevent abnormal behavior. It only punishes the person who commits the infraction, and that person may not have had the capacity to avoid it in the first instance. Normal parents who desire to apply hard and firm discipline that may work and prevent children from becoming wards of society are restricted, because the laws of society have determined that some discipline methods used in previous generations are considered child abuse today. Many of the parents of my generation, my parents' generation, their parents' generation and prior generations would have been considered child abusers by today's standards. But those parents considered what they did to be raising children properly, and the fruits of their beliefs are evident in the caliber of children they brought to adulthood.

Many of the old-timers who are running today's institutions are products of that type of so-called harsh, strict discipline, and it didn't kill them. It made them better men and women, and society was better served thereby. Yesterday's society could probably not have been built with the caliber of some of the individuals being nurtured by today's standards. What it took to survive in those days was probably more than what most of the children of today's society have. We are required to use human resources made up of those who can't read, can't write, can't spell, can't concentrate, can't show up on time for work and have no desire to give an honest day's work for an honest day's pay. That's the result of the nurturing process of today's parents. They weren't in control, and the results speak for themselves.

Our society, along with the help of the Civil Liberties Union, may have helped to bring some parents to where they are today. However, no society, nor the Civil Liberties Union, told future parents to do drugs or engage in promiscuous sex or to accept a gay lifestyle, but the society set the type of climate that indicated it was okay to do those things. The Civil Liberties Union was partly instrumental in taking prayer out of schools, and any society that abandons God abandons good moral persuasion and direction and is headed toward moral collapse.

At this point, the visible parallels are frightening, and I'm afraid we are almost there. Our founding fathers had some religious principles that, at the least, included God. Our present society (in America) is afraid to mention God, for fear of offending someone who doesn't want America's God, someone who worships a god that is a product of where they came from. There is nothing wrong with our country being a melting pot, but should we allow those in the pot to make us abandon all of the things that were once dear to us? We seem to be doing just that, and our children are suffering because of it.

We are also suffering, because we are losing our children to the streets. However, those parents who have not yet entered the nurturing stream or who are just entering the nurturing stream (parents of a one-year old) have a chance to get control and keep control of the child. If you want to be in charge of your child tomorrow, you must take charge of him today. You don't have the luxury of waiting until tomorrow. You must take charge from the cradle, and this applies to any child.

A child is a child, and has the tendencies and makeup of a child. It doesn't matter who you are. You can be black, white, yellow, red, brown or any other color, but the offspring you produce will still be a child possessing the instincts and characteristics of a child. You can be American, European, Asian, African, Australian, a New Zealander or any other nationality on planet Earth, and your offspring, when he or she enters the world, will be a child.

Hopefully, the child will have normal development of sense mechanisms. This child, just as all other children, will be labeled as a child within the human family structure and will need the same direction, guidance, discipline and care as any other child within the human family. Guidance is both physical and verbal and involves speaking, teaching, demonstrating, helping, leading, loving, approving, disapproving, compelling, restraining, punishing and sometimes ignoring. But there are two basic things that all of the children will need, and those are love and discipline.

The proportions must be measured, and how you mete them out depends on the personality of the child. All of the other basic and enhanced needs will grow out of the fact that you love them, and the degree of exhibited love will grow out of the extent to which you need to discipline them. Love can't be shown in the place of necessary discipline, and discipline can't be shown in the place of love.

Discipline comes in various forms, and those forms may have some relationship to ethnic and cultural background. However, the end results must be the same, and that is to raise a child who is capable of making the transition from childhood into adulthood intact.

You must start early. Your authority must be asserted at the earliest possible stage of development in a child's life. The child must understand from the beginning who is in charge, and thereafter until she reaches the point at which she is on her own. The child must be directed by you, not you be directed by the child.

2. Who Is in Charge?

Children aren't born belligerent nor obstinate nor difficult. They may possess those tendencies, but they're allowed to get to that point by parents who fail to take charge forcefully and early. Children are allowed to take on those characteristics by parents who fail to apply enough disciplinary pressure. Parents should be able to make an early assessment of the disciplinary needs of each child, and the needs of each will likely be different, because of personality differences. God made us that way as children, and that is what characterizes us as individuals–each uniquely different.

In a multi-child household, each child is different than each other child, and the parent must recognize the differences early on. In the neighborhood, your child is uniquely different than the neighbor's child in many ways, and especially in his or her personality and temperament. That is why the nurturing process has to be continuously adjusted and readjusted to fit the temperament of the child, who is constantly exposed to environmental forces around her. You must recognize the existence of the environment outside of your household, reinforce the positive forces within your household and repel the negative forces acting on your child from outside of your household—if you are to keep control over the nurturing process.

Parents sometime need to adjust their temperament to meet the conditions imposed upon them by a child's temperament. A soft parent can be taken over and rendered "not in control" by an obstinate child. A parent that is too strict may damage the personality of a mild-mannered child. We must know and understand the individuality of each of our children and apply control procedures accordingly. Some children may only respond to corporal punishment to bring them under control. With other children, raising the voice two octaves will bring them under control, and with others, a certain look will give the needed message.

Parents should always be aware that corporal punishment has a place in our society, and let us make no mistake in realizing that fact. I was recently speaking to a young mother, whose children are very much under control. She majored in nursing education in college, and her husband majored in engineering. They have three girls. One is still an infant, and the other two are a bit older. The children are a model example of good parenting skills. Love and discipline engulf their entire being. They are so sweet, so well mannered that you could take them for your own.

We implied to the mother that she would make a good teacher. She immediately responded, "No, if I can't spank them, I can't teach them." She recognized that teaching and spanking may sometimes go hand in hand. At the very least, she was implying that children may sometimes need spanking. For some children, the only way we will be able to bring them under control is to execute this type of punishment on a regular basis, or as needed. Corporal punishment should not and need not be abusive, but it should be meant to make a child feel uncomfortable. It should hurt to the extent that the child would rather not commit the infraction, if it subjects him or her to the pain borne out of the punishment.

Some children are difficult and determined. I know because I came from a family of twelve, and we all had various personalities, as would be expected. Some of my siblings were very difficult and determined, but my mama and daddy were even more difficult and determined. Some children may be able to bear the pain of corporal punishment once a year; others may be able to bear it once a month; still others may be able to bear it once a week and I've heard of difficult children who needed that form of punishment every single day. The extent to which a child is willing to suffer the pain of punishment depends on the trade-off he or she is trying to obtain for getting her or his way or in controlling a situation. My response is: "Whatever it takes!"

It is strange that some laws attempt to legislate how we can punish our own children, but they permit law enforcement officers to do to them what we are not allowed to do. This implies that parents don't have the sense, or common judgment, to properly discipline their child. Some parents may not, but law enforcement officers certainly can't know our children's needs better than we do. Some parents may be mentally compromised, but so are some law enforcement officers. Some of them suffer from the same psychosis as some parents, so they aren't in any better position to discipline our children than are we. Discipline should be left to competent parents.

I've witnessed small children acting completely out of control, and the parent smacked them lightly on the backside over a padding of clothing. Obviously, that wasn't painful and didn't serve to bring the child back into line. Parents who do this as punishment are only playing games with themselves and the child, because as one of the sayings of life states, "No pain, no gain." When my father executed punishment, he only needed to do it once or twice in your life. That was enough for you to know beyond any reasonable doubt that you didn't want it again. And you knew that the only way to avoid it was to not commit that infraction or not be out of control in that area.

My mother and father were always in control of us and never had any qualms about executing whatever punishment they deemed necessary—corporal or otherwise. I think if one of us had done something bad enough, my father would probably have just killed that one and put him or her in the grave. In stature, I stand about five feet, ten and a half inches, and weigh in at about a hundred and sixty-five pounds. My father was that size or maybe a bit smaller. Still, I can recall that he was quite a strong individual and could "beat the devil out of you."

We thought he was a giant. It wasn't until I got to be an adult that I realized my father wasn't very big. Still, he wielded power and respect in his household. My father would deal with you in whatever area you got out of control—unless my mother dealt with you first. And even if mother dealt with you first, my father would sometimes add a little reinforcement to let you know, in no uncertain terms, that they (not you) were in control.

Our parents always controlled their children. You were never in control as long as you lived in their home. If you were out of the home and came back into their presence, they still exercised some control over you. If you wanted to be in control of your life as an adult, you didn't come around my parents with behavior they didn't agree with. You didn't drink alcoholic beverages around them, you didn't smoke around them, you didn't curse around them, you didn't dance around them (unless it was as worship to God), and you didn't gamble around them or bring another man or woman around them who wasn't your husband or wife (if you were married). When we were growing up, we couldn't lie to our parents and hope not be punished if they found out about it. They had control, and they were in charge.

When you're in charge in your parenting, you should know what's going on in your household and have a good idea what your children are up to at any given time. Nothing should be private and off limits to your awareness. There should be no "closed door" policy in your house.

There are some things which may not be readily discernible, but in most cases there will be signs alerting you to what is going on—especially if you are parenting as you should be and are properly monitoring your child's life and activities. If you are not parenting in this manner, you may one day live to regret it. You may one day exclaim, "I didn't know that!"

This brings to mind various accounts of teen pregnancies, where children resided in the same house with a parent, progressed to a term of eight to nine months (and some to the point of delivery), and yet it was said that the parent was not even aware of the child's pregnancy. That's really "out of it." The parent or parents *should* have been aware. These parents (without a doubt) had to be completely "out of touch" with reality. How, on God's earth, could a parent interact with a child in the same household, virtually on a daily basis, and not know that she was eight months, five months, or even three months pregnant?

Pregnant woman usually always have some symptoms that are quite noticeable and don't fit into any normal category. I'm neither a doctor, nor a female, but my common sense tells me that "all" pregnant women must have some symptom or symptoms that gives them away. They may not all be physical, but there must be some indicative changes in the physical, the dress, the moods, the attitude or any number of other signals that would indicate something unusual is going on. The signs may not say, "She's pregnant," but they should say something is going on which requires looking into. Not all pregnant women may have all of the same symptoms or in the same severity, but do any of them not have any symptoms at all? What happens when your child says, "I don't want to eat because I don't feel well?" Do you just say "Okay, you can be excused to go to your room?"

When we were growing up, if a child expressed feelings of some type of illness, our parents wanted to know what was going on, and if it persisted, the child was taken to the doctor. If the child was female and showed or expressed any signs of nausea or upset stomach (especially if she was at childbearing age), the primary suspicion would probably have been pregnancy. That would surely get the female a trip to the doctor's office. I've known of accounts when a girl was taken to the doctor by her mother, and after examination, the mother was told that the child was pregnant. Some children still tried to deny it—even after the doctor had confirmed it.

In reflecting on this pregnancy situation, it was said that one child wore a certain style of baggy clothes the whole time, and this clothing concealed the evidence of her pregnancy. That should be another reason to condemn those ugly, baggy clothes. I don't care who designs them or who they are designed for. Today's children would say individuals like me are "behind the times." I could very well be, and I don't mind accepting that label. These same children would say you're behind the times if you're not in agreement with all of their other bad behavior—exhibited in song, dress, language and other antisocial activity.

Should not the parent have asked the child why she always dressed in that manner—especially if it was a change from her prior norm? If you're a guardian, witnessing a change that is negative and constant, how could you not ask what it means? If you're a mother, and your daughter is not showing any evidence of having a normal, expected menstrual cycle, do you have no way of knowing it? Can your daughter be impacted by the usual accompanying discomforts and mood swings, and you not wonder what's going on?

The parents in this particular case didn't know, and the child refused to admit to having done anything that would bring about pregnancy. Maybe she wanted the mother to think she was very holy, as was Mary, the mother of Jesus. Some children denied it all the way to the strap, and even after every blow of the strap.

A TABLESPOON OF LOVE, A TABLESPOON OF DISCIPLINE

In most cases, they surely got a strapping, for this behavior was considered to be "gross misconduct." In the old days, very few parents took that sitting down. In today's society, parents (like children) seem to have no shame. Nothing embarrasses them. The love for the "darling daughter" outweighs any feeling of shame or regret for what the child has done. In generations past, that type of behavior would have brought tears to most mothers' eyes, and most mothers would have hung their head in sorrow. This doesn't mean it didn't happen, and it doesn't mean it should have been the end of the world. But there was some redeeming value in feeling remorseful over such behavior. Today, it has come to be so commonplace that it is looked upon as just an ordinary process of living life.

Some women actually make conscious choices to have a baby by a man they neither love nor desire to marry. There seems to be something not quite correct in this thinking. Maybe it points to the moral position of today's society, and maybe that position isn't all good. For our part, there is some redeeming value in being forgiving and understanding. God wants us to be, but maybe our understanding has reached the point of condoning. Looking at the moral condition of our society today, should we not, at the least, wonder if we should be so accepting of bad behavior?

None of us should attempt to play God or be judges, but I wonder if it is positive to be so understanding. Where should we draw a line? All families won't be "atomic" families, and we should not cast out any individual who bears a child, void of being part of a conventional marriage. However, the practice of doing this has become so ingrained in our society that it has virtually come to be acceptable social behavior. So-called "role models" are doing it, and the behavior is being repeated generation after generation after generation.

Having children out of wedlock has become an integral part of other morally misdirected behavior, and that's a problem. And, when a problem is presented, everyone wants to know what the solution is. The solution is for parents to begin properly parenting again. If we don't start, I'm afraid our society may be finished. The American society is gradually getting to the moral point of no return. This came about because parents lost control three generations ago. Great civilizations have crumbled under the weight of moral degradation, so we must wake up before it's too late.

We endeavored, with all of our being, to keep control of our parenting requirements in raising our child. We endeavored to be on top of things, and our child had no cause to rebel against our directing her life. Celeste, our child, was easy. I'm not saying she was a totally docile child with a totally agreeable personality. She had her ways, and she will tell you she inherited a hot temper from her father. It may be true. I certainly had a temper that, more than once, put me on the verge of going to jail, but when it was our turn to parent, we could not allow Celeste to act out her hot temper at our expense, and my parents had not allowed me to do it to them either.

Celeste was obstinate at times, and had a determination in her personality that had to be directed by a greater sense of determination in her parents' personality. We had to be in control of her, because you can't direct what you don't control. Celeste received corporal punishment, maybe twice from me and maybe once from her mother. That was all she needed in that area. It wasn't abusive, but it sufficiently addressed the behavior.

As children growing up, we didn't get many bouts of corporal punishment from our father. We probably could not have withstood any more than he had to administer. We received more from our mother, because she was around more to witness our infractions. And she didn't play either. She was on your case and was always in control.

Because they were firm with us, most of the time, my father only had to speak the word, and the message was loud and clear. Whatever it was about the corporal punishment worked in us children. The elements contained in the act of corporal punishment embraced discipline in keeping a child on track, and that was necessary in the process of successful parenting. It kept us from a life of crime and drugs, created in us a fear of God and His wrath, and gave us a respect for our elders. It gave us a strong drive, a sense of determination, and those of us who duplicated the process were in control of our children. We also gave them the same sense of focus and direction.

Control directs, direction shapes, and shape determines. You may wonder what all this means. It meant that most of us twelve children finished college, all but two came to know and serve God, and none of us served time in jail for committing a crime. That's a good record of parenting.

3. All Social Systems Dictate

Controlling or being in control isn't unique to a parent-child relationship. It is existent in all of the entities within the systems of our society. Even in a democracy, the people don't rule, although they are presumed to have input into the laws and ideals that mirror our wishes and desires. In our democratic society, we elect others who are supposed to speak for the majority opinion, but quite often the legislation that comes out voices the desires and opinions of the legislators, and not the desires and the opinions of the people. This should not be and is different than the family unit, in that the family unit has hands-on control, and is intended to serve absolutely the good of the one being controlled or directed.

For any social system to function properly, it must have rules and guidelines that must be adhered to and followed, because if it doesn't, the system will fail and not be able to satisfy the need for which it was established. Many, if not all of these social systems affect our lives and the lives of our children in some way and at some point in our lives. Some of these systems are established to nurture us and prepare us for success or well-being in the other areas of our lives. They are intended to put us on track. Others are intended to punish us for not staying on track, and maybe to call our attention to the error of our ways, so that we may be able to get back on track, if we find ourselves off track.

Among the social systems our children may encounter in growing up are: caregivers (other than parents), preschools and kindergartens, elementary school, high school, college, the military, jobs, law enforcement, the streets and life in general—for all who live to face it. All of these systems operate in a dictatorial manner, in that they are all inclined to dictate, or command. That is what the dictionary says *dictatorial* means. In addition, it is a reasonable assumption that they must be in absolute control of what they are doing, so as to achieve desired goals. This is true with some of these entities, more so than with others.

We must be in control of our children, to prepare them for a smooth interaction within the system of those entities mentioned, which they may need to pass through. All those systems have rules, and if a child resists playing by the rules of some of them, she may find herself at odds with that entity and may be unable to reap the benefits needed or expected to be derived. If the child resists playing by the rules of others, she may find herself up against a system that can turn her life upside down and cause her more pain than she is prepared to endure.

There are certain modes of behavior and demeanor that speak an international language. If a child is raised with and by those, she will possess the ability to traverse the road of life in good form. That mode of behavior is what a child might get from a parent who is in control of the child, rather than the child being in control. A child who is raised in an environment that is controlled by her or his parents or guardians may have what will be necessary to successfully pass through the institutions of life and come out in good form, equipped to live life in a positive mode. That child will be prepared to navigate the systems of life and acquire those things that will be of great value to her or him in future years.

4. The Systems of Life

The systems of life begin with God—whether you choose to believe it or not. God was there before the beginning and in the beginning. He is there now, and will be there throughout all of the ages of eternity. He is the author of and the ruler over the universe. He gives us rules and dictates a code of behavior through His Word, the Bible. For those who are disobedient and fail to adhere to the dictates of His Word, a price is paid, and the punishment can hurt severely.

His dictates are as true as they are spoken, and to go against the dictates of God is to operate within the realm of sinful man. The Bible says, *"The wages [or payment] of sin is death"* (Romans 6:23). This means, not only, that we can die today for our sins, but also that we will die throughout the ages of eternity.

The second of life's systems is the family. Each family member is an individual, and each has her or his own set of rules for another person or child to play by, or that child will not be able to interact in harmony with the other members of the family. Some of the family members grow up and obtain their own space. If another child enters the space of this family member, he or she has to play by the rules. Otherwise that sibling may prefer the child not come around again. Therefore, the child must be well-behaved and respectable of others and their property.

The third of life's systems can be those in the care-giving area, other than a parent or guardian. This person would have no desire to care for a child who is out of control. An out-of-control child has poor discipline habits, which includes disobedience, disruptive and destructive behavior. That child doesn't follow instructions, causes trouble and destroys property. That type of child doesn't fit well in another person's space, nor is she or he easily managed by the caregiver. The caregiver would probably not be desirous of overseeing the welfare of that child.

5. SCHOOLING

Moving out into the public system of life, a child's first encounter will be with the school system. This is one of the larger of life's systems, and has a strict set of rules and guidelines that vary from institution to institution, but all having basic rules that require a child to, at the very least, be manageable or controllable. An out-of-control child would so disrupt the system that she or he would not be able to remain in mainstream education. Since a child under a certain age is required to attend school or be home-schooled, there is no choice but to school the child, if you don't have the aptitude to home-school her or him. Since the child must be schooled, she should be prepared to do it in as smooth a manner as possible.

If a child doesn't properly and successfully negotiate the school system, she or he may, and usually does find herself or himself outside of mainstream education, in trouble with the law and unsuccessful at making the transition from childhood to adulthood. A child entering the school system must be prepared to obey the rules of the institution, be attentive to what is being taught and strive to obtain a successful transition from grade to grade until the cycle of required education is completed.

The school system begins with kindergarten. This is a preschool format that is meant to prepare a young child for the transition into the main school environment—the first grade—emotionally and academically. It is somewhat of a midpoint between a child leaving the confines of his parents' or caregiver's all-day-care environment, and the mainstream school environment, which usually takes the child away from home all day. The overseer of this environment is likely to be a total stranger and less involved with loving care than with the desire and responsibility of getting a job done. The kindergarten environment is meant to slowly wean the child from the need and desire to be around the parent or caregiver and cause her to function comfortably in another setting—the first-grade setting.

In this kindergarten environment, children are also exposed to some of the basic things that will be a part of the everyday environment when the child reaches first grade. Some children may leave home and go directly to first grade. Most others go through the kindergarten process. Whether a child does or does not, the most important thing is that the child is ready for the first grade experience and is able to handle the challenges it may present. The purpose of the school environment is to teach the child the basics of interacting with others, the skills needed to continue in the learning environment until enough intellect is acquired to satisfy her or his own needs. The school environment also introduces and reinforces those things that should be introduced at home, such as basic hygiene, caring for one's own property and the property of others, sharing and interacting with other children and a mutual respect for those who share her or his surroundings.

The focus is to develop a child mentally, physically, emotionally and socially. In addition, there is a creative side to every child, although the nature of the creativity varies from child to child. This creativity must be nurtured and developed. It is therefore important for a parent or guardian to have begun introducing these processes to the child before the child enters first grade, otherwise the child may find herself unable to adjust to the foreign atmosphere at the expected pace. A parent who is in control will probably have prepared the child for this first-grade transition.

The child should have the necessary independence at this stage to be able to exist away from the parent without crying and to settle down in the teacher's care. The child should be trained in the basic functions of eating habits and bathroom requirements. The child should know the basics relative to respect and obedience to those who will have authority over her or him. She or he should also know the basics of following instructions. Knowing these basic skills will enable the child to smoothly make the transition from the parents' home to the school or the first grade.

As the child progresses from the first grade through the upper grades, the basic teachings above will be reinforced and enlarged to fit the needs of the growing and developing child. The home environment is the place where children should be taught the basics of life. The purpose of the school environment is to educate the child in the skills of reading, writing and arithmetic. Those were once the building blocks of the learning process, and are still the most necessary requirements—if a child is to be prepared to master the more advanced levels of education. At one stage, schools endeavored to move away from the basics, but the caliber of children exiting the educational system told educators they needed to begin getting back to these basics.

Educators have now introduced calculators for use in the school system, and children can use them to figure out the needed answers. We weren't even allowed to use calculators in college. Was the introduction of calculators intended to make children brighter and more scientific? Or was it expected to make it easier to teach math? I tutored children who had access to these calculators, and I'm here to report that they were no more advanced then we were three or four generations ago. The mere fact that they were in a math "help" class is evidence that the scientific approach didn't help much.

I took these children back to the basics of math—the multiplication tables and other basics, and it proved more helpful than the calculators. The problem with the world is the fact that everyone is trying to get away from the basics, especially in America. The problem with children is the fact that the basic parenting techniques are no longer employed. You can't spank children, because it damages their self-esteem. That is nothing more than a lie from the pit of the psychology books. I was strapped when I needed it, and my self-esteem is very much intact.

As a matter of fact, I think my self-esteem is better for my having been raised as I was. All of my siblings appear to have very high self-esteem, and we were all whipped. Rose, the parent mentioned in the earlier part of this book, strapped her son, and it didn't appear to damage his self-esteem one bit. Even at a young age, he is an animator of note and has demonstrated his abilities in various well-known films. He feels great about himself and has given motivational talks to other striving young people. It wasn't just about him; he had on-track parenting.

I was reflecting on a politically-savvy grandmother who raised four sons virtually alone (as the story was told), and one grew up to become a presidential spokesman, two are attorneys of note, and the other headed up a large and important government agency. That success has to speak to good parenting, and good parenting comes without a price. It only requires a desire.

There is nothing wrong with the past three generations of children that fell apart—except the fact that poor parenting was in charge. Parents got away from the basics and became too scientific and too psychological. They tried to raise children by the science and psychology books. Three generations ago many parents could hardly spell nor pronounce "psychology" —not to mention using it to raise their children by. Psychology seemed to have been unable to speak to where good parenting could go, but spoke to where bad parenting had been. And even then, the real issues were not addressed. It appears that we are living in an era when children are being shortchanged from the cradle to the grave, and they are also reaching the grave much earlier through self-destruction.

BE IN CHARGE OF YOUR CHILD, NOT THE OTHER WAY AROUND

I believe, beyond any reasonable doubt, that parents bear the greatest responsibility for what children do or do not become. I'm a living example and can point to many more from my parents' generation and even from the generation of today. If the parents do it properly, children will do it properly. Parents must believe this and stop the "blame game," passing the buck and making excuses for the failure of their child.

Things outside of the sphere of educational skills should need only to be reinforced at school. Teachers are operating within a limited time frame and have neither the time nor the patience to teach those things that should be taught at home. Parents, who have been in control of the child from the beginning, have given the child discipline, among the other basics, and this discipline is likely to and expected to carry through, as the child negotiates the systems of life. A disciplined child is more easily taught than one who lacks discipline, and a disciplined child integrates more smoothly into the social and learning environment.

As the child passes from grade school and junior high (if this is the case) to high school, he or she will need to have the basic disciplines intact, as well as others that are introduced at different levels of maturity. These will include the ability to get along with others in the spirit of team play. In high school, a child is being introduced to life's requirements of being able to be part of a team, because in life "No man is an island." The idea of persistence and determination will begin to come full circle in high school, because all children will be challenged in ways they may not have encountered before. It is only the child who has been strengthened with an attitude of persistence and determination who will succeed when the chips are down and the odds are against her. Life determines that "only the strong survive."

An undisciplined child may have her or his learning direction severely compromised. A selfish child will have fewer friends and associates. A child who has been permitted to have his way at home may become totally frustrated and disappointed, because the environment of life is not the environment of home, and the child may find it difficult to have her or his way. Those in life may not give in to the child, as a sibling or parent would. Others in life may also wish to have their way, and it is impossible for every person to triumph in her or his own will in the same environment, because forces are all pulling against each other.

A child who has not been disciplined in truth and honesty will likely run into conflict with his peers, and those responsible for his intellectual development. Dishonesty threatens to surface every time one needs a prop to get by, through a road block or beyond a challenge. At a juncture such as that, one grabs for any available source of help. Cheating, lying or stealing always seem to be available options for a person inclined toward that type of behavior. They appear to be the easiest way out of a situation. Though it appears to be, it is probably not, because the price paid, if one is caught, usually far outweighs the benefits to be derived, and the odds of not being found out in dishonest endeavors are very slim.

Children, over the years, have been caught cheating on exams and even pilfering exam papers. They never expected to get caught. Very few individuals (if any) have ever been able to plan the perfect crime, because none can ever know the subtle ramifications of his actions. Part of the subtle unknowns has to do with what others may think or do, and one cannot always predict another's response to a given situation. Honesty is a discipline and a strong virtue to be taught and reinforced by parents. Those who have authority over children, beginning with parents, don't like to be tricked, fooled or misled.

A child who has not been taught good virtues and to care about herself in the areas of upright character will often be shunned by peers. Manners and appearance are essential in character building and in the establishment of good self-esteem in a child. The lack of self-esteem can weigh heavily on a child and often lead her to compromise other values. Some institutions require children to demonstrate, in their appearance, that they take pride in themselves. It is often one of the rules and requirements of attending such an institution.

Leadership is another virtue that will go far in the development of a child for the successes of life. If a child has not been disciplined in the qualities of leadership, she will either be a follower or sit on the sidelines. There are only three courses to take in life relative to getting things done: You either lead, follow or watch. Some people make things happen, others watch things happen, and still others ask what happened.

Why should a child develop leadership qualities in the final stages of education? It will have much to do with the leadership qualities she or he will carry onto the stage of adult life. If a child has leadership qualities, they will likely have manifested themselves in one way or another by the time she enters and settles down to college life. Many of the leaders of yesterday and today exhibited their leadership potential in college. Some were former class presidents and vice-presidents, and others headed various college or-ganizations and groups. Others got involved in things that were new to the surroundings, taking on the task of being a forerunner of change. Those individuals took these same qualifications to the post-college job, and the promotion and eventually the summons to become department head, or to be in some other position of leadership in the private or government sector.

Discipline your child in leadership. Stress the importance of being a leader. It's a worthwhile quality to be out front in positive matters. Those who can lead do lead, and those who can't follow.

The transition from high school to college is the prelude to the last stepping-stone prior to walking into the circle of adult life. College is the forum where all of the discipline and prior acquired learning will come together and be tied neatly in one bundle. This can be the setting for life's final proving ground. At no other place, except maybe the military and in life itself, will the disciplines of honesty, perseverance and leadership be more meaningful.

Many students have been known to virtually copy their way through college. A part of these will end up as incompetents in their profession, and another part will be discovered and thrown out of school for lack of integrity and a breach of the rules. This may follow them through life and prevent them from ever reaching the pinnacle of life's possibilities. It could prevent them from achieving that one accomplishment, which may have otherwise been there for them.

Perseverance is the one quality that is most needed by all students. For those who are striving to just get by, they need to persevere to complete the endeavor. For those students who are striving to be at the top of their graduating class, perseverance is needed to stay in the top competition, because the one you're competing against is always striving to beat you to the goal. You aren't allowed to slack off in the striving, because the other person will not likely be slowing down. It is only through perseverance that you can have the possibility of achieving your desired goal.

6. THE MILITARY

Not all children will grow up and become a part of the military. The modern-day climate of the military consists of a virtual all-volunteer armed forces. That may likely be the climate for the foreseeable future, unless world ideology changes in such a way as to put nations at each other's throats again. Since the military is pseudo-voluntary, it is likely that those who feel a common connection with the ideology, discipline and requirements of the military will be the ones who will become a part of it. However, these children should be aware of the fact that the military can make a person or break a person.

Those who have the discipline to undergo the training and accept authority (virtually without question) can possibly go through a stint in the military, come out with an honorable discharge and add a positive flavor to life's opportunities and possibilities. Others, who may not be able to do this, could end up with "bad time" or be dismissed from the military with less than an honorable discharge, maybe causing a blight to hang over their career for the balance of their life.

There are some glaring qualities a child must possess that speak loudly and are absolutely necessary, if a child is going to successfully negotiate a career in the military. Without a doubt, a child must be able to take orders and not question the authority of the one giving the orders, or the source of the orders—if that person has charge of him or her. If a child has not been taught to respect authority and obey the one who has rule over him or her, that child is likely to have a difficult and unsuccessful stint in the military and will, more than likely, leave it a failure.

Another positive, but not required discipline is leadership. A child who has been disciplined in leadership will likely accomplish more, and go further in the military. In the military, you can be a good leader or a good follower, and being either, you will likely exit the military with honor.

There are some other subtle qualities a child may not have been taught, that may seem unimportant to the child, but could prove to be the very things needed to make a military life less challenging. They are qualities such as neatness, organization and good moral direction. The military is an institution that stresses neatness, and organization is required to meet the standards expected and demanded.

In the area of neatness, periodic inspections are conducted, to make sure uniforms are neat, clean, in order and serviceable. For a child inclined toward this type of behavior, the efforts to meet military demands in this area will be less challenging.

Organization is also of utmost importance in successfully training for the myriad of tasks and assignments that may be put upon one to perform as a part of his or her military profession. The military requires one to be organized and orderly, which are interchangeable disciplines; to be organized means to be orderly. A child raised to be orderly would find the task of making the transition from civilian life to military life easier than it would be for a disorganized individual.

I guess one would wonder what moral direction has to do with the military. After all, one of the reasons for joining the military is to see the world and get the chance to meet different people. Well, as you're touring the world and meeting all those different people, bad moral direction can get one negatively involved with the wrong individual, and that could render one seriously ill or even dead from disease or treachery. Good moral direction teaches one to mind his or her moral business and steer clear of health troubles and safety issues.

High moral standards can go far in maintaining the health and well-being of a military person. An individual entering the military may not give much thought to moral behavior, but it can sometimes make the difference between life and death or sickness and health. Military personnel travel quite a lot, and sometimes to many different countries during a career. They may come in contact with many different people of the opposite sex. Often these individuals are thrust into situations in which, unless one is morally disciplined, he or she can be overcome with lust and desire. This can pose a dangerous situation, because diseases spread, and the more morally reckless one tends to be, the more promiscuous one will be.

People from a different country may have diseases common to that country, and these diseases may not always prove to be as harmful to the natives of that country as they would be to a stranger. The natives may have built up a tolerance, or resistance, to certain germs that would make others, who have less resistance, seriously ill. If we could see the rash of military careers that were sacrificed in exchange for a few hours in bed, we could readily see the value and importance of moral integrity.

The ability to resist temptation is ideal. We realize that we are all human, and some of us are not as strong as others. On the other hand, some don't desire to exercise strength. They merely give in to their desires, not considering the potential consequences. These types of individuals sometimes fall into the "pit." I'm sure that many of these military men and women whose careers were ruined and whose families were shamed wish they had had the ability to say *no*. Give your child good moral direction, and it will serve her or him well in the military or in life outside of the military.

7. IF YOU BREAK THE LAW

Many of our children will never have an encounter with law enforcement, but many will, and if they do, it can be less than a pleasant experience. It can even be deadly sometimes. A simple, legal infraction can end with someone being dead or a person's life being turned upside down.

Teach your child to obey the law, because lawbreakers eventually encounter "the long arm of the law." As the saying goes, "You can't outrun 'the long arm of the law.' " At the end of the arm, is a law enforcement person—a marshal, a policeman and sometimes a judge—that is, if you make it to the judge's presence alive. Individuals don't always become policemen because of a desire to help mankind and bring order to society. They often become policemen because of an egotistic desire to wield authority and/or take out other frustrations against a group or category of people they dislike. Some of these policemen are aggressive, power-hungry and trigger happy, and they will seek any excuse to beat upon your child, to give your child the corporal punishment you never gave her or him.

When your child is at the mercy of a police officer, it can be unpleasant and dangerous. You must first teach your child to obey the law and, if at all possible, to avoid being at the wrong place at the wrong time. Teach her or him to steer clear of other children who are inclined toward trouble. Many children have ended up in serious trouble, just by being in the company of the wrong individual.

If your child has an encounter with the law and is in the wrong, and sometimes even if he is in the right, he should have been taught to keep his mouth shut, because "mouthing-off" to authorities can only exacerbate the problem. It can further lead to a confrontation that may become violent and deadly. It's beside the point that this is a free country, and we have freedom of speech and all of that. Don't take it for granted, when it comes to dealing with law enforcement officers. Some policemen will look for any excuse to batter your child, or even you.

If your child is confronted by the law and is in the right, he or she may protest, within reason, but if the situation shows signs of turning ugly, your child should have been taught to stop the protest and let the settlement take place in the court. Obedience to the law and discipline are the key.

8. THE WORK WORLD

Another of life's systems is the work world. The workplace is a part of the work world, and the workplace is governed, or run, by an overseer known as a boss, manager, supervisor or whatever other designation given the person in charge. That person usually operates within a set of guidelines that are handed down from the top, and these guidelines usually mirror the ideas and desires of top management. Businesses are usually managed from the top down. That means, the impetus for the action taken was conceived at the top of the management hierarchy.

A business environment is meant to constitute a team and requires the coordinated efforts of all team players to get the job done. Anyone who plays on the team must play according to the rules of the team leader or management—as the case may be. The company dictates the policy. If one desires to work for that entity, she or he must be willing to adhere to the rules of the game.

A child must be taught, and made aware of the fact that if she or he wants to play on the team, she must be willing to play by the rules of the team, or otherwise she can't play. Many individuals go through life, not understanding this or adhering to this fact. They are constantly being put off teams or are unable to remain, due to the pressures of adjusting.

Playing on another person's team isn't the only choice in life. There is also the option of forming your own team. In this situation, you can make the rules and give the orders. If you prefer calling the shots, rather than responding to others calling the shots, then the best alternative is to form your own team. However, the idea of forming your own team has its challenges. They may be different from the challenges of playing on someone else's team, but nevertheless they can be challenging.

The bottom line is that a child must be able to adjust to the dictates of the social entity, if she is to function successfully within its framework. Just as a parent takes charge and directs his or her child, so also do social systems operate within the confines of their system. So children must be taught to abide by the rules of the entity within which they are functioning. The best place to start teaching a child this is in the home, and the best time is as early after birth as plausible.

To teach, you must be able to direct, and to direct, you must first be in charge, or in control, of the one you're directing. You can't direct the one who controls you; you can only direct the one you're in control of. Your child needs direction from the very beginning, so take charge, and be in control.

Sooner or later, your child will be on her own, out in the arena of life. She will be responsible for her own actions and behavior, and everything she does (right or wrong) will have repercussions. Positive actions usually reap positive benefits, and negative actions most often reap negative benefits. Life has a way of rewarding an individual for her actions—good or bad. Life also has a tendency to be real and most often awards the prize promised or earned. When one goes against the rules and dictates of life, the just reward will surely be forthcoming. From the cradle to the grave and all along the way, we are encountering systems and entities that demand something of us, and if we are to reap the benefits of what we're seeking to get from that system or avoid the punishment meted out for not playing by that system's rules, then we must adhere to the dictates of the systems of life.

9. A Good Child

Parents like to think they have raised a child they can refer to as "a good child." Don't make the mistake of thinking your out-of-control child is "a good child." If you convince yourself that such a child is a good child, you're likely to fail in executing discipline and control. That child will tend to grow more and more out of control, and you may not be able to bring her or him back onto a path of disciplined direction.

As a child continues along an undisciplined path and reaches the arena of maturing life, his or her ways and actions will cause life to exact a severe beating upon him or her. Some parents have a strange sense of what constitutes a good child. Some children are young tyrants. They hit, they kick, they spit, they scream, they disobey, they attack other children, they destroy everything in their path, and they don't do one thing they're instructed to do. Still, the parent says he or she is "a good child." Some of those children grow up to be rapists, murderers and thieves, and the parent still insist: "He's a good boy [or good girl]. I don't know what went wrong."

The parent visits the boy or girl at the jail cell and comes home and says, "He's a good boy [or she's a good girl]." That same parent mortgages the house to put up bail to get the child out of jail. The child skips town, and the parent loses the house. She still says, "He's a good boy. I don't know what got into him."

The child shows up again one day and threatens to kill the parent, who thinks he's a good boy. The parent says, "He was a good boy before he started running with that crowd [or before those men got him hooked on drugs]." The truth of the matter is that the child wasn't good from the age of two years and upward, and it was the parent's fault.

Does this sound like you or does it sound like someone you know or have read about in the newspaper? Is that parent merely in denial or just has erroneous values concerning good and bad?

Children such as the one described above were never directed in good behavior. The parent was never in charge, and that was evident from the time the child turned two years of age. The behavior of such a child can never be stretched to fit into a mold that could be labeled "good."

A good child is taught to obey the parent or parents and wants to please the parent or parents. A good child is obedient and abides by the rules. A good child is not apt to break the law and is considerate of others. A good child wants to make the parent happy and proud—not unhappy and embarrassed. A good child is unselfish and understanding and would not hesitate to sacrifice or give of her or his resources for the parent's well-being, just as parents may have done for her or him. A good child recognizes a parent's vulnerability, understands and does what she or he can do to make things better. A good child inquires about a parent's potential need, even though it may not be obvious. A good child strives to see what she or he can give to the parent, not seek what she or he can get from the parent. A good child is there in a parent's twilight years, to see what can be done to help make life more comfortable and bearable. They're not born bad or good. You must raise them to be that way.

10. SOCIETY IS GLOBAL

With the advent of supersonic jets that can negotiate continents in a matter of hours, communication networks that can connect you to distant lands in a matter of seconds and the relaxation of travel into and out of different countries of the world, individuals are getting greater exposure to the peoples and cultures of those in other parts of the world. That exposure often fuels the desires to visit those faraway places. With the financial affluence that abounds in many of today's societies, the desire is more than a possibility; it is a probability. Society has become global.

A TABLESPOON OF LOVE, A TABLESPOON OF DISCIPLINE

The likelihood of most children traveling outside of their place of birth is very real. It is, therefore, in the child's best interest for parents to instruct and direct her or him in some of the ways and customs of societies other than her or his own. People no longer "live in a shoebox." They travel, if not as children, then certainly as adults, to other parts of the world. Parents should make children aware of the type of behavior that should not be exercised in another country. Other peoples' societies should not be subjected to the bad influences and behavior of ill-trained children from other countries. It doesn't give the other country a good name, and it gives the host country a distaste for those of the other society.

It is disgusting and unfair for an individual to go to another country and violate the laws and customs of that country. Children should be raised to respect the laws and customs of other countries, where they are allowed to visit or live. If the child can't be controlled in his own country, he or she should stay in that country.

In New York, I noticed teenagers (and adults) sitting on the back of the subway bench with their feet on the part where people are supposed to be sitting. Based on the language heard from time to time, some of these individuals may not have been native to this country. And what about those who go to other countries and run scams or other racketeering activities? And then we have the proliferation of drugs from other countries. People come to America from other countries and deal in drugs, get themselves addicted to drugs and often deal in theft and murder, with no compunction concerning the fact that they are guests in a foreign country. I'm sure Americans in some instances go to other countries and exhibit similar behavior, and when they do, they should be justly punished.

Parents need to teach their children proper behavior at home and abroad. Parents who can't control their children should keep them at home in their own house, in their own country. All parents, everywhere in the world, should be in control of their children; children should not be in control of their parents. Proper discipline and behavior cuts across all boundaries and ethnic barriers. It's international; it's global.

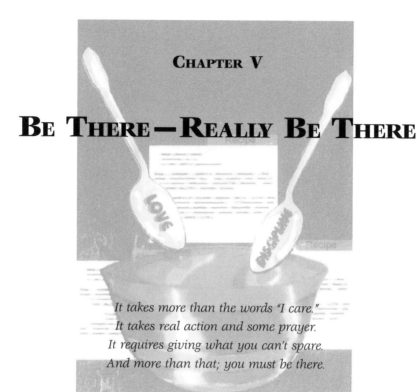

CHAPTER V

BE THERE—REALLY BE THERE

It takes more than the words "I care."
It takes real action and some prayer.
It requires giving what you can't spare.
And more than that; you must be there.

1. WHAT DOES BEING THERE MEAN?

Some mothers leave their children with a baby-sitter much too soon after childbirth and are away from them much too often when they are growing up. In some necessary circumstances, it is expected and acceptable for a mother to make an early return to her business, if the economic needs demand it, but the business should not be such as would preclude her from spending quality time with the child during the formative years. It is vitally important for you to forego all but necessary and unavoidable activity related to your work and or social encounters to come home and spend quality time with your child during the formative years and beyond, but especially during those formative years.

You must be home to spend time with the child or children during waking hours, so the child can get to know you and establish a parent-child bond. Nothing else should be more important than this, except when the ordinary and necessary requirements of the job demand and require your time, in order for you to maintain your financial livelihood. If you don't come home after business, and the father is also absent (or is the not-always-there type of father), this leads to a developing child missing the presence of both parents. The early years of the child's development are the most important years, and if you lose the child during these years, you quite often lose the child forever. Being there is a part of the love, which is one of the main ingredients in successfully raising a child.

I know many individuals who have now reached adulthood and beyond and are yet harboring the effects of absent parents. I know one individual who was put in a boarding school while her parent pursued a medical profession. That individual still suffers from the feeling of not being loved, as well as from low self-esteem. The mother has a thriving medical profession, but she really doesn't have the child; she lost the child years ago and is constantly trying to buy her back. However, it is a bit late. Money can never buy back lost years; the damage has already been done. I wonder if the parent thinks the trade-off was worth it. Parents don't always realize the damage that can be done by their absence from the child, and in many cases, the damage is never mended during the child's lifetime.

I know of another situation in which two sons were boarded off to live with a relative, while the father pursued a law career. The law career was consummated, and the father is now a judge, but the son I'm familiar with has extremely low self-esteem, abuses drugs and alcohol, abuses women and is unable to maintain a lasting relationship. He blames his parents, and it is right for him to do so. It would have been fine if the child could have put aside the fact that the parent was not always there and go on about his life, but some children are unable to do so. Some can weather the storms of various parental mistakes, while others cannot. Personalities react in different ways. We have weak and strong, and we have optimist and pessimist. That's the nature of the human spirit, reacting in accordance with individual makeup.

I know of another case of an individual whose father was always out drinking, while the mother was pursuing an advanced education degree. The child is an addicted drug abuser, unreachable by the mother or any one else. The father has long since died from the effects of alcohol abuse.

We have all read the long list of children from financially-affluent families who have fallen by the wayside because the parents were not there for them. The parents provided all of the necessary material things and thought that was sufficient. But it wasn't; the child wanted the parental presence.

I still reflect on the character in one of America's long-running sitcoms whose son was in and out of drug rehabilitation centers most of his adult life and eventually died from the effects of the substance abuse. The father admitted his fault of not having spent enough time with his son. The son was always desirous of the father's presence, but the father was always on his way to shoot another episode of this well-received sitcom, or to show his presence at some other unrelated social function. The son waited and wished, but the father very seldom came. The son had a nanny, the best of clothes, cars and money to spend, but he was void of the father's presence.

Enough examples are all around us that we need not cite names and families. We've heard it said far too many times: "My parents were not there for me." By now, parents should have come to realize that it is not merely an accident that absentee parents lose their children. It's not speculation, and parents don't really need a sociological study to be convinced of this fact. The parents who are absent from their child would probably not care to believe the study anyway. The parent's absence is usually for some selfish reason of their own desire, and rarely for the benefit of the child. If you asked the child, I believe most of them would rather have the parent's presence than the material things given in place of their presence. If you, as a parent, have a problem making this decision, ask the child what she or he would prefer.

I know what I felt growing up, and my mother was mostly there for us. I felt unhappy even when she went out to shop or to church and left us at home. I could hardly wait for her to return. The joy of having her around was beyond my ability to express. If this was the case in my childhood (and I'm sure I could have been considered an average reflection of most children), picture a child who waits every day and every night, and the parent seldom shows up. At the very least, this could lead the child to think she or he is unloved by the parent. I came to realize later in life how important an ingredient it is in the life of a developing child. So you need to be there— mothers or fathers, if it's a single-parent household, and mothers and fathers, if it's a two-parent household.

Children can survive with the presence of one loving parent, but not with the absence of both. This doesn't mean you must take off from work, when it is not necessarily practical to do so. Practicality dictates that parents who are required to work must be absent from the child to go to work, but after that, a parent should dedicate all of the other time, within reason, to be with and nurture the child. To the greatest extent possible, all activities after work should be planned to include the child.

In a single-parent household, the social relationships may need to be curtailed or even put on hold in some instances; the child should be considered first. Take the child to church with you, grocery or clothes shopping or any other place where the child would not be endangered or disrupt the purpose for which a parent finds himself or herself at a particular place.

Your being there isn't the same as a nanny or baby-sitter being there. Neither the nanny nor the baby-sitter is the parent of the child. There is a special natural bond that binds the child to the parent, and this bond is conspicuously absent in the temporary caregiver. Don't confuse your presence with the other caregiver's; the two are not the same. If you are a kind and loving parent, your child will always prefer you to the temporary caregiver. It is natural.

What does being there mean? It means being there for the first cry on the first moment of the first day the child enters the world. It means being there to change the first soiled diaper, to fix the first formula, to open the first jar of baby food, for the first Christmas, to see her take her first step, for the first vaccinations, for the first day of school, for her graduation from preschool to the first grade, for her graduation from grade school and high school and from college and for all of the many school plays and speeches and awards ceremonies in between. It means being there for the wedding and for all the times thereafter when she has questions she can't answer and problems she can't solve, and for all the times for the rest of her life when the need to call on her parent may arise. That's what parenting is all about, and that's what being there means.

I heard a parent remark once, "You worry about them from the time they are born until the time you die." If the child abides in your household, you often may stay awake until late into the night, waiting for her or him to arrive, and all the time until the child arrives you're wondering if she or he is safe and well. We all know so well the experiences of someone answering the door to find a stranger standing there with an "I-don't-know-how-to-tell-you-this" look on his or her face. Some know from firsthand experience, and others of us know from sharing the grief of others. At some time in life, most of us have received that dreaded phone call that we knew may come some day. It was concerning a loved one, and sometimes that loved one was a child.

If a parent had a child away on a distant battlefield, the appearance of a military officer at the door told the story, even without any words being spoken. If your child was a policeman or fireman, the unexpected appearance of an officer at the door often spelled bad news. On other occasions, parents have received upsetting news on the evening news report or from another source. A child is always the source of a parent's worry and concern.

Can you recall the first Christmas your child was old enough to walk and was able to come to see what Santa had brought? I can, and I can also remember the night before Christmas, when Celeste hardly wanted to go to sleep, because of the childhood anxiety of it being Christmas Eve. I wanted her to hurry off to sleep, so I could go and begin setting up the toys. I didn't have a great mechanical aptitude, so I needed a lot of time to assemble the things that required assembly.

We finally got her to sleep, after what seemed like an eternity. She fought sleep as long as she could, until it finally got the best of her. I pulled the covers up around her shoulders and tiptoed downstairs, to begin setting up the toys. It took me the better part of the night. Her mother assisted me, as she could, but the greater burden was on my shoulders. It was challenging, but I finally got everything assembled and set up for the morning surprise.

We probably looked forward to Celeste coming downstairs to see what Santa brought more than she did. There isn't a much greater joy than to see the look on a child's face when she or he wakes up on Christmas morning, comes in (in pajamas), because a child can never seem to wait long enough to go through the ritual of getting dressed. When the child begins to look around at all the Christmas presents, the eyes go from one thing to the next, not knowing what to play with first.

Children can bring you such joy when they are small, and it takes such a small effort to make them happy. If you raise them properly, they can bring you an equal amount of joy as adults, because you will witness accomplishment after accomplishment, as each one unfolds. Celeste has brought us such joy in her endeavors and accomplishments. On the other hand, if you don't raise them properly, they can break your heart, mind and spirit over and over and over again.

A TABLESPOON OF LOVE, A TABLESPOON OF DISCIPLINE

The Christmas mentioned was the one just prior to Celeste's third birth-day, and since then we have celebrated thirty-five others, each bringing as much joy as the one before. On Celeste's fifth Christmas, she got a self-propelled car, one she could get in and drive herself. It had a motor that could be recharged from the house current. Every time I took her outside to run it up and down the walk, other children would come around to stare. But she treated it like just another toy. It had no special meaning to her, other than the joy of having a fun toy.

The Christmas of her twenty-eighth year we opened presents on the telephone. That was also joyous. She was grown and married, and we had given them their presents a few days before Christmas, knowing that Christmas would find us both going in different directions. We got on the phone and announced the opening of the various presents. That was just a part of the joy of being there.

And then there are the birthdays; don't forget the birthdays. We gave Celeste a birthday party every year from the time she was two years old until she turned eight, and I'm sure they all left some lasting, cherished memories. Her fondest memories are probably of her parents being there when it counted most. That sent the message that we loved her, which made all the difference.

We were typical middle-class working parents. At this time in life, I was a postal clerk, and my wife was a secretary/billing clerk. And when I speak of being middle-class, I am referring to an economic state, as opposed to an educational or intellectual state. The state of middle-class encompasses the largest sector of the American populace, or at least it did in the 1960s, the time in which Celeste was born. Therefore, our child-raising could be considered typical of the great majority of families across the United States. So the parameters considered in raising Celeste could have had practical application in most American families.

I had decided, prior to the time I got married, that when and if I fathered a child, I would always be there for her or him. I had vowed in my mind, from the time I was a teenager, that if I ever had a child or children, I would never leave them or fail to take care of them. My child's mother and I separated early in the child's life. And even though I was leaving the home with a heavy heart, I was determined to still be there for Celeste. I decided that I would still love, nurture, oversee, provide, participate and discipline my child until she became an adult, became independent and even beyond that. I also vowed that I would do whatever it took, within the law, to equip my child with the necessary tools of life to enable her, at the appropriate adult age, to go out of her parent's household and function independently on her own.

2. FROM THE CRADLE

As soon as I set up the cradle, I decided that since child development starts at an early age, the development of Celeste's cognitive skills should begin very early. So I went out and bought crib objects which could be mounted over the crib for her to watch. They were in the form of brightly colored birds that moved back and forth. She paid a lot of attention to these objects and their movement, and this served to enhance the development of her attention span, alertness and concentration. This was a part of being there for the beginning of her intellectual development.

Another part of being there was the stage in which a child would grab both your ears and pull on them. I guess she could not resist the fascination of those two objects protruding from either side of her father's head. And there were the facial slaps. It seemed that Celeste had nothing else to do with her hands but to slap my face.

I remember how I would carry her in my arms, and she would hold on tight for dear life for fear of falling from my grasp. That was typical of most young children who saw and felt love in the parent. That was all a part of the love connection, the making-sure-you-were-there connection. If you missed being there for these little events, you missed one of the better aspects of the beginning of your child-raising experience.

About the time Celeste reached six months of age, her mother was returning to work, and I took on the task of daytime care. I worked nights, leaving for work at about 9:30 to 10:00 P.M., and returning home the next morning at about 8 to 8:30 A.M. My normal working hours were 12 midnight to 8:30 A.M., but I had my hours changed to accommodate the care of Celeste and to allow her mother to leave for work as early as she could.

My wife would be waiting to leave for work when I arrived home in the morning. I would walk in the door, and she would walk out. I would come in, wash up, awaken the baby, bathe her, feed her and remain up for her until after her noontime feeding and nap. When she laid down for her noontime nap, I would lie down and sleep for a few hours, and when she woke up, I would wake up, dry her and change her and perform the other necessary care chores, until her mother arrived home in the evening. I would then lie down again to sleep and get up just before the baby's bedtime. I would read her a bedtime story, give her the usual hug and kiss and tuck her into bed.

We had a set routine: she would give her mother a hug and kiss, then give me a hug and kiss, and I would read the bedtime story and tuck her in. Her mother would have taken care of the evening feeding and bathing and have her in her little pajamas ready for bed. Then it was my turn.

By the time Celeste had reached fourteen months of age, she was out of her crib and sleeping in a single bed. We redecorated her room. I painted it in bright, pastel colors that were intended to add excitement to the child's room. We added a bookshelf and stocked it with children's books. We bought picture books for her, some with thick cardboard pages, and others with rag pages, which a child could interact with and not destroy. We were there in the development stage. She learned to stand alone, crawl and walk at the normally-expected age.

She had begun to walk, and during this period, a child will go wherever her little legs will carry her and explore every bit of undiscovered territory. This was also the age in which I crawled around the floor with her sitting on my back. She called this "giving me a horsy ride." She looked forward to this almost on a daily basis. That was okay with me. It was all part of being there and all part of the love connection.

As Celeste began to walk almost everywhere her feet would carry her, we began to notice the pattern of her walking with her feet turned slightly outward. She was about two to three years of age then. This was one of those walking patterns that parents often overlook, or consider not important enough to be concerned about. We were concerned, because we believed children should walk with feet in a normal walking posture.

I can recall some children around me, when I was growing up, who had various types of abnormal foot growth. With one pattern, when the child walked with the feet pointed inward, and we, as children referred to it as "pigeon-toed." Others had a pattern of walking with feet pointed outward instead of straight ahead. We referred to that as "slew-footed." Don't ask me where we got those names from, because I don't have the faintest idea. Others had a walking pattern in which the knees tended to hit together, and we referred to that as "knock-kneed." I don't know if these descriptions had any basis in medical terminology, or even if they were fitting, but these were descriptions we used as children to describe what were really growth abnormalities that may have emerged from the position the fetus assumed in the womb before birth.

In the days when I was growing up, many parents overlooked these abnormalities, and children often came to carry these conditions into adulthood, and most often for the rest of their lives. That need not have been, and after seeing these conditions when I was growing up, I was determined that my child would not go through life with any such condition. Many or most of these conditions could have been corrected without unnecessary pain or inconvenience to the child. However, the situation had to be tackled early.

We thought it important enough to consult an orthopedic specialist. Looking through the yellow pages, we came upon a specialist skilled in the area of reshaping bones, especially in developing children, and we took Celeste for an examination and evaluation. The doctor prescribed for her a set of metal braces that were strapped or screwed to her shoes and adjusted to redefine her pattern of walking. She had to walk in them and even sleep in them.

At this point in her development, we had began to see a pattern of strength and determination emerging in this child, which pointed to the fact that you would not be able to keep her down. She walked in those braces, fell down, got up and walked again. They served the purpose of reshaping her foot bones, so as to bring her feet back to a normal walking posture. The problem was corrected, but many similar problems in other children were not corrected because the parents were not there for them.

There is no need to enter into a discussion of whether a parent or parents can afford such corrective procedures, because many families spend money on things that do not have equal importance. When it comes to the child or children, they simply are not there. One of the most important ingredients of successful child-raising is being there. Many of the problems some children take into adulthood that grossly impact their lives in a negative way could have been reversed earlier if the parent or parents had been there.

3. Preschool and the First Babysitter

About the time Celeste reached the age of three, we made a decision to send her to a babysitter. We came to know the family through a mutual acquaintance. The wife kept children on a daily basis and had three young children of her own. She seemed qualified enough, upon talking with her, and we decided to take the child to her. By this time, I was back working my regular shift, which began at 12 midnight and ended at 8:30 A.M. My wife would drop Celeste at the babysitter in the morning on her way to work and pick her up in the evening on her way back home. Sometimes I would drop her off and pick her up, especially on my days off.

On the day when I would be picking Celeste up, I would call the babysitter to prepare her for my coming, and Celeste would be so happy knowing that she would be going home with her daddy. When she saw me, she would start jumping up and down. Reflecting on those times, I can remember the joy my daughter would feel when the babysitter would say, "Celeste your father is here." Celeste would grab whatever she had and run out the door with me, hardly even stopping to say good-bye in her haste. We would walk off hand-in-hand toward home.

Those were such wonderful times, witnessing the love and trust a young innocent child had in her parent. Parents should never compromise that trust by doing anything to negatively impact the lives of young children. This is the code loving and caring parents lived by then and still live by today. Those who violate this code aren't loving and caring, and down the road they will pay dearly. A child who may be a product of the violation of this code of love and caring can go on to suffer a wrecked life and a distorted personality.

This ritual of getting my daughter from the babysitter was merely another aspect of my parental presence—the act of being there for her. Little did I know then what an impact that aspect of being there would have on her life. What a bond of love and caring this type of interaction creates in a child, and such a bond as this helps to shape a child's life in very positive ways.

Children can sense your love by your presence, so a parent should never take lightly the aspect of being there. It can be more important than any ambition you may be pursuing. You will never know just how important it is, until you experience the loss of the connection to your child and the distance created between you and your child, by your not being there.

Some parents take time off from their children to consummate a professional ambition, such as pursuing a law degree, a medical degree, or a Masters degree, and once that is accomplished, they go back to the child or children to pick up where they left off. But when this is done, the child is not there mentally, and sometimes not emotionally nor physically. You must work your career or ambitions in between the needs of your child, not work your child's needs in between the needs of your career or ambition.

Children often don't buy the philosophy of you leaving them to consummate a career in order for them to have more things. They could care less about those things. They would much rather have you. Love, caring and being there can go miles further in the life of a child than can expensive toys and baubles. A child will sit and eat bread with you and even suffer with you and love you more for it.

I've seen far too many adults whose parent/s neglected being there when they were most needed by their child, because they were working two jobs, nurturing a romantic relationship, pursuing a college degree or just hanging out in the streets. These children often found other things to fill the void left by the parent's absence. Some died in house fires, others invited friends and associates over against the parent's wishes and got into other types of trouble, and others chose to hang out with friends rather than go home to a house always void of their parent's presence.

Hanging out in the streets has gotten some children in trouble with the law and others involved in illicit behavior, including drugs and sex. You cannot control what your child may or may not do when you are not there, especially if your not being there is the norm rather than the exception.

Celeste's time at the babysitter was play time, and she could always look forward to being picked up every day at about the same time by her mother or father, and sometimes by both together. She knew her mother or her daddy was going to come and pick her up, take her home, feed and bathe her and spend some time talking to her and doing little, special games or other fun things before her time for bed. If, for some reason, her mother was unable to pick her up, her father would be there, and that was just as well, because she loved both her parents. And they both loved her and took care of her.

Celeste continued to spend the entire day at the babysitter's until she was four years old, and at that time, we began to seek out a preschool or nursery for her. She was a bright, alert four-year-old, and we had her tested for one of the local preschools. She passed the necessary testing, and we enrolled her in the preschool program. She looked forward to this, because she was never a homebound child. She was a child who had been on the go since she was old enough to leave home with an attending adult. She was always happy to see her parents, but she was equally comfortable when going off to spend the night somewhere. So going off to a day school was no problem for her.

Celeste would get picked up in the morning and get dropped off at the babysitter's after school. Her mother would pick her up from the sitter on her way from work. Sometimes, just as before, I would pick her up early and sit with her until my wife came home.

During this period in her life, I had begun pursuing a college degree and working full time, but I was determined to take time out to sit down for dinner with my wife and Celeste, after I got up in the evening. Before I left for work at night, I would give her a bedtime snack, usually consisting of some frozen dessert or juice. I remember that little voice saying, "Mommy, come and give me a hug and kiss." Her mother knew she was getting prepared for her bedtime story and to get tucked into bed by her dad.

On my days off, I would sometimes put Celeste on the school bus in the morning, when it didn't conflict with my school classes. By evening, I would often be home from college study. I picked her up after her preschool and interacted with her until her mother came home. We would play little children's games, do jigsaw puzzles, or I would read to her.

After I finished my college studies, my schedule was similar to her mother's, so her mother or I would put her on the school bus in the morning, and usually her mother would pick her up from the sitter in the evening. Whenever I would be arriving home a little earlier than usual, I would get her from the babysitter. We were both there working together for the child's well-being. When her mother wasn't there, I was there, and when I wasn't there, her mother was there.

Whenever there was a need to be present, concerning school-related matters, we both considered it our obligation to be there and involved in the matters together. This pattern continued throughout Celeste's entire school career, until she was out of college.

She spent one year in the preschool program, the school had its graduation exercise, and the little children received their certificate. Celeste was ready for the first grade. She began first grade in September at the age of five. Her sixth birthday would be in January. She could already perform beyond the first-grade level.

4. Grade School

During this development period, between completing a year in preschool and entering first grade, we focused our attention on her growth and intellectual development and bought her various types of books, puzzles and anything else that would enhance her intellectually. She was a little genius at putting together puzzles. We would give her any type of puzzle, and she would stare at it with a sense of concentration and fixation, as if she had some sixth sense about where the pieces belonged. After staring at it for a minute or two, she would take her little skinny fingers, pick up a piece and put it into place. She seemed always to have been able to choose the fitting piece.

When she was tested for the first grade, one of the tests given was concerned with putting objects of different shapes into their proper holes, and she could perform the task in a snap. She could also read, do some counting and knew part of her multiplication tables. I had been bent on teaching anything she was capable of absorbing at her age and development.

Since she was advanced enough, by virtue of the tests taken, we began seeking a school for her to begin first-grade study. We knew we didn't want to put her in a city school. After all, it was the era of the 1960s, when institutions and their students were failing. Drugs were being sold on gradeschool campuses to grade-schoolers. Many of these children, by this time, had addicted parents. I also felt I didn't have the patience nor the restraint to deal passively with children who might have been inclined to get physical with my daughter. Those were the days when children were beating up on other children, taking their money and jackets, and exercising all types of other negative behavior. To keep Celeste away from this potentially-negative behavior, we decided her schooling would begin in a private institution.

We were prepared to do whatever we deemed necessary, even if it required sacrifice. We had heard many positive things about the Montessori method and decided to investigate the Montessori Schools. We visited one of the schools, checked it out and concluded that we would take her to be tested there. We took her, the necessary tests were administered, and she passed the requirements set forth. At the age of five years and eight months, Celeste entered first grade at the Montessori School.

Things started off well, and Celeste immediately plunged into the learning experience that lay ahead. She enjoyed being a part of this new beginning in learning and moved ahead at a rapid pace. She quickly adjusted to her new part-time guardians, the process of doing school work and bringing home homework. We were there to interact with her on a daily basis concerning the homework. We watched her form the "a," the "c," and the number "3," watched her draw the line under 2 + 2 and do all the other things peculiar to a first-grader.

After the end of the school day, the bus would drop her off at the babysitter, as before, and one of us would pick her up in the evening. When I picked her up, I would ask her how her day went, and she would begin to tell those long, drawn-out stories that meant nothing to anyone except little children. I would listen attentively, as if it was the most interesting tale I had ever heard. After she finished relating her tale, I would ask specific questions just to get her accustomed to responding to detailed inquiries. I didn't know it at the time, but this ritual would possibly be instrumental in helping her during the debate sessions she pursued in high school years later. (Celeste was on her high school debate team for a couple of years, and I was on my college debate team for a couple of years.)

On one occasion, I asked Celeste what her teacher was like and then asked her to describe her teacher to me. When I asked her if she liked her teacher, she said, "Yes, Daddy; she is very nice." Then I asked her to describe her teacher. She said, "She is a little brown, like you and Mommy. She wears her hair pulled back like this (and she drew her hands back on both sides of her head). She's about old like Mommy. She has big eyes and a thumbtack in her head." The "thumbtack in her head" made me chuckle, until I came to realize that her teacher was a Hindu and thus had the symbolic red dot on her forehead.

Celeste was always quite descriptive, and if she got to know you, she would talk to you forever. She was very withdrawn and uncomfortable around those she didn't know as well. I recall the time her mother took her to the doctor for a cold she had acquired. When she came home, I went through the usual questioning ritual. I asked her what the doctor said. She replied, "She gave me a shot right here, and it hurt." She pointed to her backside to show me where the doctor injected her. I said, "She didn't mean to hurt you. She just wanted to make you well." She said, "There was nothing wrong back there." I laughed and thought to myself, What a skewed sense of relationship children have, with their limited sense of knowledge.

BE THERE—REALLY BE THERE

As Celeste began to settle deeper into her school regimen, I began to introduce her to more advanced reading and math materials. I was of the belief that a child could learn anything you taught her, if she had normal learning capacities, and you had the ability to impart the information. When we were together, our environment became an extended classroom and another learning experience.

I took Celeste with me everywhere that it was convenient to take her. When she was not in school or spending the weekend with her cousins or a classmate, she was with me or her mother—or both of us. We took her to church, to the supermarket and on shopping trips. On some school holidays, her mother would take her to the office with her. During this period, I had a boat, and we often got in the car, went down to the boat dock and got on the boat. We would sit there at the small galley table, holding small conversation and drinking soda pop. Those were fun times for her, as well as for me, and all of those times added to the growing bond between father and child that often lasts for a lifetime.

Celeste was an only child, and I had always heard that only children turned out to be selfish. Children who were selfish were often excused for being that way, because of the fact that they had no siblings, with whom they had to share things. It was understood that everything which wasn't for Mother or Daddy belonged to the only child. Since I was determined to break the normal pattern of negative behavior in parenting, I decided if only children are selfish, my child would not be selfish, even though she was an only child. I was determined to break this pattern by teaching Celeste and requiring that she share with her friends and playmates.

Celeste's great uncle had a maintenance contract with one of the well-known ice-cream companies in the city and was able to buy ice-cream in bulk from the plant. We would order five gallon containers in several flavors and stock them in the freezer for her. We also kept a supply of ice-cream cones. When she wanted ice-cream, we would go to the freezer, take out a couple of flavors and scoop her up a double dip. Whenever she had playmates over, we would require her to share cones with them, if they wanted ice cream. This was one of the ways of teaching her to share what she had with others, and this attitude was strengthened and developed at every opportunity.

I came to realize the fruits of our teachings when Celeste was a junior in college. She went back to school with a sizable amount of money she had earned over the summer and more than an abundant supply of clothing. She always had more than an adequate supply of clothing. We bought her good quality clothes, and she took good care of them. During the school year, she gave away some of her nice pieces. When I asked what happened to certain pieces of her wearing apparel, she told me she had given away some things to one of her classmates. She said "Dad, she didn't have a lot of nice things like I have." I thought it so honorable that she had done that, so I didn't even scold her. I merely smiled and said, "That was very nice of you." After all, my intention was that she grow up an unselfish child, even though she was an only child.

We watched her grow and develop, all the while teaching, nurturing, hugging and directing. She was progressing at a pace that was always a grade or two beyond her present placement. We bought her lots of little books to read, and she became an avid reader. I bought her word flash cards to help increase her vocabulary. She progressed to the second grade, while at the same time reading and doing math at fourth-grade level. Then she progressed to the third grade.

After finishing the third grade, Celeste was testing on a sixth-grade level, and it was suggested that she could bypass fourth grade and go on to the fifth. Since she was advanced, we decided we would allow her to skip a grade. So she went from the third grade to the fifth grade.

At this point, she was performing some basic algebraic functions that I had taught her and devouring almost every book she picked up. She was now eight years of age, had been in grade school for three years and said to me, "Daddy, I can read anything I see." And she could. She would read road signs, billboards, building signs, truck signs and practically anything else she saw. Sometimes I would have to admonish her to be quiet. She could virtually drive you up a wall reading things.

She could read light stories in the newspaper. One day, while we were riding the bus together, I handed her a copy of the *New York Times*, to keep her occupied while I concentrated on the events ahead of us for the day. She was holding the newspaper in front of her face, and a little old lady sitting nearby looked at her, as if to say, "She can't read that paper." But she could. After all, she was going on nine and had the face of a nine-year-old. When she looked up and began asking questions concerning what she was reading, the little old lady tucked her head in surrender.

At this point, we began looking for a more challenging school for Celeste, feeling that she was outgrowing what her school was offering. We inquired, sought out and settled on a small private school in Hollis, Queens, New York. We didn't know, at the time we enrolled her, that her stay there would be brief. There seems to have been a discipline problem at the school.

We had put her in a private school precisely to avoid discipline problems, but one of the boys at the school made it his business to tease her on a regular basis, and that all but drove me up the wall. When I brought it to the attention of the school administration, the answer was, "Mr. Gandy, boys will be boys." I immediately decided I would move my daughter out of that particular school.

One of the most memorable things about Celeste's stint at that school was the evening I and another parent were waiting for our children to return from a school field trip. The students always seemed to be out of control, and we had to wonder why their parents had sent them there. It didn't seem to be to learn. Had they sent them there just to have someone to babysit them?

As the children began to arrive at the building from the field trip, many came in running and screaming in a boisterous manner. I looked at the children as they entered and shook my head in disgust. Turning to the other waiting parent, I said, "I know my child doesn't behave like that. I taught her better." A few minutes later, the door opened slowly, and two young children entered, talking quietly to each other. Celeste was one of them. We were standing on the side, and Celeste didn't notice me standing there. So the two of them quietly walked down the stairs, got their belongings and headed back up. It was only on her way back up the stairs that Celeste noticed me. "Hi, Dad," she said in greeting. I was so proud of her that day.

Since the teasing incident at the school, we had begun searching for another school to enroll her in. She was completing the sixth grade and testing two to three grades above her present grade level. We had her tested and interviewed at several private schools. All met our environmental standards, the curricular standards looked good, and they all appeared to be about the business of teaching children. Celeste was now ten years of age and headed for the seventh grade. However, after undergoing the batteries of academic, psychological and maturity evaluation tests, she was deemed ready for eighth grade in all categories. She tested psychologically very mature for her age. Based on these tests, we decided we would let her skip seventh grade and go from sixth grade to eighth, and we made the choice to enroll her in a new prep school.

A TABLESPOON OF LOVE, A TABLESPOON OF DISCIPLINE

One thing about Celeste: she was a child with strength, independence and perseverance. Whatever environment she found herself in, she quickly adjusted, made friends and associates in the new environment and went about her life without missing a beat. She had a solid personality, embracing high self-esteem. She believed in herself and must have felt she had parents who loved her, were watching her back and would always be there to see her through. She seldom complained about anything. She adapted and went on about her life.

Celeste is a leader at heart. She always remembered what I said to her when she was at a very young age. I admonished her to never be a follower, to be a leader. "Followers," I told her, "tend to get themselves in the most serious trouble. If you follow anything, it had better be something smart." I guess, since she considered herself smart, she had to lead because she construed my remarks to mean she should only follow someone smarter than she was.

She thought herself as smart as most of her peers, so she was quick to take a leadership stance. Her daughter has some of those same traits, and must have come by them instinctively. She is now four years of age, and when she pulls out a computer game, she admonishes you to just sit down and watch her. She'll say to you, "No! You don't do this; just I do this." She is a little four-year-old "Napoleoness."

Celeste also showed leadership qualities when she made a decision to join the Girl Scouts of America. When she voiced her desire to be a girl scout, we were in favor, because we saw nothing negative surrounding it. It was an honorable desire, so she joined. She wanted to go as far as she could during her scouting stint and became a first-class scout. We sold cookies for her and supported her in every way we could.

Then there were the uniforms, the pins and the scouting programs we attended. I often took her to Girl Scout meetings at a place some distance from her home, but it didn't trouble me much. I was happy to have taken the time to help her in pursuit of the things she considered important in her life. The group she met with embraced a nice bunch of children, and the parents were equally nice and supportive of the children.

We relished every little pin and advancement Celeste received. We were happy for her accomplishments. She wanted to master all she surveyed. She persevered, and she accomplished, sometimes with effort and sometimes with setbacks. Everything was not always as easy as she would have liked. She was challenged at times, but she met every challenge without any thought of not succeeding. Celeste became a first-class scout, which was probably the goal she had set for herself. Then she moved on to other things, as she was apt to do.

One of the highlights of her girl scouting period was the Halloween costume party given for her scouting troop. She needed a costume for it, and I had to put something together. I wanted her to have a great costume, and I wanted it to be different. She had told her mother she needed the costume, and her mother said, "Tell your father." When those types of words echoed from her mother's lips, I knew I had to get involved to accomplish the mission.

I spoke to the young lady who worked with me in my boutique. She was a very gifted seamstress. She said she had about two hundred and fifty Tastee Bread wrappers that had been saved for "who knows what," and she could make Celeste a costume from them. And she did. She made a dynamite costume including a jumpsuit and matching hat. It was truly uniquely different. Celeste went to the costume party in one of the most exciting and original Halloween "get ups" at the party. I had to be there, because I had to take her and pick her up. She was very happy that her parents were able to come through for her in another time of need.

The girl scouting stint was merely another piece of the puzzle of Celeste's developing life. She had pursued this activity after school at the required time of interaction, and this activity didn't require her to miss a beat in her school life. She was now on her way to the eighth grade. She would be attending a new school, making new friends and acquaintances and blazing new trails. The school of choice to begin her eighth grade year was a multicultural prep-school in Flushing, New York. It exemplified a prep-school in both student body makeup and campus surroundings.

On the day I was to take her back for the preschool interview, I had to make a business stop in Manhattan, and she was with me. It was a bright spring day, probably in late May. Her mother had dressed her in white pants, white sandals and a brightly colored blue and white top. She put matching ribbons in her hair. I finished my business and decided we should get a little lunch prior to going to the interview. We had lunch and topped it off with cherry pie for her.

After that we went to the interview, and everything went in a positive direction. I and her mother were pleased that she would be attending that school. I'm not quite certain why we selected it over another, but I think it was because it had a greater infusion of children from various ethnic backgrounds. We felt this would be a great climate for broadening Celeste's views relative to ethnic diversity. We also thought the diversity would bring challenge. We were wrong.

As it turned out, this was a school of affluent preppies who didn't need to work very hard for their good grades, and who probably did more socializing than studying. Still, in this school, Celeste was virtually a straight A student. She spent one year there, completing the eighth grade with very high marks. The challenge, however, wasn't great enough, and it was time to move her along.

She was leaving junior high and entering high school. She would begin her high school career at another school. It was a small school in Jackson Heights, New York. From there, she would graduate high school and move on to college, and out of there to her career and the challenges of life, for which parents are supposed to have prepared the child. Again, she settled in, underwent the adjustment, made new friends and went about the business of learning.

5. High School

The Garden School was a fine small school with an air of academic seriousness and challenge. The environment was a mixture of urban movement and suburban local. It was borderline Manhattan in Queens, Long Island. At this school, Celeste would find as much challenge as she needed to keep her constantly on her toes. She was twelve years of age and beginning her ninth-grade study. She was one of the two youngest in her high school. She had begun school at five years of age and had skipped two grades.

This school had been chosen over another prep-school in Manhattan to which she had been accepted. That school was the *alma mater* of the young man involved in the "preppie murder case," involving the murder of a young girl in Central Park, during a so-called lover's tryst. We decided we were not very excited about the idea of our daughter riding the subway from Queens to Manhattan every day at her young age just to attend high school, so we opted for the closer one in Jackson Heights. There, she would be able to get a well-rounded and challenging education.

She was enrolled and went about the business of school and the direction toward which high school pointed a student. At this school, field trips abounded, and after each, I was waiting outside to take Celeste home. This seemed to have been an almost every week scenario. However, the field trips were rich in cultural and educational benefits for the students.

Then there were the PTA meetings her mother and I attended. We never missed one during her entire school career. We were both there to ask questions concerning her progress, her behavior and her attitude, and we never got a bad report. She never wanted to miss a day from school. She received perfect attendance certificates throughout her entire school career, because she loved school. We made it convenient and comfortable for her to attend, and she did her best to be there every open school day. One day (long after she had finished college) she remarked to me, "Dad, I had one of the best school careers a kid could ask for." She was indeed a happy child, always striving and doing her best. At times, various subjects would challenge her, and I would be the first to tell her when she had to do better. I would always try to give her self-assurance.

One day she came home upset over a paper she had written. The teacher had marked it up with corrections in red. Celeste was adamant, for she thought she had written a masterpiece. I looked at it and said, "I don't blame the teacher for marking this up; this is nothing." Her head was down. The paper may not have been all that terrible, but it didn't come close to the acceptable quality expected of our daughter, so I couldn't let her go away thinking she had already arrived. I guess she figured that when both the teacher and her father said it was bad, it must have been bad.

"You can do better than this," I said, and after that, she did come to do better in that particular area of study. She always hated to be defeated. She was the type who couldn't stand to lose a game without remarking that her opponent may have done something unfair to win. She was somewhat of a "sore loser." However, she must have come about it honestly, because I am a bit that way myself. Whatever I play, my determination is to win, and if I don't, I will go back and practice until I can defeat my opponent.

She continued in her studies, raising and leveling off, sometimes making the honor roll and sometimes feeling thoroughly challenged. She exhibited an all-around high school spirit. She made friends and participated in those extra curricular activities we thought she could handle along with her studies. She kept her eyes on the future that lay ahead—college and her career.

A TABLESPOON OF LOVE, A TABLESPOON OF DISCIPLINE

Celeste and her school mates had a lot of fun together. It was a small intimate school atmosphere. In tenth grade, they were allowed to go off campus and purchase their lunch like grownups. Celeste had her allowance and managed it like a frugal banker. She enjoyed going off campus for lunch with her fellow classmates. The student body allowed for close knit friendships, because it was not huge and overwhelming, where hardly anyone knew anyone. The high school graduating class was to have only thirty-two students, and all of them except one went off to college.

Every evening after school, Celeste would pop into the boutique I owned and do a few chores, wait on a few customers or both. After that, she would go home, which was just around the corner. Then, she would call her mother, get herself a snack and do her homework. If she had a problem with any of her homework, she would call me, and I would walk around the corner and help her resolve the problem. When she had pressing homework to do, she would go directly home. She always called me and her mother to let us know she had arrived safely.

On Saturdays and some of her school days off, Celeste often spent time with me in the store, and at other times she would tag along with me to the designer houses to order stock for the store. I often bought designer pieces for her, sometimes jeans and sometimes other items. She was one of the more fashionable, unspoiled students in her high school class. She was always low-key and caring of others who might have had less. She never said, "Dad, can I have this?" or "Dad can I have that?" One thing I loathed was to see a child ask her parents to buy things that, quite often, they simply could not afford.

I often saw that very thing in my store. Sometimes a parent would come into the store with a child. The child might desire a particular outfit, and if the parent could not afford it or would not buy it for the child, the child would "get an attitude." Sometimes a parent might have felt badly if a child wanted something that he or she could not afford to buy. I felt bad for the parent. So I adopted a policy with my child that made it better. She was not to ask for anything, other than those essentials I may not be aware that she needed, and I would get her what I could. I often used the expression, "My child is rich, but I'm poor."

She attended school with a few children from upper-class families, economically speaking. Her high school was small, and I guess the administrators didn't deem it feasible to get involved in a prom scenario. One of her classmates was like "Richie Rich." He sponsored a prom party for the kids in his class, had it hosted at a fancy restaurant, and he arrived in a chauffeured limousine. His father was a large construction contractor.

Another of her classmates' parents owned two fancy East Side eateries, and he had his birthday party hosted at one of them. The parents closed the restaurant for the day, had the jukebox records changed to music familiar to the children, and had a professional artist come in and draw a birthday greeting book for the "birthday boy." The children had their own private party in the fancy restaurant with all of the fixings. Another child's parents owned several Chinese restaurants, and the daughter often took Celeste with her to one or the other of the restaurants to eat.

As Celeste began to approach her junior year in high school, I decided it was time for her to have braces put on her teeth. She had a couple of crooked teeth that made her smile a bit less than perfect. The family, on her mother's side, had very strong teeth, and so did Celeste, except for the couple of teeth which needed straightening. I sought out a highly recommended orthodontist, took Celeste for a consultation and subsequently got her fitted for braces. She wore them with a smile, very seldom complaining.

I was there for the beginning of the initial procedure, and she had to have a couple of teeth surgically extracted to make room for the others to move over after installation of the braces. I remember her lying her head on my shoulder on the way home after the surgery. She left my shirt very bloodstained. After the numbing wore off, she experienced a great deal of pain for a child. However, she bore it like a real trooper. She never complained about the discomfort.

I was there for the initial fitting of the braces, and during most of the periodic visits, in order to be informed of the progress or problems, if any. Eventually the period of time was full, and the braces came off. It was a happy time. She had a beautiful set of straight, white teeth. This is but another example of how parents can be and should be there for the child, through many events in life.

Something was always going on in Celeste's life, but I guess that was "par for the course." Something was always going on in our lives also, when we were children, so her life was no exception. The exception is when the parent opts out of all of these growing-up events. One day during the summer, she accidentally pushed her arm through the glass storm door, sustaining several minor cuts. Her mother called me in a panic. I rushed over and took her to the hospital. Her mother had a tendency to panic at the sight of blood.

On another occasion, during the high pollen season, she experienced itchy eyes. She began to rub one of them to ease the itching. She didn't realize, in her little child's mind, the damage that could be done by abrasively rubbing your eyes. The rubbing irritated the eye and caused a slight cornea abrasion. Again I had to rush over to take her to the hospital. It was all about being there, and thank God I wanted to be there and could be there.

During this period in Celeste's life, her mother and I weren't living in the same house. We had been living apart since she was nine years of age, but her care continued just as if we were living together. As a matter of fact, one of my associates said to me, "You take care of Celeste better than other fathers who live in the same house with the child." Every chance we got, Celeste and I would spend time together going to McDonald's, Burger King or the movies. As the holidays began, we would attend the annual Macy's Thanksgiving Day Parade. In preparation, we would dress warm in layered clothing, and sometimes we would carry a thermos of hot chocolate or purchase it on the way to the parade. We always got there early enough to get a seat on the front row.

I always carried a stool for Celeste to stand on, and she would alternately sit and stand while watching the parade go by. Sometimes I would have her allow another little child to share her stool, a child who otherwise could not get a good view of the passing parade. We had fun enjoying those special events together. Those are the things children remember most. They are the most prized moments, and they leave the most cherished memories.

You must take time out to enjoy some of the special occasions with your child. That will make all of the difference in the world. Those are the times that make a child know that you really love her and are there for her. Those times together were really special. When Celeste knew she was going to do something with her father, she would be excited for the entire day. She often told anyone who would listen that her father was taking her here or taking her there.

On those special occasions when we would go to Burger King, we would have our Whopper with cheese, french fries and a soda pop. Celeste loved french fries, as I guess all children do. She would always say, "Dad, can we have french fries?" I would say, "Sure, we can have french fries." If she ever thought I didn't have enough money, she would let me know that she had some money we could use. I would always say, "That's okay. You keep your money." After Burger King, we would stop at Baskin Robbins, get a double scoop cone of ice-cream and eat it while we walked slowly toward home.

I can recall a time when she was much younger, and I took her to the annual boat show held at the New York Coliseum. We would be constantly getting on and off the fancy boats on display. She would say to me, as I looked at a particular boat, "Dad, you like that kind of boat? I'll buy it for you. I have money in my bank." She would be talking about a boat costing $65,000.00, and her bank had every bit of $39.00 in it, but she was so caring and giving and so willing to share. She was always looking out for her father, and (I'm sure) equally so for her mother.

I remember one day when she and I went roller skating together at a local roller rink. We were leisurely skating around the floor and having animated conversation, as we often did. She was a much better skater than I was, since I probably hadn't been on roller skates in some twenty-five years and may have been a bit out of shape. As we were skating around, I suddenly experienced a freak tripping accident and fell to the floor, sustaining an ugly gash over my eye. She must have been very frightened, after seeing the blood. Being as young as she was, she may have been worried that I could die. At her age, she was probably unable to assess the extent of the injury. However, she took charge, once we reached the hospital, telling the doctor everything he needed to know concerning who I was, how old I was, where I lived, etc. She said, "That's okay, Dad. You don't have to talk. I'll give them the information." Even at that age she was quick to take charge, whenever the occasion required her to do so.

That ordeal marked the end of my skating, because the thought always lurked in the back of my mind that I could fall again and break a limb or sustain some other injury. By this time, I was past forty-five and nearing the age where breaking bones was not the thing to do. Celeste went on to continue her roller skating every chance she got and to engage in ice skating also.

She had been ice skating from a young age, and I got her fitted for custom ice skates, when her feet finally stopped growing. She often skated at the Rockefeller Center Rink, and I would go there and watch her glide around the ice. She actually worked at the rink part time as a rink monitor and instructor. She invited many of her friends and acquaintances there to skate and sponsored several skating parties. She has also gotten her little daughter into skates, and those who didn't know her well were surprised to see how well she could skate. She was always a bit low-key, a modest child, and that didn't come from me. It probably came from her mother, because in most instances, I let people know what I know and what I can do.

At one time in Celeste's life, you couldn't convince her that her father didn't know everything. One day one of her little friends asked her something she didn't know the answer to, and I heard her say to her little friend, "I don't know; ask my father. He knows everything." There is an age at which a child thinks her parent knows everything, and my daughter was no different.

The time came when Celeste was well into her junior year in high school, and it was, for her, a time of serious concentration and planning. This was the beginning of the home stretch, the period when everything she did in school would impact her future. These last two years would make the difference; they would help determine if college, what college and what major. They would actually determine what she may have been capable of becoming.

Personally, I wanted her to be an engineer. At the time, I felt that the real money and rewards were in that field. This was the dawning of the technological revolution, and technical knowledge would go far in the professional world far into the future. The horse and buggy days in America were virtually gone forever, never to return. We were at the edge of a dawning, new century—the year 2000—ushering in a virtual explosion of technology. She somewhat agreed and began setting her sights on the engineering field. I think she felt her father knew what he was talking about. After all, her father knew everything. If she had any misgivings about becoming an engineer, she never expressed them to me.

Celeste began shaping her future by focusing more sharply than ever on the pre-college scholastic requirements. She listened to her high school guidance counselors and to her parents, and as best she could, she channeled her energies and efforts into setting the stage for college acceptance. As the junior year began to draw to a close and the senior year came clearly into view, she had put most of the pieces of the puzzle of her pre-college preparation into place. Her grades were well above average, she had extracurricular activities to her credit, and the other schools and school years showed evidence of a young lady whose parents had prepared for her future beyond high school.

BE THERE—REALLY BE THERE

As she entered her senior year, we began poring over college catalogues, which were collected from various colleges of interest and from the library. We began sending out applications to those which seemed to best fit the career choices she had in mind. As time wore on, she began the process of narrowing down college choices to a few she may have had an interest in attending.

There were also some that we were not specifically *disinterested* in her attending. Any good learning institution would have been acceptable to me, whether it was local or in some distant state. I was confident that Celeste had been prepared and conditioned to stand on her own, at home or away from home. She was a self-starter, and a self-motivator. She sought help when she needed it but did not wait for anyone to get her on track. She took personal initiative at all times, as long as it was within the guidelines which her parents had laid down for her. She didn't usually make rash, dumb decisions and especially without speaking to her parents first. She sought out enough information beforehand to bring to her parents to help them help her to make reasonable decisions.

She brought the applications, and her mother and I gave our input, as needed. I had broad-ranging insight concerning the college selection and acceptance process, because I had once traveled that road. It all came back to me, the page that says: "In two hundred words or less, tell us why you would like to attend Green Campus College," or "What are the most recent ten books you have read, and which one had the greatest influence on your thinking?" We helped her through all of the application procedures, as required, and she put the ones in the mail that had priority in her selection.

I'm not quite sure how she came about desiring to attend the college she actually graduated from (Rochester Institute of Technology in Rochester, New York). It was a college I didn't know a great deal about. Nevertheless, it was a fine institution that got much of its support from the Kodak Corporation. The institution had been around for quite some time and had graduated a host of quality engineers in all areas of the engineering discipline. I was happy she had selected that institution, because the more I came to know about it, the more I came to respect it as a noteworthy institution of higher learning. In addition, I believe she formed some lifelong friendships with individuals she met during her college career. She even met the young man there whom she later married. He graduated as a very bright, proficient computer engineer, who went on to become a team leader for a large niche computer company.

A TABLESPOON OF LOVE, A TABLESPOON OF DISCIPLINE

Her high school guidance counselor wasn't altogether keen on the idea of her pursuing the engineering field. I don't know exactly why, but maybe (mere speculation) he could see a creative part of her that wasn't so technical, and maybe he could have also been a little old-fashioned with the idea that the field of engineering was a man's domain. A part of Celeste is creative, and another part of her evidences the thinker, the analyst and the technician. All of those characteristics of her makeup finally merged to get her settled into the engineering discipline she has come to make her career. The discipline is packaging engineering, which lends itself to some creativity and much technical discipline.

I'm sure her high school guidance counselor was surprised, if he saw her name in the wedding section of the *New York Times,* with her job title being the packaging engineer for a major pharmaceuticals company, or when she came to one of the high school reunions with her business card reading "Packaging Engineer." Children always surprise high school guidance counselors, don't they? They surprise them in positive ways, as well as surprising them in negative ways.

During this period, there were also other things and other lessons that Celeste had to learn. It wasn't until her twelfth year that she was old enough to get a learner's permit for driving. I wanted her to learn to drive at an early age, because I felt it very important to get her involved early, so she could grow into the requirements of the road experience, before any form of nervousness set in. I also felt it was another aspect required for her complete preparedness for life and living. I saw so many who reached adulthood and beyond and never learned to drive. Some tried to learn in later years, but found themselves too nervous to take on the task of interacting on the high-speed roads of modern society.

I felt it an absolute requirement that all modern-day children learned to drive, when they came of age. In times past, parents didn't want to risk possible damage to their vehicle, while teaching the child to drive. I refused to fall in love with any auto to the extent that I coveted it and worried over it. No auto would be too good or too sacred to use for teaching my child to drive. My only concern was for her safety. So, she got her permit, and I embarked upon the task of teaching her how to drive.

I would take her out at my every possible convenience. This continued until such time as I felt she could safely handle a vehicle on the road. I felt that the perfecting of driving skills would come about from the frequency of her driving. I was also intent on her becoming a driver who could park the vehicle well. It always appeared that most women drivers had a problem parking well, and I didn't want my daughter to fall into that "most" category. I've seen women attempting to back into a space long enough to fit a tractor and trailer into, and finally drive away believing the space to be too small. On the other hand, I've seen women struggle (for what seemed like forever) to fit into a smaller space and end up getting into the space, but leaving the car parked two or three feet from the curb. I would look at the woman, shake my head and say to myself, "Where did she get her license?"

My determination was for my daughter to be able to handle a car well, and (above all) to be able to park well. In the process of teaching her to park, I had a routine that required her to make three perfect parks in a row before we quit for the day. If she made two and fouled up the third, she had to start over. If she got the first perfect and missed on the second, she had to start over. This may not have been easy for her. One time she said to me (in frustration), "I don't want to drive anymore." I said, "Yes you do. I'm giving the lessons, and you'll quit when I say we're finished." After all, she was still the child, and I was still the father. She wasn't supposed to tell me what to do. I couldn't let her quit because the endeavor was frustrating her. Life wouldn't let her quit if she got frustrated. Sometimes in life you won't be able to quit, regardless of how frustrating the endeavor may be, because the need may demand that you keep going. There may be too much riding on the finish.

When she said she wanted to quit, I was reminded of the time when she would come into the boutique. There were certain things she enjoyed doing and others that she didn't enjoy. One of the chores that she didn't like much was cleaning the display counters. One day she came into the store, and I said, "Celeste, get the glass cleaner and some paper towels and clean the counters." She cleaned one counter, and said, "I'm going home now." I said, "No you're not. Keep cleaning the counters until you finish them all."

She thought she could escape the chore she didn't like by going home. Children will get around you if they can, but you must stay on top of your game and the child's game. I didn't let her quit, just as I didn't let her quit in other situations. I'm glad I didn't let her quit, when it came to the parking lessons, because she can park very well today, as a result of my perseverance and her not quitting. I remember her saying that the driving tester complimented her on her parking, when she took her road test. I'm sure she's glad I didn't let her quit on any of those various occasions when she felt like she was ready to throw in the towel.

It finally came to the time when Celeste was getting her program in place for high school graduation and college acceptance. Her mother was preparing to settle into a new residence for herself and the child. She, as well as I, had the child in mind in many of the decisions we made after she became a part of our lives. We decided, out of necessity, to make many sacrifices and undergo many inconveniences, if necessary, for the benefit of her well-being. We decided that, in all circumstances, we would be there, giving our all for our daughter. Her mother grasped the opportunity to purchase an apartment in a luxury high-rise cooperative apartment building. It was located in a very desirable area of the city. It had most of the conveniences of luxury living, including the circular entranceway, twenty-four-hour uniformed doorman and private swimming pool. Celeste and her mother were settling into the new living quarters just as the child's senior year was drawing to a close.

Celeste had made her grades and had been accepted into RIT, to begin working on her engineering major. She'd also had acceptances from other colleges and universities she had applied to, but her decision was to attend RIT. We were comfortable with the choice, seeing no reason to oppose it. She was happy about the choice and was looking forward with great anticipation to attending.

We were looking forward to her graduation from high school, because that represented the culmination of one of the most important legs of the educational journey. To many of us, it is the expected or is an accepted conclusion that children will complete high school. However, based on the statistics, many fail to complete that leg of the journey. Celeste was almost there, and there was no question as to whether or not she would graduate. After almost ten and a half years, five private schools, hours of worries, times of discipline, times of joy and pride, periods of disappointment and tens of thousands of dollars, she was at the threshold of embarking on the second most important leg of her academic journey. She was getting prepared to set the stage for how she might support herself as she traveled through life.

As parents, we could not help but be proud and happy. We were in the process of relieving ourselves of one of life's heavy financial endeavors and about to take on an even heavier one—college tuition and it seemed to have gone through the roof. In addition to tuition, Celeste would require housing, food, allowance, books, fees and all of the other extras that become a part of a child's college pursuit.

As she approached high school graduation, we began to put all of the final pieces in place. There were the final graduation fees to be dealt with and the graduation dress and accessories. This was a small school, and it opted out of the cap and gown regimen. I took Celeste to one of the upscale department stores in Manhattan to purchase her graduation dress. She selected a pale pink dress, slightly "A-line," with puffed shoulders. Then I took her somewhere else for shoes. She selected a pair of medium high-heeled, white pumps that complemented the pale pink dress. They went well together, because Celeste is somewhat on the tall side for a lady. Her mother did whatever else there was to be done, relative to the dress, and now Celeste was ready to take the graduation walk down the high school auditorium aisle.

It was a fine June day, and there we sat, proud and beaming parents, patting ourselves on the back for a job well done. Our daughter was completing high school and had been accepted into a very fine institution of higher learning. There we sat, waiting for the graduates to march in. There would be thirty-two of them, thirty-one of which would then head off for some college or university. One or two of them went to MIT, the top engineering school in the country. It was a moment to remember, and I had my camera loaded, sitting on a tripod and waiting to snap the graduation picture.

And then the well-known graduation song, "Pomp and Circumstance," began. The graduated came marching in two-by-two, and each couple marched to their final destination on the auditorium stage. Looking into the audience, the students could see a sea of proud faces: parents, grandparents, aunts, uncles, sisters, brothers, neighbors, friends and others, all expectantly waiting to hear the name of his or her favorite graduate called and to see that graduate step up to receive the reward toward which she or he had so diligently strived.

Whether it came hard for some or not so hard for others, it was all the same—just as well deserved. There were scholarships and grants for most, if not all, and Celeste was among the recipients. After all, this was a private school that stressed academic excellence, and going on to college was expected from students who are nurtured in that type of environment.

Celeste received some grants and fellowships, but above all that, she received an award given for the first time. This award was being given by a family to honor their son who had passed away in his final year of high school, and it was to recognize the student who most exemplified the high school spirit. Celeste was chosen.

I considered this to be one of the greatest honors a student in her graduating class could have received, to go through high school and blend into the high school atmosphere in such a way that the faculty considers that you most exemplify the high school spirit. This was evidence of a student who had showed temperance, was well behaved, friendly, outgoing and one who put her best academic foot forward. I'm sure if those parents could meet Celeste today, they would be proud to have made her the first recipient of that award in honor of their son. She is now a senior packaging engineer for a major pharmaceutical company, she married a computer engineer who led a technology team at one of the major information systems companies, and they lived happily in suburbia.

After graduation from high school, the students went their separate ways, some off to vacations in far-flung lands or exotic hideaways, some to summer jobs, some to early college and some off to some place of rest to savor the joy of being relieved from the rigors of so many years of academic endeavors.

Those who were friends, I'm sure, kept in touch and met from time to time. Others sauntered off into the atmosphere of life, never to be seen again by their fellow classmates. That's the way life is. Many of my high school classmates have never been seen or heard from in the general high school graduating community.

Celeste spent the summer working at her mother's place of business and having lunch from time to time with one of her high school friends who worked at Tiffany's for the summer. The places they worked were in close proximity. On other weekend occasions, she got together with others of her high school classmates with whom she had become close during their high school days.

6. COLLEGE

After her graduation from high school, we, as well as Celeste, were busy making preparations for her college beginning. We had to put financial wheels in motion, and she had to put intellectual wheels in motion. When the time finally arrived for her to go off to college, it was late August.

Celeste had been given all the instructions concerning directions, arrival procedures, dorm assignment and roommate. She was anxiously looking forward to this new beginning, and so were we, but as parents, we could not help but have anxieties about the new life upon which our daughter was about to embark. At the beginning, you could never know the final outcome of such a journey. Some kids went off to college and never came home again. Some met with traumatic experiences or serious accidents. Others got in trouble with the law. Some got mixed up with other children of a completely different background and persuasion, and came to make a three-hundred-and-sixty-degree turn in family outlook and family values. Some females came home pregnant, with ruined careers and lives.

In reflecting on the circumstances of two college kids' dilemma, they could have possibly faced the death penalty for the murder of their infant child, conceived while they were away in college. The parent or parents had sent their daughter away to college to study, and she ended up in an undesirable pregnancy. The son of the other parent or parents was a willing participant in this behavior, and as such, could have been required to pay with his life. The act of sending them off to college was innocent enough. The outcome resulting from their behavior was far removed from what the parents expected. The outcome could have stretched even beyond their wildest dreams.

On the other hand, some children drop out of school and come to disappoint themselves and their families. The possible outcomes of sending children off to college are many and varied. So, for us, as parents, this was a new journey, the beginning of an end we could not see nor predict with certainty.

We knew we had parented well, we had disciplined well, we had loved and we were there—really there for our daughter. And we knew our daughter. We knew many of her strengths and, I think, many of her weaknesses. We had a pretty good idea of what she was capable of and what she was incapable of doing or being. But we didn't completely know who she was.

No parent completely knows his or her child. No husband completely knows his wife, and no wife completely knows her husband. No individual completely knows himself or herself. Given different times and different circumstances, one may act or react in a way that is completely contrary to the way they would normally act. The person you think you knew (even self) can be a "Dr.-Jekyll-and-Mr.-Hyde" personality. A part of the child is a façade, and the other part is the real child. A child is human; she's an individual. No individual shows the same side of herself to every other individual in the same way. There is a side she shows to parents, a side she shows to her teachers, a side she shows to her male friends, a side she shows her female friends, a side she shows her close friends, a side she shows society and a side she holds dear and private that she and only God know.

This brings to mind a situation involving an acquaintance of mine and her daughter. She was of the opinion that her daughter always told her everything, and she expressed that opinion loud and clear. She said, on one occasion, that if her daughter had a sexual encounter, she would tell her that also, because her daughter confided in her about everything—even her most personal and intimate encounters. I countered, "No child tells everything." But the mother insisted that I was wrong about her and her daughter on that point.

One day, subsequent to her mother expressing this opinion, the daughter was having a disagreement with the man she was in a relationship with at the time. We were outside, and the mother went inside to see what was taking them so long to come outside. When the mother went inside to see what was going on, she found the daughter and her friend in the midst of a misunderstanding concerning something the male friend had innocently failed to do. In the process of the daughter's friend explaining what happened, he was trying to assure the daughter how much he cared. He just forgot to do what she had expected him to do.

The mother chimed in to indicate to the daughter's friend how much the daughter cared for him, because, she said, "You are the only man she has had sex with." Well, he was the only one the daughter had told her about. But the daughter's friend retorted, "Mother, she told me about two others." Obviously, this man was the third person, but the daughter had not revealed the other two to her mother. The crux of the story is: no child tells all.

So because we don't completely know our child, we can't always know what decisions she or he might make and what path the decisions might take. Yes, we give our child directions and values (our values), but sometimes, against our direction and our values, she or he may choose to take her own direction, adopt some other values and discard some or all of ours. She may adopt some she feels more comfortable with.

A college is a shaping ground for ideas and a melting pot of races, religions and personalities. Your child can be completely reshaped in the atmosphere of college. However, if your discipline was consistent, and your love was balanced and unwavering, your child's desire will be to make you proud and happy, and not do anything that will cause you undue hurt or disappointment. Hence, "The apple will not fall far from the tree."

Finally, the time to leave for college was upon us. We packed Celeste and all of her needed (and maybe some unneeded) college gear into the car and left for Rochester. It was a brisk day, with fall slowly dawning down-state and virtually in full bloom the further we got from the city. After some four to six hours of driving, we reached the college campus.

The atmosphere was congenial, the surroundings were rustic, and the air was a bit nippy. We were directed to the building and the dormitory where she would be bunking. Celeste immediately began to settle in and unpack her things.

Shortly after our arrival, her roommate and parents arrived. We looked around and examined her living quarters and the surrounding area. We spent a bit of time talking and getting her comfortable in her new environment. She assured us that she would be fine. That was typical Celeste—always looking at things optimistically and if otherwise, you would never know. After making sure she had all of the basic necessities she needed to begin her college life, we departed. After all, this was not her first time away from home. However, it was her first extended time away.

On our way back home, there was a lot of silence, which is often an indication of the thinking processes going on inside of the minds. There were the "ifs" and "what ifs" and the "suppose this's" and "suppose that's." By the time we reached home again, we had all but put our fears and anxieties to rest for the time being, to let the future take its course. We spoke with Celeste on a frequent basis, and she informed us of her intentions, her course selections and her progress. She told us when she was doing well academically, and sometimes she told us when she was not doing so well. And there were times when she did not shine as we thought she could or as she thought she could.

There were times when I could help Celeste surmount academic hurdles over the telephone and other times when I seemed unable to help her, even with all of the possible talk and instructions I may have been able to give her. Sometimes she was seriously challenged by the requirements of a particular course, and I guess that is not unusual. All students struggle with some course. It could be one she found difficult or one she might not particularly like. It should be expected that a student will not usually excel in everything all of the time.

There was one occasion when I felt very powerless to help her in some course obstacle she was encountering. I was very sorrowful and virtually in tears. I felt I could do what she was trying to do, and seemed not to have been able to do. Have you ever tried so hard to help your child through some difficult circumstance, and no matter how hard you tried it seemed you couldn't help her or him? Isn't that a tough one? Well, in this instance, I virtually threw up my hands and said, "Celeste, I've done all I can do on the phone to help you. If I could come up there and do it for you, I would." That is just how I felt. I wish I could have gone there to sit in that course in her place to get her through the difficult challenge. I could not. However, she persevered somehow, overcame the challenge and moved on toward accomplishing her goal.

She started out majoring in electrical engineering, but down the road she switched her major to packaging engineering. I told her, before she began college, that she could switch her major once and only once. There would be no dabbling in college courses at our expense. We talked about the switch we were contemplating. She seemed to have felt that electrical engineering was too structured and did not leave room for her creative side. Based on the discussion, I agreed with her desire to slightly modify her major. The challenge was still in the engineering discipline, but a different aspect and focus. This major would better lend itself to a balance between the technical and the creative. I'm glad she made that decision, and I'm also glad I supported her in it, because ever since she began working in her field, she has done well, and feels very good about what she does.

She continued to move ahead, focusing on the things surrounding her major and keeping the objective in clear view. This saw her well into her sophomore year. She continued along her path of focus, but not without some bumps and obstacles here and there. I interacted with her from time to time with her studies and plans in any area I could be of help. Some of her subjects were outside of my realm of knowledge, because even fathers don't know everything. She studied (I'm sure) as hard as she could and got rest from the stress of school by returning home from time to time, especially on non-school days and holidays.

She seemed always happy to be home. Her mother was always there, just as I was. Her mother provided a good home for her to come to, one with pleasant surroundings and lots of good home cooking. I'm sure Celeste always felt special, coming home to a big welcome by the building doorman, who often addressed her as "Madam," even though she was only seventeen or eighteen years of age. That was a bit young to be a "Madam." On holidays, the building she came home to was festively decorated and very cheery, and from time to time she brought home friends and classmates who also got the VIP treatment.

Of course, on the trips home we would spend time together. When she came in by train, I would often go to the railroad station to meet her and bring her home. When the holiday was Christmas, it was always celebrated together as a family unit. We always began Christmas morning together, opening presents and sharing refreshments at her and her mother's home. Since the time Celeste was small, we both saw to it that she had a present for her parent on that special occasion. On the other special holidays, such as Mother's Day and Father's Day, we also made certain she had a present for her mother or her father, on whatever holiday it was.

Most of her years, from her pre-teen and onward, Celeste saved her money to purchase a present for her parent on the appropriate occasion. I can recall one occasion when she should have had money to buy her mother a present, but didn't have any. She came to me, and I gave her the money, but not without a scolding and a stern lesson in unselfishness. I admonished her to always save money out of her allowance for these types of needs.

For her, the months of college seemed to creep by. For me, they also didn't seem to pass fast enough. When she had her challenges, I wished the more that the period of pursuit would come to a speedy end. It couldn't have happened too soon for me. However, the challenges she was experiencing were just "par for the course." College challenges most students, and Celeste was no exception.

Knowing Celeste as we did, we knew she would overcome any challenge and go on about the pursuit of her goal. She's not the type to fold her tent and quit. She knew she had to succeed for herself, as well as for her parents, who so believed in her. She knew we had done so much and had so much confidence in her that she probably felt hard-pressed not to ever let us down. I'm sure she wanted to do something to show that she appreciated us being there for her.

In her second year of college, she had decided she wanted to live outside of the dorm setting, in a housing complex nearby, and she decided to share an apartment with two other students. I had misgivings about it, because in that environment, they were responsible for preparing their own meals. When she resided in the dorm, the meals were included and paid for, along with the cost of lodging. Living in an apartment setting required more discipline. We sent her a food allowance, but worried a great deal about the possibility of her spending all of the money prematurely and going hungry, rather than telling us she hadn't managed her finances well. The thought never ceased to bother me.

Now, as I look back on the situation, we never knew if she ever did that or not, because she never told us. When I visited her on one occasion, I wanted to see what she had in the refrigerator and in the cabinets, and I wanted to know what she had eaten at mealtime. She almost convinced me that she was eating well and never went hungry. We always tried to be diligent about sending needed funds for food and other college necessities. Sometimes she would run up large telephone bills that had to be taken care of and, as with other things, we had to be there to take up the slack.

I baked her cookies and cakes and chocolate brownies, and her mother sent her care packages of other needed and wanted items. It was about not forgetting the necessities, about not letting her down and about always being there.

The third year brought other challenges, and other decisions had to be made concerning finals, major subjects and making sure everything was in perspective for the soon-to-be-coming graduation, because the following year would constitute the wrapping-up procedure.

By this time, Celeste had made many close friends and acquaintances. Some of them came home with her on various weekends and some of the other school days off. I was happy to see them studying hard together and enjoying themselves, as opportunity permitted. Some of her friends were photography majors, and some were newspaper printing and production majors. The school curriculum covered a wide spectrum of industrial majors. It was a technology institute, just as the name implied.

Her third year in college was highlighted by a summer job program, whereby she was able to work in her field of study. She was employed for the summer in a large computer manufacturing company and got the opportunity to utilize some packaging engineering skills on an actual job project. The job was located in the Massachusetts area, and getting her up there and settled in was quite a feat. It required finding a suitable place for her to live and buying the necessary comforts.

She needed a TV and a fan, for starters, because the living quarters turned out to be an attic apartment. However, we didn't "sweat it" a lot, because it was only temporary. We also had to work out the plans concerning getting to and from the place of employment on a daily basis. This really required "being there." I managed, and she managed, and when the summer work was over, she came home with about $2,800.00 she had managed to save after paying all her expenses.

Celeste also got a job offer to work with that company after she had completed her degree, an offer she later chose to opt out of. Maybe that job didn't offer the glamour she was told existed in her field, which could be found in the likes of cosmetic packaging, cereal packaging or others.

The summer passed. She was back in school, and this was the beginning of her senior year. The time was fast approaching, and all of her pre-graduation requirements were falling into place. The required courses were under her belt. She had survived the rigors of the four-year curriculum, and now her eyes were toward graduation.

It all seemed like a lifetime in coming. She had reached the point of focus on the cap and gown, the invitations and our thoughts for a graduation present. Her mother and I were busy getting our responsibilities in focus. It was, indeed, a joy to be at the point of paying for the cap and gown and all of the other related graduation requirements, because I knew that what I was now paying for was a successful college completion.

She had surmounted the second most difficult and important of life's hurdles, and I was glad just to have been able to be there for her throughout this experience. These are the types of times and circumstances when your being there matters most. They are the ones that most children remember, even after you're no longer around. Being there when times are easy is easy, and being there when times are hard is hard.

My baby was graduating from college, and the exhilaration I felt was beyond words. To see her finally reach the finishing line of this endeavor was one of the happiest days of my life. I was not only happy for me and her mother; I was equally happy for her, because I'm sure she often felt the strain of the struggle, and she may have sometimes wondered if she would ultimately triumph. Such doubt is not unusual. I went through similar emotions, and so did many others. But we had confidence in her. She is not one who always discloses her plans or her frustrations, but she always seems to have a plan and doesn't let frustrations take over her plans. Most importantly, she doesn't quit until she wins.

I decided I would give her a thousand dollars for a graduation present. That was about the extent of what I felt I could afford at the moment. After all, we were on the threshold of completing fifteen years of private schooling, and that was no financial picnic for a middle-class family such as ours. Out of the thousand dollars I was giving her, I told her she could spend five hundred on whatever she wanted to, and the other five hundred should be invested in something. It turned out that the five hundred dollars invested, plus whatever returns it yielded, was later used to help her buy the apartment she lived in for four years prior to getting married. Since then, the market value on that apartment has more than tripled.

On the night before graduation, I spent the night in Rochester in order to be up and about for the early morning graduation preliminaries. The anxiety was high, and I was so full I felt almost as if I would burst wide open. I could hardly contain my joy at the fact that she was graduating from college. It was finally happening. I had waited years to witness this event. I'd had no doubt about her reaching this point, but feeling that it would happen and witnessing the occurrence are two very different things. It just doesn't happen until it happens, and it was now happening.

I rose early, cleaned myself up, got dressed and went to the college campus to look for Celeste. When I arrived at the campus and the site of the graduation ceremony, there were throngs of students and relatives milling around, all waiting for the fateful moment. I'm sure they were as joy-filled as I and her mother were. This was the culmination of one of the most important educational endeavors in the life of a child and the parents of the child. Finishing college wasn't new to the family. I also finished college, but I did it as an individual thing.

Obtaining a college degree is still a major accomplishment, because, even today, the high school dropout rate is very high. A college degree (at the least) gives a child a profession, an opportunity to compete, and it opens doors to possibilities, although it may not always get you inside. Whatever it does or doesn't do, it is akin to a basic necessity in today's society. This event would represent the finality of all of the efforts put forth, even from the beginning. It would be the high mark of all the coaching, nurturing, the tuition and fees, the books, the food and lodging, the clothing, the allowance, the phone bills and all of the various other expenditures required in seeing a child through school. We had done it. We had arrived at the point that tied all of our struggles, anxieties, hopes and dreams neatly together in one big package.

We spotted Celeste among the crowd, and she saw us coming too. She is tall and so she towered above many of the others and was rather easy to spot. She was smiling broadly and seemed as happy as we were. My thoughts immediately flashed back to the time some four years prior when we had dropped her off at her dormitory to begin her college pursuit. The time seemed to have crept by, but it had now come full circle, and she had now qualified for the degree of Bachelor of Science in packaging engineering.

Celeste hugged us and then proceeded to lead us around, so she could introduce us to her friends and schoolmates with whom she shared a common interest. After this was over, it was time to go in, take our seats and wait for the graduation exercise formalities to begin. And what a procession it was! There were thousands of graduates, majoring in every conceivable engineering discipline, as well as in various other fields. It was a long, drawn out process. We just wanted to hear her name called; the rest of the roll calling didn't make a great deal of difference to us. However, we had to sit through it all, because the others had to sit through it too. There were other proud parents and relatives waiting to hear their graduate's name called.

So we really didn't mind the wait; it was all a part of the gaiety of the event. We had patience. After all, we had waited almost fifteen years for this day to come. From the first day Celeste had started school, we had anticipated the day she would be graduating from college.

After all was said and done and all of the degrees were awarded, the graduates streamed out into the open. They said what would be the final "hellos" and "good-byes" for some and proceeded to join their relatives, to prepare themselves for what could very well be the final campus exit. We gathered Celeste and two or three of her friends together to go for a late lunch.

After that, Celeste bid her friends adieu and departed with us for her living quarters. We had to be about the business of clearing out her belongings before embarking on the trip home. We had been there for the start, and we were there for the finish. That's what being there is all about; it's about hanging in from start to finish.

This represented the passing of another milestone. The next big event would be giving her in marriage. After that, the hands-on, day-to-day parenting would be done. But there would certainly be other events to be encountered in between the college graduation and the wedding ceremony, events concerning jobs and independent living quarters. Those would constitute two of the last big challenges that required being there, prior to relinquishing my role and her mother's role to her husband.

7. Post-College and Marriage

Many things happened in between the time Celeste finished college and the time she got married. One, the after-college job that she would have liked to get didn't materialize immediately. She had turned down the job offer at the company where she had interned for the summer, obviously not thinking it would matter and wanting to get immediate employment in an area she liked. However, it did matter, because the type of job she wanted, much to her surprise, was not readily available. She ended up taking a position outside of her field of study to earn money in support of her financial sufficiency.

I helped her to acquire the position, because I was keenly aware of what her financial needs would probably be. She took a glorified secretarial position, and before leaving the firm, she had parlayed that position into a substantive permanent offer. In hindsight, I was so happy she turned this offer down, because a position in her field was now on the horizon. I would have been the first one to advise her not to take the offer, even though the pay and all other pertinent perks were enticing. I'm glad she made that important decision on her own. It's a big negative to spend valuable time working in an area outside of your field of endeavor, only to discover later that when you're ready to work in your field, you have no valuable experience and will, more than likely, have to start at the bottom—much like an apprentice.

It was not at all surprising that Celeste would accomplish what she did on that first job, because she was parented to have good work ethics, to be punctual, to manage time well, to give a good day's work for a bad day's pay (if necessary), and to be the ultimate professional in all of her interactions, whether with superiors, clients or customers. Most workers in her age group had long since lost the positive work ethics battle, because most in her age group were not raised to even have these qualities. They were spoiled, given too much, and not much was demanded of them.

Those qualities were all a part of the "bad parenting" syndrome. As parents we didn't fit into that mold, and as a child, Celeste was not a product of that outcome. She had acquired a keen sense of business from a young age and came about it honestly. I was always involved in some type of business enterprise, and she got an opportunity to witness business operations firsthand. She wasn't keenly aware of it, but her grandfather was also an entrepreneur of sorts, having run a grocery store, a candy store, a printing business and a small construction operation. The business bug just sort of rubbed off on her through osmosis.

I taught her how to count and handle money, make up bank deposits, and take them to the bank at an age when she could barely see the top of the teller's counter. She would go into the bank, and the tellers would say, "That's Don Gandy's daughter." She also knew the importance of organizing her time and keeping appointments.

Along the journey of travel that took her from college to marriage, she paused at several stops. One stop gave her an honor for being deemed an outstanding young lady in her community and church circle. It was awarded by the "Helping Hand Club" of her church. The occasion was inspiring, and the joy of being there to witness my daughter being thought of in such a manner was a testament to our parenting success. She shared the dais that day with four other honorees, the local senator and the borough district attorney. It was a banquet affair, and her parents were there.

This was just another one of those special occasions and another opportunity to be there to help celebrate another one of life's joys of accomplishment, as our daughter continued her trek toward adulthood. A properly raised child, by God's grace, had been equipped to pull together the requirements needed to carry her through life in all of the various areas previously mentioned.

Celeste was arriving. She was daily asserting her ability to survive independently as an adult. She acquired her own apartment, took on all the chores of house furnishing and decorating, housekeeping, preparing her own meals and paying her own bills. She acquired her own car and took on the task of learning how to get from point "a" to point "b" and how to keep this required survival necessity in good working order.

Throughout most of this period, she was keeping company with the young man who would later become her husband. I'm sure she learned the art of give and take from the relationship, and without a doubt she learned and practiced the art of caring and sharing and being there for someone to make his life better. She had to do and be all of those things to her husband in his final years, just as life had required her parents to be there for her, to make her life better. It has been required of Celeste to be more than a hill; she has had to be a mountain at times.

David, her husband, was a giant in his young years and transitioned into eternity at a very young age. During the long term of his illness, she showed herself to possess boundless love and caring and "being there." On occasion, she spent nights in his hospital room with him, she fluffed his pillow, and she made the doctor visits with him, to hear the sometimes not-so-good news about his illness. She even went from full-time work to part-time, so that she could be there for him.

But David had earned that support by the way he lived his life. He tried to make everyone's life better with a word of advice, with money (if needed) and with shared knowledge at every opportunity. They were both so much alike in many ways. They were both only children, both strivers, both "doers," both possessed a sense of caring and sharing, both were unselfish, both graduated from the same college, both attended the same private school for a period, both had good business sense, and both exuded a boundless sense of strength—even when the chips may have been down. David was a "Mt. Everest." In reflection, I can't think for one minute that they just happened upon the planet and that their ways and habits just dropped on them. The same is true in the life of any child; they must be taught and nurtured "to be."

Celeste has a close set of friends, all of whom seem to fit together very well. They did parties, trips and other recreational things together. Many of those friendships grew out of their college days, and many are still alive and well today.

The transitional period from college through job stability, independent housekeeping and social survival led to the final step of the transition into adulthood—marriage. This only says that the finality of a child becoming a woman or man is partly evidenced in marriage (especially when one reaches a mature, or marrying, age). Marriage usually breaks any dependence on parental guidance for everyday direction and evidences how successful the child-raising process has been.

The idea in raising a child successfully is that the child will have the ability, through legal and honest means, to provide for her or his financial well-being, to be morally equipped to live life and interact with one's fellow-man in an atmosphere of congeniality and respect, and to find a suitable mate (if that is one's desire), who has a similar vision and goals. Then, between the two, they can help to comfort and bear each other's burdens, they can have a family (if life and circumstances dictate it), and can go on to love God for who He is and for the support He can give them throughout their lives.

After all of the post-college events were said and done and after all of the pre-adult lessons were learned, the next step, as desire dictated, was the preparation for sharing life with the man with whom Celeste felt compatible. She and David made a decision to enter into marriage. As her future husband, David discussed their decision with us and we gave our feedback, and upon our approval, they went about the business of planning the occasion.

They didn't need us for the nuts and bolts of the pre-marriage planning, because their intelligence and ability gave them all that was needed to get the required things done. However, we were both there for them when and if they needed us at those unexpected times that required a little additional effort or assistance. We did small things that we were asked to do and gave some financial support that helped to lighten the load. They bore the brunt of the financial requirements of the wedding, and that was as they wanted it to be. Whatever the cost, they did it as they desired to do it. We were there for the support—if they needed to lean on us.

After all of the planning and the leaning, the day of the marriage finally arrived. We were still there, as was David's family. As the ceremony required, I was there to give Celeste in marriage. This was an anxious occasion, because they were both embarking on a journey, not knowing where it would take them. Nothing about their future was "written in stone."

After one finishes the parenting process, and the child is ready to transition from childhood to adulthood, few joys are greater than giving your daughter in what you think will be a caring, nurturing and being-there-for-each-other marriage. The man she married was all of that and more. He was truly capable of taking on the challenges of a husband and father, and he did.

Beyond the joy of giving your daughter in marriage is the joy of knowing that you were not just there for the wedding; you were there for the first steps, the smiles, the tears, the vaccinations, the skinned knees, the bumped head, the other hurts, the schools, the academic challenges, the graduations, the honors, the illnesses, the needs and for all of the other "before-and-after" and the "in-betweens." I am glad I could be there, because so many fathers wanted to be there for their child and could not be, and so many others didn't care if they were there or not. There is a special pride that goes with the thought of knowing that I did the hard stuff, and even when I couldn't, I did it. When the chips were down, I did it, and when it required more than I was or had, I still did it.

Seeing the results of our being there for Celeste and who she now is, I'm grateful to God for keeping us there by her, to see her grow from a child to a woman. If I had to do it all over again for her, I would, because she is my child. I owed it to her, and she made the journey easier than it could have been. Look around at some of our adults, and you can understand what I mean. Not only were we there for her; she was also there to help us be there. Thus, our journey was made worthwhile.

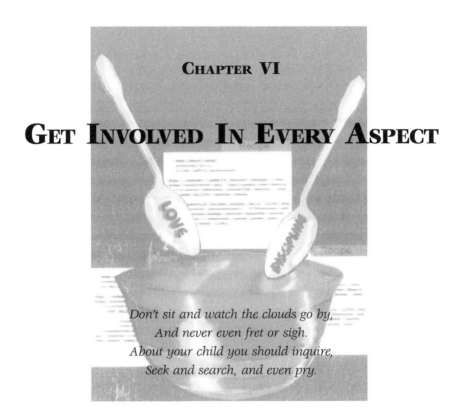

CHAPTER VI

GET INVOLVED IN EVERY ASPECT

Don't sit and watch the clouds go by,
And never even fret or sigh.
About your child you should inquire,
Seek and search, and even pry.

1. IT IS OUR RESPONSIBILITY

A child is an individual—boy or girl—who is in a stage of development wherein he or she needs the guidance of a more mature person, due to his or her inability to make adult decisions. *Child* denotes a stage of development or underdevelopment in both a physical and mental sense. Because the child has not yet reached the stage in which he or she is expected to be capable of making adult decisions, that child needs the guidance of a guardian or more grown-up individual. At this stage of his or her development, the child needs to be (and must be) directed by a more mature individual, capable of steering him or her along a course designed to effect a smooth transition into adulthood.

If the transition is to be smooth, the child has to be directed in the proper mode of behavior. He or she has to be directed in taking on the things that will enhance life in a positive way and omitting those things that

175

will influence life in a negative way. So we, as guardians of the children, are responsible for properly directing their behavior. We, as guardians of the children, should exercise some control over many (if not every) aspect of their lives, especially in the areas that require decisions to be made that cannot be properly made by them, with the immature mind they possess in their childlike stage of development. As a matter of fact, we, as parents or guardians, are responsible for making the decisions that will steer children along a right course and keep them on track.

This is our responsibility to them, as their overseers. We are responsible for guiding their decisions and behavior, until they reach a point wherein they can be responsible for the outcome of their own decisions. Prior to the time the child reaches the age in which she or he is responsible for her or his own actions, we, as parents or guardians, must endure the consequences of their bad decisions or their indecisions. That is why parents or guardians came into being. It is assumed, and rightfully so, that guardians, in their adult minds and with their adult state of development, possess the maturity to steer a child along a proper course of behavior and development.

Do guardians always make the best decisions concerning the child's direction and development? No. Could the child make a better decision concerning her or his direction and development? Sometimes, maybe. However, guardians, with their mature minds are more likely to get it right more often than a child will. Some guardians make terrible decisions concerning a child's growth and developmental progress, but given the overall perspective of guardian decision-making, more guardians are more likely to make the better decision more often than a child would.

Individuals usually become guardians only because they have traveled a path in life that the child has yet to travel, and the guardian supposedly knows of the dangers and pitfalls to be encountered along the journey through life. For those dangers and pitfalls of which guardians may not be aware, they usually possess a better sense and ability to scope out the potential snares that may lie ahead than would a child. We, as guardians, must carry out the responsibility to the best of our ability. We must not shirk that obligation or grow weary in the process. If we don't quite get it right every time, it is still presumed that we will, more often than the child, get it right, and that is what can make all of the difference between successful development and failure.

If we, as adults, can't get it right, then what can we expect of a child? We must, therefore go about life, directing and involving ourselves in every aspect of our child's development. The responsibility for misdirecting is mostly ours, and if we do misdirect, the child, as well as all of society, can suffer from the results of our misdirection. The responsibility for what our children become is mostly on our shoulders, as their guardians.

2. The Clothes and Things

We must exercise control over the clothes our children wear and the haircut or hairstyle they get. We must take responsibility for decisions concerning the schools they attend, and we must exercise broad, discretionary powers over their social life and the company they keep. Parents should also have strong input (to the extent of their ability to do so) into the course of study a child may desire to pursue, and that should relate more to the child's ability and fitness than to the desires and hopes, because a guardian may be partly responsible for what a child may become or may not become. Guardians should give instructions and make demands upon children, because this is an integral part of shaping their direction.

Guardians should have specific influence concerning the music children listen to, the things they spend the guardian's money on and the source of funds that didn't come from the guardian. The control and direction should begin at the youngest age at which a child is capable of understanding what yes and no mean and right from wrong. It should continue until such time as you, the guardian, are no longer responsible for the outcome of a child's decisions and behavior.

Parents or guardians should direct what a child eats, what she or he watches on television, what movies she attends or whether or not she should be allowed to go to a movie at all. In a final thought, parents or guardians should exercise as much influence as possible over the place a child may choose to live and the person the child may choose to marry.

The clothing children wear, when they are under parental control, is usually purchased by the parent or guardian, and is either paid for by the parent or accepted from someone else by the parent. These clothes either denote a behavior or influence a behavior. The clothing individuals wear tells a great deal about the person wearing them. A child's style of clothing and maintenance tell much about the wearer, as well as the provider. They may also give a clue concerning the direction toward which a child may be headed. Don't allow your child to set a mode of behavior by a style of clothes.

Sometimes one has a tendency to become what one exhibits. Quite often the outer manifestations are mirroring inner desires. Sometimes, if the child dresses like a sophisticate, she or he will act like a sophisticate; if a child dresses pretty, she may act pretty; if a child dresses in a seductive way, she may desire to be seductive, and if a child dresses like a street dude or gangster, he may act or desire to act accordingly. The biblical saying, *"As a man thinketh in his heart, so is he,"* goes far to depict the man.

Just as it is with clothes, a hairstyle says much about the individual sporting it. Individuals often endeavor to depict an inward feeling by an outward display. There are times when an individual may present herself or himself in a certain light in which she or he thinks she wants to be seen and may refrain from ever doing that again. The remark may say, "That wasn't me." The person thought that was the wanted look but decided, after seeing the look, that it was not. However, when the presentation is continued and consistent, it is either mirroring who the individual is or who the individual wants to become. Be aware of what your child is displaying, because it may be a preview of what she or he is already endeavoring to become. The "look" will sometimes indicate a direction and a destination. Do you recall the old saying, "If it walks like a duck, looks like a duck and quacks like a duck, it probably is a duck"?

A child's social life should be closely monitored and directed. If you ever lose control of what a child is doing, you have lost control of the child. Where your child goes and what your child does should be of utmost concern to you as a parent or guardian. You must realize that the environment within which your child circulates will have a great deal of influence over the behavior your child will come to exhibit, and behavior may ultimately direct what your child will become. I heard a saying once and don't know the original source from whence it came, but it goes like this: "Sow a thought, reap an action; sow an action, reap a habit; sow a habit, reap a destiny."

Don't accept or permit your child to participate in or go around in any circle or group that tends to promote or embrace bad habits or values contrary to your good beliefs and teaching or that promotes behavior that would impact your child's life in a negative way in the future. Children have ended up in cults and gangs that promoted violence, sexual misconduct, lawbreaking and many other forms of social misconduct, because not enough attention was given to the monitoring of the child's social activities. Many such activities have led to an early untimely death for the child and caused untold suffering and grief for the parents or guardians. The annals of the past are filled with such accounts. If you are "on top of" and monitor your child's social life, you can often get an inkling of some of the negative, or destructive, habits or behavior that may be taking shape.

A part of the social patterns and behavior is the company your child keeps. Do you remember the saying "birds of a feather flock together"? When you see your child around an individual or alone in that individual's company more than once or twice, you should find out something about that individual. Associates tend to influence the individual with whom they are associating. One initially picks an associate because one thinks that individual has something in common with her or him. If she or he finds out that this is not the case, she will either sever the association or find some common ground for continuing the association. When this happens, the associates begin to take on each other's ways and habits. After a while, one will begin to behave like the other.

The company that a child keeps could possibly influence the child's goals and aspirations. My mother used to say, "If you want to go some-where, you must get with the people who are on their way there." Obviously, the one who isn't going can only hold the child back. So monitor and have direct input into whom your child can and cannot keep company with. Demand and insist on her not keeping company with an individual who may influence her or his life in a negative way.

When it comes to schools that children desire to attend, guardians should have direct involvement and feedback. Children have various reasons for wanting to attend a certain school, and many of the reasons are not because the academic standards are high or the discipline is strict. Often the desire to attend a certain school is because a friend or friends attend and/or a certain known type of behavior is permitted or goes on that is conducive to a child's behavioral desires.

Children presently attending a particular school are aware of behavior patterns and activities prevalent in that particular school's environment. This information and feedback has been filtered down from other children who have attended or who know someone who has attended. This pertinent information is all over the landscape. As a guardian, you may want to know as much as possible about the school, the behavior exhibited there, the quality of students graduating from there and the percentage of students graduating who are likely to go on to institutions of higher learning. This is important to know prior to your child's potential attendance.

A guardian can tell a great deal concerning a child's focus by the school she or he desires to attend. A child with an academic focus will desire a school atmosphere that is known for high academic standards and disciplinary controls, because the two seem to go hand in hand. A child who seems to desire a school known for higher emphasis on socializing probably has less of a desire for academic fulfillment. Children get feedback on the climate in particular schools, and other children will or will not want to attend based on this feedback. Therefore, if you visit and/or get feedback on a school your child wants to attend, you may be able to discern a great deal relative to the direction the child may be headed. This is especially true if a child knows someone who has attended or is attending and is able to get information about the climate in that school. So we, as guardians, must take the responsibility for a child's decision concerning the school she or he desires to attend.

In addition to the desired school, the desired course of study will also give input into a child's desired focus. The guidelines are elementary and can prove worthwhile, if considered. You can tell if a child doesn't mind being challenged, has lofty ambitions or wants merely to get out of school and get it over with. When and if you discover the reason, and the reason seems contrary to normal desires and expectations from a child, an attempt can be made to steer a child in a more positive direction. In some instances, a parent or guardian can save thousands of dollars that may have been spent toward a college education for a child that has shown signs of not being college bound or college material. While you are being prudent about looking into the school or schools your child desires to attend and the reason the child wants to attend, you should also be applying the same standard of inspection in looking into a child's intended curriculum.

Another element surrounding a child's environment that may predict where a child is or is not headed is the music the child listens to. A child with godly desires and direction will desire to be surrounded by and inspired by the type of music that has its roots in godly inspiration. The devil's roots aren't in Christ, and he will not seek to attract with sacred music. On the other hand, Christian roots aren't grounded in Satan, and individuals will not be drawn to Christ with demonically-inspired music. That which is not centered in the positive is centered in the negative. There can be no middle ground or fence straddling. Music can inspire one toward higher positive values or lower negative values, and if it means enough for a child to spend her money or your money on, it is enough to get your child's attention.

Parents should pay close attention to non-Christian music, because much of it has subtle satanic messages. It is very important for a guardian to monitor and direct the type of music the child can and cannot listen to in your house. Sometimes you are at a loss to monitor that which the child may listen to, when she or he is outside of your listening ear. You must have this type of control, and if you are in control, you should be able to have some say in what's done on the premises where you pay the rent or the mortgage.

When we were growing up, the only acceptable music, as far as our parents were concerned, that could be played in our home was gospel or country and western. Country and western used to be clean, and is still one of the cleaner versions of acceptable music. The above two types of music were the only forms of music considered as having lyrics clean enough to be played in our home.

You cannot follow a child around twenty-four hours a day, to monitor the type of music she or he listens to, but you can monitor the type that is being played in your house and the type of music your child is spending your hard-earned money to buy. Parents must keep in mind where a child's monies and support are coming from. Would you give a child your money and not have any input or say so over what the money is being used for? I would not. If you would, you'd be a very foolish parent, who may live to regret the error of your ways.

3. Where Things Come From

If a child is buying things with money that wasn't supplied by you, you need to immediately get specific knowledge concerning the source or sources of the money, before a drug lord or racketeering element comes into your house and brings harm or kills both the child and you. There are and can be many ill-gotten sources of money, and any or all of them can lead to a child's undoing. Don't sit idly by and watch a child bring things into your home or presence that could not have been obtained with the funds you supplied and not ask the child where the thing or things came from.

I can reflect on a made-for-television movie about a young girl who got entangled in an affair with an older man. The affair reached epic proportions and made national news headlines. One scene I remember quite well, that has relevance here, showed the young fifteen- or sixteen-year-old high school student working as an escort to older men and being paid as much as $100.00 or more per escort to do things for their entertainment and enjoyment. The significance isn't only what she was doing, but the type of money she was getting. The parents didn't have a clue as to what was going on in her life.

She was using these funds to pay a car note, among other things. They knew about her having the car note, but they thought she was working an acceptable, part-time, after-school job. They never diligently and seriously looked into the job situation, so they never knew where the money was coming from. They made assumptions that were far from actuality. This account was based on a true story, and the details mirrored a real-life situation.

Some parents are passively going about life, while children are spending money on clothes, records and tapes and other materials that could not have possibly been obtained by funds given them by these parents. Other children are exhibiting wares and life-styles obtained through illegal drug sales, theft and the sale of stolen goods. Can you, the parent, see the changes and never bother to ask the child where the money came from that purchased those things or that life-style? Many parents accept gratuities and favors from such ill-gotten gain and never inquire about the source.

Other children's favors and life-styles are being financed by a more mature individual who may be "keeping them" in exchange for intimate favors. Some children are even being kept by homosexual lovers, also in exchange for intimate sexual favors. And all of the above can lead to death at one extreme, or physical and social ruin at the other extreme. That is why it is in the parent or guardian's best interest to inquire about the source of money used to finance unusual purchases, such as those that could not have been obtained with money afforded by them personally. As a parent or guardian, you should and must be concerned. If you have a child who is still a minor in age, still being supported by you, under your roof and who is too grown to give you an account, you have already lost control and have done a very poor job as a parent or guardian in raising the child.

4. THINGS CONSUMED BY BODY AND MIND

Are you concerned about your child's health? If so, then you must have direct parental input into the child's eating habits. The eating habits formed early in the child's life will often be the eating habits a child will carry with her throughout life. A balanced lunch or dinner meal, usually consists of meat, a starch (maybe protein based) and a green vegetable. It is better if the frequency of the vegetable served consists of a green leafy vegetable. Children should have balance in every meal, and such balance should begin with breakfast.

Don't send your child off to school or permit your child to go off to school with no breakfast or the wrong type of breakfast. Some of the wrong types include: sodas, sweets and unhealthy snacks such as potato chips, popcorn, cheese doodles, pretzels, Doritos and the like. The sodas, the sweets and the latter items provide virtually no nourishment for a child's body and may even set a pattern that can possibly lead to obesity and some of the other physical ailments that a youngster can be prone to. If you are not in the position or are not home when your child leaves for school, you should leave specific instructions with the child, the older sibling or the caregiver as to how you desire the child or children to eat. Put the proper type of healthy breakfast foods in the home for the child's consumption, and give specific guidelines on what and how the foods should be prepared for consumption.

Tell your child; don't let your child tell you. Yes, there may be certain things a child may not like or certain things that may not agree with a child's metabolism. That is not at all unusual. Find a suitable alternative, and keep the health direction in focus. Also direct, by words and instructions, what your child should spend her lunch money for. The lunch may not be and need not be a study in the healthy food chain, but can be a healthy consumable, as opposed to a non-nutritional snack. That eliminates candy bars, potato chips, popcorn and the like.

The dinner should be the premier health-balanced meal of the day and should definitely embody healthy proteins, carbohydrates and green vegetables. It can also include a balanced serving of dessert. A salad, in addition to the above, can go a long way toward enhancing the health-worthiness of a meal. These aren't words that need come from a nutritionist or a dietician. They are merely common sense conclusions about directing your child's eating habits and are coming from a parent who parented, based on sound information that was in print at the time we were parenting. This information was "all over the landscape" for parents to benefit from. So I am not suggesting this from the point of view of an expert, because healthy eating habits don't require the input of an expert.

When my child was growing up, health-worthiness and balanced meals were always stressed and adhered to in our household. One of the favorite green vegetables in our home was green peas. In additional to this, we often had green leafy vegetables, such as collard greens and spinach. My daughter will not eat many green peas these days, because they were not her favorite growing up. Nevertheless, she was required to eat what was prepared and what the rest of the family ate, as long as she could eat it, and it didn't prove disagreeable to her body system. A balanced meal was the order of the day in our household.

Parents should never fall into the habit of catering to a child's contrary eating whims, just to please the child. If it is convenient and time permits, it is okay to prepare something special for a child now and then. However, you should not allow your child to usurp your time and energy, by demanding special attention when it comes to meals. If you have more than one child and each child demands something special every day, you could virtually go off the deep end in an attempt to meet those demands. In most instances, you should require the child or children to eat what the family eats or go hungry, until she decides to not be so picky. On the other hands, you should avoid preparing meals that may not be acceptable to the entire family.

Eating habits may tell you a great deal about the quality of the individual with whom you may want to have a relationship or even marry. Children of a positive parenting experience tend to have positive concerns about when they eat and what they eat. Children raised eating fast food and junk food will probably continue the same type of eating habits and will be less inclined not to allow their children to do the same. If they ate that type of food, they would obviously see nothing wrong with it.

Quality parenting is usually concerned with the whole child—including the quality of the foods the child is allowed to consume. Quality parenting addresses the notion of balanced meals at organized mealtimes. Children raised eating balanced meals will usually desire and prepare balanced meals throughout their lives. An individual who is quick to settle for fast foods and detests the idea of eating vegetables and salads was probably not well parented, because feeding a child properly is an integral and important aspect of quality parenting. Mind that individual well, because she or he is likely to show evidence of other parenting shortcomings as well. Quality parents know and understand the benefits of giving a child balanced meals. Parents with no regard or understanding of quality parenting don't tend to care as much about what they or their children consume, just as long as the appetite is satisfied.

If you're dating an individual, take note of their eating habits. Those habits may very well give a clue concerning the quality of their upbringing or where the child came from. Quality parenting has no direct relationship to financial status but is more directly related to nurturing the whole individual. Quality eating can be done on a budget and is probably cheaper than fast food consumption. Some of the more nutritious vegetables are reasonably priced. Peas and beans are quite healthy and can be purchased for next to nothing. I came from a family of modest means, but my, did my parents feed us healthy food: peas and beans, leafy green vegetables, fruits, oatmeal, sardines, milk, freshly-brewed ice tea from "scratch" and so on.

My parents insisted on us eating this way. They left off the fat meats, the pig's feet and the ham sandwiches, and I fed my child in like manner. Dinner was never served without a vegetable. Individuals who eat all manner of unhealthy things at all times throughout their waking hours are studies in poor eating habits and poor discipline. Those types of individuals are likely to have serious health challenges down the road of life. So if you are not anxious to nurse your mate's future obesity, diabetes, high blood pressure, stroke, cancer or heart disease, take note of the eating habits before you decide to say "I do."

There are lots of positive vibrations behind a person who stresses eating green vegetables, fruits, organic products and healthy salads, and who avoids eating junk food frequently, avoids eating between meals and steers clear of fatty foods that are high in cholesterol. These positive vibrations can, at the very least, speak well for the individual in the area of health.

It often follows that a person who cares about her or his body will care about the mind. One cannot be healthy on "bread alone." This reminds one of the analogy that one who will take the time to clean and shine his shoes will usually do likewise for clothes and body. When you meet an individual who looks trim (not necessarily slim), whose skin looks clear and healthy, who goes out of her or his way to consume an abundance of fresh fruits and vegetables and who takes quality vitamin and mineral supplements, he or she is probably an individual who has had health challenges in the past or wants to avoid having health challenges in the future.

Proper nourishment of the body can help to reverse negative health effects. Who we are has much to do with where we came from, and eating habits can do much to change where we may be going health-wise. When I think of the fact that I gained five pounds in twenty-five years, I can say that I am a testimony to the control one may have. I came out of the military in 1963 weighing 147 pounds. Now, in 2007, I'm weighing in at 166 pounds. Everyone says to me, "Don, it's your metabolism." That may very well be a part of it, but I have a thirty and one-half inch waist and a forty-two inch chest. I know many individuals who are my size but are sporting a "pot belly." Metabolism didn't accomplish that; good eating habits did.

We must strive to avoid polluting the child's body as well as the mind. There is much to be said these days concerning what children watch on television and what they're doing on the Internet. I cannot understand a parent's "inability" to direct and monitor what a young child watches on television. There appears to be an ingrained psychology against invading a child's privacy. What privacy? Parents, don't be silly. Get on the case. If you don't invade their privacy now, one day you may wish you had done so, but it will be too late.

If a parent is having a problem controlling what a child watches on television, maybe the child's television should be removed from their room. If you can't do either of these things, then you're afraid of upsetting your child, and you are likely to be a parenting failure. Evidence of this type of parenting is "all over the landscape," and that is part of the problem with our society today—poor parenting.

Parents should give strict instructions and guidelines as to when and what a child can watch, and if the guidelines are disobeyed, suitable punishment should be exacted. Do you, as a parent, go around giving orders and instructions that the child routinely disobeys? If that is the case, you're on a very slippery slope. You are not in control, and your lack of control indicates that you have not properly parented your child. If you're not in control and cannot direct what your child watches, maybe you should put the television under lock and key.

On occasion, programs that are acceptable to be watched can be watched together as a family. That would give the parent or parents another opportunity to spend quality time with their children. The same applies to the movies. Parents or guardians should not give children money to attend movies with themes considered unacceptable for their viewing, given a particular age and theme.

Sometimes a child misbehaves and acts contrary to a parent's instructions, when she is away from the watchful eye of the parent. That child can only be left to God. Her or his behavior will be discovered, sooner or later, and the child may end up paying a dear price for disobedience. Quite often, even to a parent's own sorrow, the child suffers repercussions relative to the disobedience exhibited. These repercussions, in some instances, teach a lesson that the child learns well, and sometimes it helps them to get back on track. At other times, the lesson isn't well learned, and the child may continue down a road to ruin. This would be an example indicating something the parent didn't do or didn't do enough.

It is imperative that we, as responsible parents, uphold our obligation of raising the child properly. We must give right direction, discipline and instructions—even when it hurts to do so. And if we do this, even if the child goes astray, we can find some comfort in knowing, beyond a shadow of a doubt, that we did our best in properly parenting the child.

5. WHERE THEY LIVE AND WHO THEY MARRY

When our child or our children reach the age or stage at which she seems mature enough and financially stable enough to go out on her own, we should be concerned about the place the child desires to live. At the very least, we should try to avoid being burdened with the thought of staying awake nights wondering if our child got inside of her living quarters safely. Sometimes the child may not realize it, but the environment can positively or negatively influence the outcome of her or his life.

As parents, we often have a better insight into the makeup of certain environments and the influences that exist there. If necessary, we should make the child aware of these influences and attempt to steer her or him away from living in an environment that may impact her or him in a negative way. When a child is independent and on her own, we cannot demand that she reside in a particular place, but we can suggest it—if it is for her or his well-being. If you, as a parent, have been a good role model, have given your child positive instructions in the past, have nurtured her in a positive environment and have been a positive influence in her or his life, the child may take your advice and direction in hand and act accordingly.

Independence denotes or signifies a breaking away from the bonds of parental ties, and marriage signifies a final breaking away into a more finite state of independence from parental ties. It does not signify family abandonment, but is an assertion of a complete desire to function independent of parental guidance.

Prior to this final decision of marriage, a parent (to the extent she or he can be heard) should have some input or opinion about the individual the child intends to marry. This can be helpful—if the input is meant to be and is objective. Sometimes parents can see things in an individual that the child is unable to see. Are you familiar with the biblical saying, "Love hides a multitude of faults"? Those faults sometimes need to be uncovered.

Quite often when faults are called to a child's attention, the child may, at least, think twice about the pending marriage. Sometimes the child getting married is too close to the individual to see the faults. Do you remember the saying, "You can't see the forest for the trees"? That saying often applies to faults of individuals in a relationship.

An old friend of mine once told me what her father said about the boy she wanted to marry: "That boy is crazy." Her husband-to-be apparently had exhibited signs of insanity that the father was able to discern but she could not. She married "that boy," and he spent the greater part of his life in a facility for the mentally ill. The father's input and discernment were right on target—even though the daughter chose not to take his advice. She quite often confessed that she wished she had listened to her father.

Parents can offer opinions and should offer their opinions, if need be, and the opinions should be objective and well intended. A parent should encourage the child to get to know the intended spouse's parents, because meeting the parents may tell a great deal about whom the child was, who she or he is, and who she or he may turn out to be. Sometimes parents will inadvertently reveal important tidbits about themselves or their child. Often, when you know the parents, you know the child. Such revealed tidbits should not be summarily dismissed without thought. Another friend said to me once, concerning her husband, "If I had met his parents before, I never would have married him." That could ring true concerning many marriages.

I advise parents to give input and exercise as much influence as they can, concerning the person their child may want to marry. After all, you as the parent, may have to share the problem that could be experienced by your child in a bad marriage. Give your objective input, for whatever it may be worth. If you see no faults, don't look to find any. No individual is perfect. It is your child who will have to live with the individual, not you. Be sure your input is objective and well intended. It's your child's future, and you may have to live it with her or him—as long as you may live.

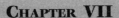

CHAPTER VII

BE UNIFIED FOR THE SAKE OF THE CHILD

If there is unity between Mom and Dad,
In raising the child, they will be glad
They worked as a team, so she will be better,
If she follows both their rules to the letter.

1. DEMONSTRATING RESPECT FOR THE OTHER PARENT

Do you want your child to respect your advice and instructions? Then show her, by example, that her father and mother respect each other's advice and instructions. Let the child know, by example, that you respect her father so much and value the instructions he gives you so much that you agree they must be carried out and *vice versa*.

One of the greatest parenting mistakes a two-parent family can make is to be in disharmony on matters relating to the child. Even if there is one parent overseeing the child on a daily basis, there should always be harmony with the other spouse, if the other spouse is around and has input into the life and raising of the child. There should be a united front on matters concerning the child.

Don't go against the other parent's decision, unless it is discussed and the change is agreed to by both parents. Neither spouse should take sides with the child against the other, for it is one of the most detrimental things you can do to the child. Don't talk to your child against the other spouse, for the child doesn't need to hear that. It does absolutely nothing to enhance the child's life and well-being.

The breakup of a marital relationship has absolutely nothing to do with a young developing child, or an older one, for that matter. That is, you cannot hold a child responsible for your not getting along with your spouse. The breaking-up point reached between spouses should not and would not have involved anything the child did, if the parenting had been positive before the disagreements. That is, you cannot hold a child responsible for your not getting along.

If it is a second marriage between the two, proper child management in coming into the relationship would render the child blameless. If both spouses love the child and have loved and nurtured her, the child sees both parents in the light of love and loves them both. Therefore, there is no need to turn the child's feelings about her mother or her father upside down. If this is done, it disappoints and hurts the child as much or more than it does the parent it is intended to hurt. A young child doesn't need to or want to feel bad about a parent she loves or about a parent she thought loved her. The least you can do, as a parent, is to leave the negative remarks about your spouse to time, and when the child comes of age, she will be able to properly assess a parent's actions and behavior on his or her own merits.

As a child is growing up, she is making assessments concerning the way she is treated and cared for: whether you have treated her well or treated her cruelly, whether you've been there for her or been an absentee parent, whether you've had time for her or were always too busy, and whether you helped to provide for her needs or never had much to contribute. Children remember everything; they remember the good, the bad and the ugly. As they begin to come of age, they begin to look back over their life and the role their parents have played and to draw their own conclusions from what has been done, rather than what has been said.

If the truth concerning your spouse is ugly, and you tell the child, it will hurt more than it will help, and the child would have been better off without ever having heard it. If the truth is beautiful, and you tell her, her life will be enhanced, her spirit will be happier, and later in life, when she comes of age, she will love and respect you more for having taken the high ground in discussing her other parent. If the truth is beautiful, and you try to paint it

192

ugly, to make the child dislike the other parent, when the child comes of age and discovers the real truth, she will not like you for having caused her all of the negative feelings against a parent that really loved her and wanted to do the best by her.

It has been said that "truth crashed to earth will rise again." Don't tell a child negative things about her other parent. If you can't say anything good about your other spouse to your child, you're better off not saying anything at all. Leave the assessment to time and the child's own conclusions. Bend over backwards to speak well of your spouse (your daughter or son's other parent) if at all possible and at all times. It is healthier for you, as well as for your child.

2. You Picked Your Child's Other Parent

Many parents are tempted to speak ill of their opposite—even when they are living together, and more so if they have separated. Don't yield to the temptation to do this. It is ugly, self serving and counterproductive. Don't let bitterness help to hurt your child; it may estrange her from a parent for life.

It would be a sad thing for a child to spend her or his life thinking negative thoughts about a parent based on an unfair and untrue assessment of the other parent. Sometimes the parent dies, with the child never knowing the truth. Sometimes this type of assessment keeps a child at a distance from a parent who has really loved her and did the best he or she could for the child. Then, in some instances, the parent dies, and the child later discovers the truth. He or she would never be able to reconcile her or his feelings with that parent, because nothing can be reconciled with the dead.

This can be a very heavy burden for a child to carry the rest of her or his life and unless she or he reconciles it with God and finds comfort, she may come to dislike the other parent for the rest of their life's relationship. Don't plant negative thoughts in the mind of your child about her other parent— be the thoughts true or false. The results you expect to get may not be forthcoming, and if they are, they may not be worth the harm caused. The price could be much too high.

Don't sit around in the presence of your child complaining about the other spouse's weaknesses, negative ways and negative behavior. Tell your spouse about the ways you don't like, but not in the presence of the child.

Remember, you married that person, and her or his negative ways, or habits, are a testament to your poor judgment. "Oh," you might say "I didn't know he [or she] was that way" or "he [or she] wasn't like that when we were dating." That's too bad, because it was your responsibility to know what you were getting yourself into.

Sometimes individuals say, "He [or she] changed on me." That's not really true. You were looking, but you just weren't seeing the real person. You were looking at the person you wanted her or him to be, or maybe what you saw was just one aspect of that individual. On the other hand, maybe what you were looking at was a façade or a temporary prop that could only be displayed for a period of time. You just didn't allow enough time for the "curtain to come down." If you're around a person long enough, the real person will ultimately show up.

Also, you can tell a great deal about a person based on where she or he came from. A pig usually comes from pig pens and is comfortable in slop. If you clean him up for a day, that doesn't convert him from his nature as a pig, and if allowed to, he will ultimately gravitate back to his environment and habits. That is where he is most comfortable. If you're paying attention, you should see lots of signs that will point you to where the person came from and where he may be headed.

Sometimes you may not see the signs, because they may be hidden behind a handsome or pretty face, the stylish leather jacket, the tight-fitting skirt, the sweet talk, the athletic build, the job position, the hot wheels, the ability to sing or act or a host of other things. Any of these may get your attention and capture your fancy at that particular period of time. Sometimes it is even called "love," and, as was stated earlier, "love hides a multitude of faults." Many of the qualities individuals fall in love with aren't lasting qualities and will ultimately fade with time.

Girls often overlook the high school "nerd" who wears glasses, dresses conservatively neat and lives in the neatly-kept house at the end of the block. You never hear loud music coming out of its walls. He doesn't hang out on the corner with the other dudes, and both his parents show up at the PTA meeting. Girls tend to overlook him when they are picking guys at that age. They're not asking questions like, "Would this guy make a good husband and father? Would he provide a good living for his family? Would he nurture his children and direct their growing up in such a manner that they will go out into life as success stories?" So the girl marries the wrong guy and realizes, after a short period of time, that the one she married isn't so smart, so neat or so ambitious, and every time the occasion arises she reminds him of his shortcomings.

If you're a parent and find yourself in this predicament, and have a child or children from this marriage, don't allow yourself to remind your spouse of what he is or is not while you and he are in the presence of the child or children. Bite your tongue, and remind yourself that you picked the person you married, and there is no need to have your child grow up thinking her parent is dumb, disorganized, lazy, not ambitious or any of the other adjective by which you care to characterize him or her.

3. OLD-FASHIONED PARENTING WORKED

I can reflect on when I was growing up and can earnestly say that I never remember my mother or father referring to the other by a negative adjective. I know without a doubt that they were not perfect. They had their faults, although they may not have been some of the glaring ones we sometimes see today. My mother was educated based on the standards of that day. She went through high school, and I'm told she also attended "finishing school," whatever that was. My father had little formal education. He was a farm boy who (no doubt) spent more time working on the farm than he did reading books. However, he had a keen sense of business, creativity, a good mechanical aptitude and a driving ambition. In many areas of intellectual prowess, he may have been very much lacking, but I never heard my mother refer to him as being dumb or stupid.

I realized in later years that my father could not solve mathematical equations, discuss the lake poets, enlighten you on Einstein's Theory of Relativity or offer an opposing argument to Kant's philosophy on knowledge or Nietzsche's philosophy about what the world is. We saw our mother solve mathematical equations, and we knew that in whatever intellectual predicament we found ourselves, Mama could tell us how to resolve it. My father never had the need to interact with us on these matters, because when it was needed, Mama was always there. So we grew up assuming (I guess) that our father was a writer, a poet, a philosopher, a builder, an engineer, a mechanic, an entrepreneur and one who could also solve mathematical problems. If he was lacking in his ability to do any of these things, we never would have known it from my mother.

What's more, we saw fairly studious writings produced by my father. He talked poetically at times, but not specifically about Byron, Whitman, Keats or Shelly. He often philosophized about life, its challenges and difficulties. He planned construction projects and built houses. He built a mechanical kitchen stove that burned oil, and he could repair almost any automobile's mechanical problem, including the changing of transmissions. He was proprietor of several businesses, including a printing business, a grocery store and a candy store. So we thought that whatever we needed to know, our father knew it. He just didn't have the occasion to tell us, because by the time he got home, Mama had already solved the problem.

Our mother could solve most of our problems—intellectual as well as disciplinary. Even after she had solved the discipline problem (if our infraction was serious enough), she would finish it off by saying, "I'm going to tell your father." That statement created a great deal of fear and anxiety in us, because we would possibly be subject to another round of discipline from him.

Boy, were they together when it came to raising us. Mama never went against his order or discipline. That was a definite "no-no," and he never went against her decision. We learned early on that if Daddy said it, there was no need to go to Mama with it, because she was not about to go over his head. If you did go over one's head and ask the other, you were subjecting yourself to serious punishment. And you knew better. If one parent disagreed with the decision by the other (and seldom was that the case), it was discussed out of our presence and seldom was the decision overruled— whether it was considered good or bad, right or wrong. If our father said it, it was like "Bible," and if our mama said it, then so be it.

The other parent never interfered when one was punishing a child. That was also forbidden. If the other parent (usually the mother) could not bear the wrath being brought upon the child, she could go and hide herself until it was finished. You see, in those days terrible behavior warranted terrible punishment, and parents had no great fear or worry about killing the child. Certain behavior warranted punishment worse than death. Backtalk in our household would certainly get you a broken lip and maybe even the loss of a few teeth. Striking a parent (in our household and many others of which I was familiar) might have gotten you killed by your parent. I never got a chance to witness such an event, because we never would have thought, in our wildest dreams, of committing such an act.

My father would say, "Boy, I'll kill you," and I believed him. To strike our father would have been worse than the act of a dog biting the hand that fed him. By today's standards, that would be considered cruel and unusual punishment and could probably get you locked up for life. I may not have thought so then, but looking back on those days I would be more prone to accept that type of discipline and the results it brought, over this modern-day discipline and the heartache it's causing. That was a better society, a safer society, and you could live in it. For the most part, parents didn't lose their children to alcohol or drugs or to the streets. Children feared their parents' wrath, and the result was that they lived.

4. Tough Love

I can recall an incident that happened when I was about fifteen years of age, and my brother was about sixteen. We were engaging in an argument in the kitchen, when my mother stepped in and said, "Shut up and cut that out." I guess we didn't stop soon enough, because she then backhanded both of us. She broke my lip and bloodied my brother's nose. He began grumbling as he walked away, so she reached around and grabbed him by the back of his shirt. She took hold of him with such force that the shirt ripped completely off of him. I'm sure she didn't mean to destroy his shirt, but the truth is she really didn't care. She wanted to get her message through to him, and it worked. The grumbling stopped immediately.

My brother had loved that shirt, and maybe, in his mind, he wished he could have given his mother a punch in the nose for what she did, but he wouldn't dare. First of all, he loved and respected her too much to hit her. Second, he knew that our father would have probably killed him, if he had even breathed the thought.

My father didn't play around. When he spoke, the entire house became quiet for fear of his wrath. He was a very big dude: maybe five feet, eight inches, and weighing in at about 160 pounds, but to us, he was a giant. And Mama: she was about five feet three or four inches and weighed (at her heaviest) about 123 pounds, but when she spoke, you moved. When she wanted us to come in for dinner or anything else, she would poke her head out the window, call us all by name and then close the window. That was all she needed to do, and it didn't ever require her doing it twice. She didn't care what you were engaged in at the time. You had to drop whatever you were doing and respond to her call.

A TABLESPOON OF LOVE, A TABLESPOON OF DISCIPLINE

But this was all okay, because along with this discipline, was love so powerful, so genuine, so unselfish and so unwavering. Whatever Mama required was wrapped in love. My mother loved us, and we knew it. We really knew it, and we still reflect on it today. She had a demeanor about her such that you could not help but love her. She did all of the extra special things for us. She went the extra mile. She hugged you; she kissed you; she scrubbed your face and neck; she washed your ears inside and outside, and she combed your hair until it hurt—especially if it was dry.

She made thirteen or fourteen cakes at Christmas, along with other fancy treats, staying up all night until she finished. At Easter she painted and decorated eggs, painting faces on them and sometimes putting cotton hair on them to make them look like some of the grand old statesmen of yesteryear. The love abounded, the upbringing was serious, and the discipline was stern and jointly coordinated. Somehow and for some reason that I am at a loss to explain, there is a great and redeeming value in a joint effort by both parents, when it comes to raising a child. What's more, you can even get the neighbor involved, and it's all right. When a child knows that all eyes are upon her or him, she is more likely to watch her behavior.

Hillary Clinton was not far off the mark when she repeated the saying: "It takes a village to raise a child." In the old days, a village actually raised a child, so children didn't go about cursing and behaving in any manner they felt big and bad enough to behave, because they were afraid their bad behavior would be seen by a neighbor or resident of the village and reported to their parents. In those days, adults would surely tell on you, because they knew your parents would believe it, appreciate it and thank them for letting them know. And once the parent knew, you would certainly get the punishment deserving of the act committed. In those days, everyone helped to raise your child: the regular school teacher, the Sunday school teacher, the neighbor, the older sibling, the uncle and aunt and any other relative old enough to give advice and correct behavior. Virtually any responsible adult was allowed to correct your child.

When my daughter was growing up, I believed in this same philosophy—that any responsible adult could correct my child and give me information concerning the infraction. I told neighbors, friends and any other responsible adult that if they saw my child doing anything wrong they were to correct her and then please inform me of the bad behavior. Today, some of the parents of misbehaving children will insist that the neighbor told a lie on their child, because they don't believe their child could do such a thing—"not my darling child."

5. AGREE TO AGREE IN SPITE OF

Even in light of the fact that my daughter's mother may have carried some bitterness after our breakup, she soon realized how positive it was to be able to call on the child's father to help keep the child moving in the right direction. She often had to say to her, "I'm going to call your father." Celeste believed me, more so than she believed her mother, because (like many mothers) her mother tended to be more emotional than substantive, when it came to raising the child. Mothers often promise the child a punishment, but then never deliver it to them, so the child tends to listen less when the mother talks. It was no different with Celeste's mother. It became somewhat of an unspoken word that her father would be involved in the parenting process on all levels and at all times, and it didn't take long for each of us to realize how necessary it was to be unified in the parenting process.

As the opportunity presented itself, I'm sure Celeste would sometimes come to me concerning something her mother had ruled on, and *vice versa.* However, we established very early that anything spoken in her mother's house remained there, and anything spoken in her father's house remained in his house. I didn't question her concerning her mother's business, and I trust that her mother operated in a similar manner. When it was child-related business, it went from her mother's house to her father's house and back there again. That was all a part of the unified process.

A child gets angry sometimes, and when she does, she can't help but be inclined to talk to the parent who didn't anger her, in opposition to the one who did. On one occasion, Celeste was commenting on a decision her mother had made that she didn't totally agree with. Maybe I did and maybe I didn't totally agree either, but I would not give Celeste the benefit of the doubt. That would have created disunity. Parents must be in agreement, assuming the decision to be honest, right and in the child's best interests. If there be any disharmony or disagreement, it should be discussed between the parents, and not with the child. When agreement is reached, it will impact the child's situation, as necessary.

On the occasion when Celeste disagreed with her mother, my remark to her took this direction: "Well Celeste, she's your mother, and she is not perfect (just as you are not perfect). She has to tolerate you in your imperfections, and so you have an obligation to tolerate her in what you may conceive as being imperfect. She may not always make the decision you consider the most appropriate or the one that may be the most appropriate, and the same may apply to you when you are making your own decisions."

"Anyway, how do you know whether the decision she made is or is not the most appropriate, based on your limited capacity to understand life? Whatever decisions she makes can be better than the equivalent one you might make, because she is older than you, wiser than you, has more experience concerning life than you and has more knowledge about the things of life. Therefore, her decisions will more likely be better than yours. You may neither agree nor understand why, at the time, but eventually you may understand and agree that it was the most appropriate decision."

On another occasion, when her mother upset her a bit, Celeste felt like voicing her annoyance. I listened, and when she finished, I said, "Look, she's your mother, and she loves you. She sacrificed a lot for you and gave of herself and her resources so that you could have. Sometimes it may not seem so, but without a doubt, your mother loves you. You have no choice; you must love her, because she is your mother, and you have no valid reason not to love her. Just because she upsets you sometimes, that is no reason for you to get 'bent out of shape.' "

"I'm sure you upset her many times, as children do, and she still didn't stop loving you. If she had done so, you would have been in a pretty bad shape. She was there from before the beginning. She didn't attempt to discard you or abandon you. She kept you, helped to care for you and nurtured you. She may sometimes make mistakes, but you have to forgive her and try to understand her."

The last time we had a discussion along these lines (and we probably had three or four) it seemed to have completely turned her thinking around, because I noticed a three-hundred-and-sixty-degree change in the way she and her mother related to each other. It was one of the best examples of how a child's perspective and outlook broadens concerning her parents, when they are in sync in matters concerning her or him. We can teach them a great deal about parent-child relationships by the way we behave with each other concerning them. Someday they may be parents, and some of the things we may say or do concerning them may prove to be valuable, when and if they do become parents.

BE UNIFIED FOR THE SAKE OF THE CHILD

I know I learned much from my parents through the way they harmonized in raising us. My mother never spoke ill of my father and would not allow us to speak ill of him either, even though there may have been instances when she could have put him down about his behavior and been completely justified in doing so. She chose to take the high road and keep her remarks about her husband and our father on a higher plane. I don't know of any occasion when my father would have been justified in speaking negatively concerning my mother. Whatever negatives that might have been known about either had to be found out by us virtually on our own. My mother was without moral fault and had very few other faults that we could observe.

It was said by my eldest sister that my mother was "spoiled," and, because of this, she may have put a lot of pressure on my father. Well, maybe she was and did. I don't know, but it is certainly something that (if it is so) I was unable to recognize, based on my youth and observation. And I don't say this just because she was my mother. I didn't love her beyond a fault. I loved her based on who she was and what she stood for, and that went a long way. Unfortunately, I am not able to say the same about my father. He had many strengths, but he also had some weaknesses, as we all do. However, this book isn't about the behavior of mothers and fathers— except as it relates to the successful raising of children.

I believe my mother and father left an important legacy in terms of how they exercised unity between them, as it impacted our upbringing. It was only after I began preparing the chapters of this book that I came to realize how much harmony existed between the two of them in raising us.

Sometimes we are "unable to see the forest for the trees." When this is the case, we need only to step back, to see clearly the thing that looked all jumbled before. I feel I may have had an ingrained belief (based on the attitude and behavior of my parents along this line) in the importance and positive power of the doctrine of parental unity in raising a child. On many occasions I found myself making harmony with my wife in matters concerning Celeste, when I might not have otherwise done so. The unity of parents, in matters relating to the children, can go a long way.

It is important to let your child know early on that she cannot play one parent off against the other. It is also important to let the child know early on that if the mother or father says "no," then "no" it will be. It is important for the child to understand that if, in the opinion of the mother or father, she shouldn't have it or do it, it should not be had or done. That sends the message to the child that you respect the other parent's decision, and this will also lead to the child's respect for the parent's opinion. What a powerful message, what a very powerful and far-reaching message that conveys!

6. Your Child Can Learn From the Way You Do It

Children make decisions and sometimes take action based on what or how they have been taught to do or not to do. The strength of what a child believes has much to do with respect for the one doing the teaching. If a child thinks her mother doesn't respect her father's opinion, or her father doesn't respect her mother's opinion, she may be less likely to respect the opinion of the respective father or mother. Whether we know it or not, we are setting patterns for our child—be it subtle or blatant. Sometimes the pattern screams at a child, and at other times it gently nudges her. In either case, if the pattern is positive, the child will be likely to adopt it as a facsimile for her own use.

After Celeste came out of college, she seemed to decide that she neither wanted nor needed any of the opinions or advice that I and her mother had given in the past. This was what I will refer to as the "pre-adult rebellious period." It seemed as if she wanted to discard "all of that stuff" and replace it with her own opinions and ideas. Everything I said was a cause for dispute. If I said, "The most important thing is up," she would say, "No, Dad, the most important thing is down." If I said, "I think you should go today," she would say, "No, I think it is better if I go tomorrow."

In the beginning of these encounters, I didn't quite get the drift, but as time went on, I began to realize that she was at the point where she felt capable of asserting her independence from my rules and live by her own—if only to show me that she had obtained that right. Maybe that was the time when she was able to say to herself, "I don't have to listen or go by my dad's rules now; I'm grown." She was at the age where she was realizing that the approach of adulthood is supposed to be the point at which you have the freedom to form your own opinions and make your own decisions as you see fit.

Whether she knew it or not, Celeste was preparing me and her mother for the time in which she would be saying, "Never mind, Mother [or Dad], I can do it myself." In other words, "I don't really need your opinion now."

"After all, I've finished college, I'm bright enough, I have a profession and can take care of myself. So, since I don't have to depend on you to take care of me, I don't have to be guided by your opinion. I can be guided by my own."

When this time comes, if you had given your child good advice, and she comes to the point where she feels she no longer needs it, I shudder to think what might be the consequences if there has been disharmony between the parents in raising her. Mothers should be especially careful in not usurping authority from the father. I have always said (on observation) that when the child doesn't listen to the father, the mother runs the house. It is likely, in that case, that neither the mother nor the father is in control. As stated earlier, some mothers tend to be more emotional than fathers, and a child does not respond readily to emotional outbursts.

Both parents should talk together on matters, as they relate to the child. Respect each other's decisions, especially in the child's presence. Don't push the spouse to make the decision you want, just to please the child. There may be such a thing as an "overabundance of love," which could be called "spoiling a child." If you do this, you may do it to your own sorrow and to the detriment of the child.

As parents, put your heads together, and help each other make the right and best decisions, based on your knowledge and experience and the circumstance at hand. That is what positive parenting is all about. Parenting involves trial and error, and however bad a parent's decision might be, it is, in most cases, far better than what could have been made by the child— considering the age of the child and the circumstance at hand. If you feel you made an error in your decision process, and you can correct it without showing weakness, do so, especially if the uncorrected decision can possibly cause the child unnecessary harm. If it won't cause unnecessary harm, but you think you could have made a better decision, stick by the one you made, and then use the better one on a similar occasion in the future. Changing decisions back and forth gives you the appearance of being "wishy-washy."

Don't be "wishy-washy." Children don't respond well to or respect indecisiveness. Wavering in decision-making suggests an inability to make a decision and suggests the lack of firmness. If you are not firm in your decisions, a child will come to question whether you really mean what you say. A child has to know you and your ways, and in so knowing, she will know what to expect and what to respect. Firmness gets more respect than mushiness.

Mark Twain made these poignant comments: "It is a wise child that knows its own father and an unusual one that unreservedly approves of him" and "When I was a boy of fourteen, my father was so ignorant I could hardly stand to have the old man around. But when I got to be twenty-one, I was astonished at how much he had learned in seven years." These two quotes probably express the opinion of many children.

In summing up the way you may be viewed through the eyes of your child, I can't help but enlist some comments I came across among other pages in my drawer. I don't know who made them or from whence they originated, but few words can more poignantly express the opinion children often have of their dad (and it may be equally so of their mother). The comments indicate what a child might be saying at various ages:

When I was four, my dad could do everything. At seven, he seemed to know a whole lot. At nine, he didn't quite know everything. At twelve, he just didn't understand. At fourteen, he was old-fashioned. At twenty-one, the man was completely out of touch. At twenty-five, he was okay. At thirty, I was wondering what he might think. At thirty-five, I just had to get his opinion first. At fifty, I wondered what he might have thought. And, at sixty, I wished I could talk it over with him just one more time.

A child's opinion of her parent and her parent's opinion and advice have much to do with the weight and respect given to that opinion. Make your opinion and that of your spouse have meaning to your child. Set the stage for mutually respecting each other's opinion, by backing the decision rendered by your spouse. Be unified on opinions relative to your child. It will make the parenting process easier and more harmonious.

CHAPTER VIII

IF YOU SEPARATE FROM YOUR SPOUSE, DON'T SEPARATE FROM YOUR CHILD

You should stop and think awhile,
And you'll realize you have a child,
To take care of, besides your wife;
You must do it, whatever the strife.

1. YOU CAN GET ALONG WITH YOUR CHILD

Society realizes that some couples will come to the conclusion that they can no longer reach agreement in their marriage. Society also understands that when this conclusion is reached, and reconciliation and counseling fail, it may be in the best interest of the husband, the wife and the children to separate. God loves marriage and the institution of marriage. If God sanctioned it, He has the power to direct the couple in sustaining it. However, if God wasn't considered in the consummation of the marriage relationship, the individuals involved may be on their own, in terms of fitting together— unless they seek God's help afterwards, to aid them in sustaining the marriage relationship. It's possible for them not to have been equally yoked in the first instance. Subsequently, the couple comes to the end of the marriage road, and there is a child or children involved. What happens to this child or these children?

Children aren't responsible for the fact that you and your mate cannot get along and must separate. You're angry at your spouse, but what did your child do to you? Do you really want to blame and punish the child or children for your failed marriage? If you do, you are acting in a very narrow-minded manner. Do you not want to support your child because you cannot make it with your spouse? If you don't want to support your child, you may be using the breakup as an excuse or cop-out for not taking care of your child.

Separation from a spouse need not mean separation from a child. Husbands, you may have to leave your wife, but don't leave your child. The judge can order you out of the house, but don't accept this as ordering you out of the life of your child. Judges don't usually attempt to prevent fathers or mothers from maintaining a relationship with their child, unless some abusive behavior took place, such that your presence around the child would be harmful or dangerous for the child. Judges probably never order a parent not to lend support for a child or children. They would be more likely to require, by law, that the estranged parent provide support for the child. Even if other things took place that preclude your having contact with the child, you should continue the support. One day you may receive help and forgiveness and grow beyond whatever the negative behavior was relative to the child, and you and the child could become whole.

I know it may be easier to pick up and leave your wife and your child and never look back. That's what a "wimp" would do. A wimp is a lesser man. A real, complete man would take on the difficult task, and that task requires supporting his child—whether or not he is able to make it with his spouse. Some wimps may have other women or some other child they have to or want to take care of. If this is indeed the case, it supports the conclusion that the man is a wimp, as opposed to a real man. Real men don't base the power of their manhood on the power of their reproductive ability. As the saying goes, "Any male can be a father, but not every male can be a husband."

This simply implies that you need not behave like a man, nor think like a man, to father a child. Real men don't go about fathering children they may grow weary of supporting. So back up man, and direct your reproductive prowess only towards fathering the child you can and will support. Your failure to support your child, because you cannot get along with your wife, is nothing more than a fainthearted excuse for not taking responsibility in that matter you're obligated to be responsible for. Don't make that excuse; the child may later hate you for it, and you may later hate yourself.

There should be nothing more important in your life than supporting the needs of the child you fathered—not supporting your girlfriend (or boyfriend), your career, your promotion, a new spouse, your social life or anything else under the sun. This includes even the church. The Bible shows that if you cannot support your family properly, then you can't serve God properly.

The separation from your spouse or a divorce should not be taken as an excuse to get out of the responsibility of helping in the raising of and providing for your child. When you use the breakup as an excuse, you're taking the easy way out, and the future may mirror your regret. You may think you're hurting your spouse, and you may well be doing that, but you are also hurting your child and yourself just as much. I can't envision what type of man could walk away from his child and the obligation for support, never look back and never feel hurt about not supporting her or him.

Don't allow any thought, or spouse, or court, or behavior pattern to separate you from your child. The lost love of your child may never be regained in the future. There will have been "too much water under the bridge." The child needs both her mother and father. If you are alive and can, by any means, get to your child, make sure you are there. Sure, it may be easier to disappear from your child's life, just as you want to disappear from your spouse's life, but the child isn't the one to blame for the separation from your spouse. In today's society, if you fail to support your child and the spouse brings it to court, the law is likely to track you down. However, the court should not have to require that you behave as a proper, caring and providing parent.

This advice is mostly for the male spouse, because (although it happens sometimes) it is not as frequent that a mother abandons her child because of a broken marriage. She carried the child for nine months, bore the agony of childbirth, and, by nature, finds it a bit more difficult to just walk away. Based on what I've often heard, the act of going through the birth pains creates a special and unique bond between the mother and child, one that tends to be conspicuously absent with the father and child. The assumption is that the father's bond isn't as deep as the mother's.

Quite often, the mother isn't the primary income provider—although that is getting to be less and less a true statement. If the mother leaves the family, quite often neither the court nor the father will track her down for reason of income. However, in today's society, when it comes to income, a mother's earnings quite often equal and even exceed that of the father. Of course there are many other reasons (non-justifiable) why estranged spouses stay away from the child or children, but don't allow any of them to cause a separation from your child. If you really love your child (and you should), you should let no obstacle, stumbling block or hurdle keep you from her.

My spouse and I separated when my daughter was about nine years of age, but I had a determination in my mind, body and spirit, that I was never going to separate from my child—except of course, by death. I had seen and heard of too much of that and refused to be another one of those statistics. No woman or circumstance was going to prevent me from helping in the nurturing of my daughter, providing for her and being there for her.

I didn't love Celeste because I thought she was the cutest, smartest and most wonderful child that was ever born. Some parents may think that about their child, and they may also be wrong. I loved my child because she was my child, I was her father, and I was supposed to love her. She also loved me. I was the only father she knew. She needed me and depended on me for my part in her support and nurturing. How could I have ever let her down?

Children don't come into the world voluntarily, nor do they have a choice as to whether or not they come here. They just open their eyes one day, and here they are, thrust into the world due to someone's pleasure, error, selfish desire, unselfish desire or because God, in His infinite wisdom and will, determined it to be so for that mother and father. It wasn't up to the child. Since that is the case, concerning her being here, we have a moral and personal responsibility to see to her nurturing and her support.

But it goes without saying that just because we have a responsibility for the nurturing and care of our child doesn't mean all of us will carry it out. It's purely a personal thing, an individual thing. The desire to carry out one's responsibility comes from within. It gets there through teaching and prior conditioning. One must desire to be responsible, and being responsible carries with it a need to sometimes get out of your comfort zone, a need to be inconvenienced sometimes, a need to be unselfish sometimes, and a need to sometimes make sacrifices beyond what you really desire to make. Being and acting in a responsible manner is something that can only be expected of a special type of individual, one who is willing to sometimes take the rough road of life, because carrying out a responsibility is often difficult. Shirking a responsibility is much easier.

A man must be awakened (if he is sleeping) to the need to be responsible to the care and well-being of the child he helped to bring into the world. He must look for reasons to act responsibly concerning his child, and not for excuses to be irresponsible. And a man must not allow the separation from his spouse to separate him from his child.

2. Your Child's Future Without You

Did you ever sit down to think about the possible future of your child, when you're absent from your spouse, and thus absent from your child? First, there is the emotional aspect for the child to deal with and adjust to, and this emotional detachment could be devastating to the child, as could be the economic aspect. Sometimes the things that work negatively on a mind are never overcome and are often carried throughout one's life as negative baggage.

Negative economic conditions can often be overcome. One of the frequent mental effects of child abandonment can be a loss of self-esteem. When a father estranges himself from his child, the child may get the feeling that he doesn't love her or him or doesn't care. The caring aspect is well taken, because a father who cares would not abandon his child. From the time a child is born, if the parent is in the family or available, there is a certain attachment between the parent and the child that grows stronger as time passes. The child grows to understand and expect this emotional support. When it is suddenly taken away, by the father separating himself from the child's presence, the child can feel at a loss to understand why and what happened. Sometimes the child may think she or he is to blame. It can be difficult for a child to understand how her father could leave and never return, if indeed that happens. It is difficult for the child to understand why the father doesn't care about her. Children often act out the frustrations of this misunderstanding in their everyday behavior. Often they may become problem children.

I was sitting down with one of my acquaintances who had a child that began acting up at about the age of ten. We were discussing the pattern and direction and that of my child. Her child lived out the years between eleven and the then-present age of twenty-one as an off-track child, and she may be off-track for years to come, unless she comes to grips with the nature of her problems and decides she is going to put them behind her. That child's family life and my child's family life had some parallels, except that the focus, goals and aspirations of those parents may have been a bit different.

Her mother and father separated when the child was about eight or nine years of age. The father went about his business, showing no desire or intention to support and nurture his child. He was eventually hauled into court, and support for the child was demanded and ordered by the court. The father never went to see the mother, and he also didn't see the child. He avoided them both because his intention was not to give them the support money.

I and my daughter's mother separated when she was eight or nine years of age, but I never abandoned my daughter economically or emotionally. I was there for her support in whatever area of need. My daughter's support never had to go through a court. The weekly support I was giving at the time took care of her private school tuition and a substantial part of the monthly mortgage payment. I contributed to extras and to her clothing needs. At that time, I was in the clothing business and had access to an upscale flow of clothing for her. My cash flow at that particular time wasn't great, because I had recently closed an insurance and tax business that had once supported a quarter of a page ad in the Yellow Book and a subway clock advertisement. At this time, I was contemplating my financial direction.

In our analysis of the difference in direction of the two children, we both came to the conclusion that the difference was in the fact that I was there for my daughter, and the other father was not. My availability for my child most likely made the difference. Some children have survived the absence of the father and continued on track, but just as many have not. Also, the survival may have a lot to do with the strength of the mother and her ability to play the role required to keep the child moving in the right, positive direction.

The other parent said her daughter had been close to her father, and when he removed himself from her life, she was unable to adjust to the void left by his absence. At one point, the child took up company with a man who was ten years her senior, while she was still a teenager. The difference in the number of years wasn't so great—unless you consider the fact that she was a child of twelve years of age, and the man was twenty-two or twenty-three. Maybe she was seeking a father image to replace that of her absent father.

Often, when a father disconnects himself from his child, it not only leaves the child emotionally deficient; it just as often leaves the child economically shortchanged. Sometimes the mother is hard-pressed to make ends meet. The absentee father must bear part of the responsibility for this type of situation. Often it is a long wait between the time the father leaves and the time he is hauled into court for child support. Thank God there is now a system in place that tracks down "deadbeat dads."

Do you want to be a deadbeat dad? Since the courts are likely to require you to support your child anyway, why not just do it voluntarily and keep the love and respect of your family? If you support your child, you can feel more comfortable, keeping in touch and interacting with the child. It will be more like you are deserving of the place in your child's life, as her or his father. You will not be a father in name only, and this interaction may be what is needed to keep the child on track.

Can you picture your child taking up company with the wrong people, just because her or his self-esteem is low, and she doesn't feel good about herself? Can you imagine your ex-spouse sitting down to the table with your child, without an adequate and nourishing meal, because the available economic means are not enough, after the two of you have separated, and you abandon your child? Sometimes that's what happens to your child after you abandon her.

Can you also picture your ex-spouse struggling to keep a warm coat, hat, gloves and shoes on the children, because her money is short of what is needed to acquire these things? Look at the picture, fathers. Is that a pleasant picture? This picture is being shown everyday. I know you may say you don't care what happens to your ex-spouse, but it is not just about your ex-spouse; it is also about your child or children. The type of things enumerated above can happen when you separate yourself from your spouse and child. Things need not be this way. You can be partly responsible for this happening or not happening.

3. WHY PUNISH YOUR CHILD?

You and your spouse couldn't make it for whatever reason. Your spouse may have done something you considered totally unfair in every way. Whatever it was may have hurt you deeply. It may have given you a reason to think you could dislike her for the rest of your life—and hers. Or you could have done something to her that was considered so hurtful she never wants to lay eyes on you again. She wants you out of the home, out of her sight and, maybe, even out of this world. These feelings are understandable, although there will always be those who feel the behavior doesn't warrant those reactions.

Suppose everyone agreed with you, and you felt perfectly justified in separating. You feel you don't want to continue the relationship, and so you leave. In man's eyes it's okay. In God's eyes it may not be, but if a man isn't following God, then he is following his own decisions. So if you feel that way about your spouse, and you're making your own decisions, I guess you must go with the decision. But what about the child or children? What did the child do wrong? The child loved you and had nothing to do with the reason you wanted to separate from your wife. How could you do something that punishes your child for the behavior of your spouse?

Are you punishing the child because the child has part of the person you no longer love or like? That child is also likely to have part of you. So when you punish the child, you are also punishing yourself. Are you punishing the child because the child looks like the one you have come to dislike? That is foolish. How can the child help it if the genes dictated that she take some of the resemblance of the person you are now disenchanted with? The look you see on your child's face is the look you once saw on your spouse's face, the one you fell in love with.

Are you punishing your child because you think that hurting your child hurts the parent of the child? You may be correct in that thought, but does that mean when the child hurts then the child's mother hurts, and you don't hurt? After all, you're one of those parents. If you don't hurt when your child hurts, there would have to be something lacking in your ability to feel hurt. Is genuine love for your child there? If you really love your child, you could not bear the thought of not being there to care and provide the necessities of life—if it is within your power to provide them.

If you fail to stay in touch with your child and provide your child with emotional and economic support, you are merely using one of the above excuses for abandoning your responsibility as a father. Do you want to support your child? If you do, then just do it. If you want to and do not do it, you're making excuses again, because no one except you can prevent you from upholding your responsibility as a parent.

4. It's All About Your Child's Life

Nothing should be more important than taking care of your child or children, as the case may be. If you're a father and you meet another woman, who becomes the focus of your life and the object of your affection, you should immediately make her aware of the fact that you have a child and the child needs your emotional, as well as your financial, support. The same applies if you're a mother and you meet a man who becomes the center of your attraction. No individual should be able to make you abandon your child or compromise her or his well-being in matters of love, proper discipline and being there emotionally, economically and physically.

Your child is a part of you and represents family. Family can leave, but can never discard the ties born out of a relationship by blood. Your child is your flesh and blood, bone of your bone and flesh of your flesh. Anyone else can leave you and never look back, because if it isn't family, the only connection is by relationship formed at a point of meeting. If the relationship goes sour, the person goes away and sometimes never returns. When you abandon your child, and all of the other relationships are done, and you're sitting there all alone (except for your thoughts), you must come to the conclusion that it probably would have been more expedient to nurture the child, rather than the other relationship.

I don't believe that properly raised children, who were nurtured and taken care of, will grow up to abandon the nurturing parents, not if the child is of sound mind and functioning as a normal human being. There is nothing constant in life except God. He will not leave you. All else may fail or forsake, but He will always be there—if you choose to take Him with you. God says in His Word that you are to take care of your family before you endeavor to serve Him. However, there should be enough time to do both—as well as the other of life's requirements. You should plan it that way. If you will notice, I said "life's requirements." I didn't say life's desires and enjoyment. There should be no excuse for not seeing after your child for any avoidable reason, not even in doing God's work. Doing His work requires that you first address family matters.

There are also other things that fathers and mothers sometime give priority to, over taking care of the child. One of those things is career. If you are a father who has a child, and your career doesn't allow you to interact with your child, it must be an extremely important and rewarding career.

But, on the other hand, you fail to give adequate financial support for your child. There appears to be a contradiction in this situation, and the contradiction is possibly an excuse for not adequately supporting your child.

Oh, you're working toward a promotion? Suppose you succeed one day, and you finally get the promotion and then look back to see that you gave neither emotional nor financial support for your child? Where does that leave you? The job may or may not be sustaining you, and your child, by the help of God and her or his mother, has gone on to success—even without you. What will you think?

Quite often neglected children and those abandoned by their father go on to accomplish great things. In some situations, this negligent parent comes to need the child to sustain his existence. Don't let that scenario apply to you. When you have a child or children, it is your duty and responsibility to take care of them. It doesn't matter that you and your spouse are separated. If you're an obligated parent, don't let anything or anybody prevent you from supporting your child. Don't allow any activity to ever come between you and your child.

You could be having the most wonderful post-breakup social life anyone could wish for. After the breakup with your spouse, you could have met your heart's desire, who made you forget you ever knew your spouse. That's good for you, but don't let that "heart's desire" make you forget you ever had a child. Your social life could be the best ever. It could be like living a dream. You could be night-clubbing and island-hopping on a frequent basis. Good for you, but don't fail to settle down often enough to see after the needs of your child.

Relationships come and go. They grow stale and sometimes fade. Sometimes the excitement dies down to a murmur. You sometimes lose the ability to physically and financially support the relationship. Those who do this are quite often left with nothing more than broken memories. All of those pleasures of yesterday are but scant memories today. Often the whirlwind of social activity draws one away from God, family and child, permitting the individual to only concentrate on the one social involvement, and when it is finished, quite often, there are no pieces left to pick up. If you must leave your spouse, stay with your child emotionally and financially. It is the honorable thing to do.

Nowadays, it is very difficult to remain in this country and not support your child. The law may not demand your physical presence and emotional support, but it does demand your financial support—and will track you down to get it. The government no longer wants to take care of children abandoned by trifling fathers. If you remain in the fifty states or in any territory where the U.S. government can reach you, you could be in for a big surprise, if you have neglected to support your child. You could even go to jail. If you ever work and get evidence of such work in the form of a 1099, W-2 or the like, the government has the ability to find you.

Since you may be forced to support your child financially, why not just continue being the complete father or mother to the child, just as you were before the breakup with your spouse? It can be so much easier and more decent, if done that way. The husband or wife will respect you more, your family and friends will respect you more, and you're likely to respect yourself more. Your child will always love you for being there. It can be a wonderful feeling to look back on your life and the life of your child and be able to say, "My wife and I couldn't make it, but I took care of my child through her financial needs and through all of the other everyday supportive requirements."

You will have no regrets, if you do it the proper way. But if you don't, sometimes your conscience will beat you until you go to your grave. I've seen too many instances of this, so I'm led to believe there is truth in it. I know of a firsthand account of a father who had been conspicuously absent from the life of his children for many years. On his deathbed, during that period of delirium between life and death (which some people experience), he tried to direct some money to his children. The money had been there, but he didn't even know where it was. He was out of touch with reality. It is probable that a guilty conscience had been bothering him for many years.

In prior years, he may have cast off and tried to ignore his feelings concerning this matter. He hadn't interacted with some of his children since they were teenagers, and some of them were now in their forties and fifties. They had grown up, completed grade school, high school and some had completed college, and through it all they had not so much as received a card of congratulations from their father. He had been too busy with his own life. The right definition, or explanation, may be: "The father had been too selfish." I'm sure this definition fits many other fathers as well, who have been too busy being about their own lives to care much about the lives of their children. Sometimes such selfishness hounds a father to the grave.

Don't assume that your child will go on loving you, if you absent yourself from her or him. She may not. Many children grow up not loving the parent or the parents who have always been there doing the best they could do. Small wonder then that a child would not love a father or mother who has removed himself or herself from the child's life unnecessarily. It takes the love of God in a child to be able to love a parent who walks out of her life, leaving her and the other parent to manage as best as they can. Too often, this has caused them to endure hardships born out of physical, mental and economic challenges. The child often despises the parent with every breath she breathes. I have witnessed many situations unfold, where the child reached adulthood, having no desire at all to know or reunite with the absentee parent she or he never knew, nor to even see that parent at all.

Another child may be curious to see the parent she never knew and see what he may actually be like. Is he nice? How could he be nice, if he didn't care enough about his child to take care of her? And the other curious question is often: "Why did he leave and not take care of me?" Children don't really understand, and the reasons given for abandoning the child don't really make sense, because there can be no sensible reason for a father or mother not taking part in the child's welfare—except if you (the parent) suffered some type of illness or legal problem that rendered you incapable of interacting with the child or sustaining yourself. A child, after coming of age and hearing the explanation, may be more understanding of the reason.

As a parent, you may think it will not matter if your child loves you or doesn't love you. I think it will matter. If you are a normal, rational human being with a conscience, it will make a big difference to you. I know that some fathers aren't considered normal, and just as many are looked upon as not having a conscience. For those who don't fit into this category, you will not likely love yourself much, if you choose to walk away from your child and never look back. You may think this behavior will not, in any way, alter your feelings for yourself. You could be correct in thinking this; it may not. However, you will probably be wrong in thinking this way, and you should not want to be wrong in thoughts on this matter. On some things, you would rather not gamble on the side of being right. If you're not, you have no recourse for your misjudgment.

This is like thinking about the Heaven or Hell God says is waiting for us after we die. Some may not believe it to be so, and some definitely don't believe it is so. Those who don't believe it is so and leave this earthly abode without being prepared for a heavenly eternity will have made the greatest misjudgment of their life. Once one breathes his last breath, her or his eternity is permanently sealed. Where it will be spent is finite, based on the life lived before dying. "Eternity" is a very long time.

Some matters, like the matters concerning your child or children, are things in which you don't want to err on the side of wrong. You will probably deeply regret what you didn't do. Your conscience may beat you to death. Don't risk living life with this type of burden of guilt hanging over you. You don't need to do that. Take the hard road of challenge, rather than the "easy street." It's your responsibility. Your child needs your support—emotionally and financially. If you must leave your wife, others are likely to understand, but few may not understand you leaving your child. Separation from a spouse should not mean separation from your child or children.

CHAPTER IX

BE AN EXAMPLE FOR THEM, AND YOU CAN DEMAND MORE OF THEM

Would you want your child to be a thief,
A doctor, lawyer or Native American Chief?
You can give him a start, if you only try
To set good examples for him to live by.
He also may want to be just like you and
Not do what you say, but do what you do.

1. WHO ARE THEIR ROLE MODELS?

Did you ever stop to think about the fact that today's generation of boys aren't often heard to say, "I want to be like my father," and today's generation of girls aren't often heard to say, "I want to be like my mother"? Almost everyone in an adult posture is admonishing children to seek a role model. I stopped and asked this question of several individuals: "Why don't children start looking for a role model in their own home? Why don't they seek a suitable role model in their parents, brothers and sisters or uncles and aunts?"

In generations prior to the 1960s, you often heard boys say, "I would like to be like my father." Today that desire seems to be an exception, rather than the rule. Children seem to have a strange desire not to take over the business of the parent, as much as children did in generations past. Maybe children have seen something in the operation of the family business that turned them off from the thought or the desire to continue that business. Children don't seem to want to follow in the footsteps of their father, as far as job or profession goes.

Parents today hold a variety of positions. They are accountants, actors, brokers, community leaders and activists, corporate presidents, doctors, delivery men, entrepreneurs, government statesmen or officials, judges, lawyers, ministers, nurses, policemen, politicians, salesmen, sports figures, teachers, taxi drivers, writers, editors, and any one or more of a host of other professions that could virtually fill a book if all the names were listed. All of the various professions, named and unnamed, are filled by someone's father or mother, and these fathers' and mothers' children had the opportunity to witness them acting in their professional capacity, as well as others who were unrelated acting in the same capacity. They watched as many of these fathers and mothers brought shame upon the profession.

This isn't meant to be an indictment of every father and mother functioning in a particular capacity. Some served in their respective professions with honesty and integrity and made their children justly proud of them. Others did not and brought shame to the profession and to the family, including the child or children. Those who did this often gave the profession a "black eye." So children sat on the sidelines listening to and watching the negative fallout from adverse behavior taking place in a particular profession that happened to be the same profession as that of the father or mother or one that involved the father or mother. From this perspective, the child decided she or he did not want to be like father or mother, as the case may be. The child settled into another profession, unrelated to the type the father or mother pursued. That perspective can partly give rise to an increase in the expression of the desire of children not to be like father or mother.

Society's children are fast running out of role models, even outside of the home, because as soon as they find a hero, who becomes such by outstanding performance exhibited in the area of her or his ability, something negative is revealed about that hero's behavior. That can cause a child to become disenchanted with that person, as it relates to that person's ability. It seems difficult for any of us to separate the myth from the man. The child may very well wonder if she or he were in the same shoes, would she or he be subject to the same fate. That could be enough to steer a child away from wanting to become what his hero became. The post-1960s generations started our society down the slippery slope we're still negotiating today, and today's children represent the evidence. Yesterday's children are today's parents, and they are operating with the equipment passed along to them.

The problem today is the notion that parents seem to be operating in a "what's-good-for-me" mode, giving little consideration to how their actions may affect their future, and hardly any consideration to how their actions may affect the future of their children. These are the generations of selfish, shameless parents, and the desire should be to put a halt to future generations of poorly-parented offspring. When it comes to what makes one feel good or happy, the decision is, "Go for it," even if the action is wrong, and is open to the possibility of yielding negative consequences.

These are generations which harbor thoughts of fatalism, and individuals seem to be convinced that they will not live long enough to witness the repercussions of their negative behavior upon the lives of their offspring. There must be truth in this presumption; otherwise those who used illicit drugs would not have done so. They were enlightened enough to know they stood a chance of producing children with an altered genetic structure, subject to birth abnormalities and substance dependency. This fatalistic attitude had to be so; otherwise alcohol abusers would not have done so, because there was enough enlightened information available, informing the users that they were subject to producing offspring suffering from fetal alcoholism syndrome. This fatalistic attitude had to be so; otherwise sexual promiscuity wouldn't have been taken so lightly. That behavior often brought about social illness and diseases that were passed along to children, who then carried the burden for the rest of their lives. They often became wards of the public dole.

These were the generations that desired their pie today; not in the sky in the great "by and by." These were the generations that wanted instant financial rewards, instant coffee, instant cereal, instant microwave meals, prefabricated office buildings and homes, assembly line autos, three-minute car washes and quickie divorces. These generations didn't want to wait for anything. They didn't want to wait for gradual pay increases, that often came in conjunction with experience and time on the job, so big unions demanded big raises, in big contracts—immediately. Big business subsequently responded with big downsizing—effective the Monday immediately following the Friday the "pink slips" were handed out.

Everyone wants so much so quickly that society has become one of "take what you can, while you can and just hope you don't get caught." Some of the licensed professional elements of society began taking all they could get away with, under the guise of legitimacy. This legitimacy extended itself to greed, and greed to corruption. Many of the lesser professionals followed, but most didn't have a license to take. They took anyhow and suffered the consequences, which often came sooner than they had expected. They only did so because they were elements of a selfish and shameless society, desiring instant rewards and instant gratification.

These are the fathers and mothers of society, and children don't see them as good role models. These are the fathers and mothers of society, who fail to set good examples for children and cannot demand anything of children. Parents of today need to change that for the benefit of today's children, who will be tomorrow's parents. Be considerate of who you are and what you are. Be careful of the example you set, because your child may view your behavior as a quick solution and decide to do as you do, rather than do as you say.

The good boy didn't want to be like his father or the good girl like her mother, because he or she didn't like or didn't desire to suffer similar fallout from the example his father or her mother represented. On the other hand, he chose to be like his father, because he thought the example his father represented was an easier road to travel. The road wasn't long and difficult, but it was short and destructive. The girl didn't want to be like her mother because she thought the example her mother represented was similar to that represented by the boy's father. Don't forget that today's children will be tomorrow's parents.

2. BAD PARENTAL EXAMPLES NOT TO FOLLOW

Bad parental examples not to follow are the likes of dishonest accountants, who compromise their profession and the reputation of their firm, as well as embarrass their child and family to earn an extra dollar; dishonest stockbrokers, who churn clients' money to make bigger commissions; unethical doctors, who wouldn't treat a dying patient unless an insurance plan was in place or the money was forthcoming; dishonest entrepreneurs, who set up scam businesses for the sole purpose of ripping-off the unsuspecting; dishonest attorneys, who file a class-action suit, receive millions on behalf of the class in question, while the members of the class receive a $1.25 store coupon; dishonest judges, who render unfair decisions for money paid under the table; greedy corporate CEOs, who can never seem to get paid enough, regardless of the amount of their annual salary and perks.

These men sit by and watch the books being "cooked" and then pretend they didn't know anything. Their resume indicated that they knew about as much as God Himself, for they were graduates of prestigious colleges and universities. Most of those executives have advanced degrees, and some boasted of doctorates in economics. Even with all of these credentials, they got caught up in dishonest corporate shenanigans and claimed they didn't even possess the smarts to appraise the events leading up to the company's fall. They were instrumental in bankrupting corporations, causing the loss of billions of dollars in devalued stock and causing employees to lose hundreds of millions of their pension and retirement funds. As a result, many employees had to go to work and continue working well into old age, because their pensions had been squandered due to the unethical conduct of the CEOs and the CFOs.

Then there are unscrupulous community leaders, who don't function on behalf of the group they represent, but pursue their own agenda; unethical government statesmen and officials, who are cast out of office for taking bribes to vote the desire of the one paying the bribe; dishonest health-care professionals, who inject their patients with drugs to end their life; dishonest policemen, who accept bribes to allow a criminal to break the law; salesmen, who would give any type of story or tell any type of untruth to convince an unsuspecting customer to buy a product; a writer, who is willing to turn out any type of writing, even pornography or smut, under the guise of freedom of speech, just to make another dollar; dishonest sports figures, who would take a bribe to take a fall; unethical teachers, who no longer have the best interest of our children at heart, but instead are more than willing to seduce our unsuspecting teenagers in order to fulfill an immoral desire; and the dishonest taxi drivers, who take the passenger over the longest circuitous route, to generate a larger fare. And the list could go on and on, embracing every meaningful work and profession performed by parents who set poor examples for their children to follow. Those types of parents will one day shame their child or children. All of these bad parental examples, not to be followed by children, are products of parenting that came of age subsequent to the 1960s.

A TABLESPOON OF LOVE, A TABLESPOON OF DISCIPLINE

What happened to the accountant of old, who wore the green eyeshade over his forehead and worked in the back office from sunup to sundown to balance the books and hardly made enough money to feed his family? Today's accountant comes out of college making money that would only be the dream of accountants of yesterday. Still, that seems not to be enough for the greedy set of accountants, who want too much, too quickly.

What happened to the stockbroker of old, whose greatest desire was to demonstrate to his client that he was proficient at increasing the funds entrusted to him in order for him to win that client's trust and to get recommendations to other prospective clients?

What happened to the doctor, who took his little black instrument bag and traveled about the countryside on call, attending to anyone needing his services, at any time of the day or night, and if the patient was unable to pay, it was all right anyhow? Now and then I hear stories told by older people of those types of doctors.

What happened to the entrepreneurs of old, who were honest and ethical to a fault? They would never trick you or devise a scheme to rip-off anyone. They enjoyed their reputation as honest businessmen, and if the money came along with the integrity exhibited, so be it. Those types of businessmen or women were more willing to give you something than to take anything from you.

What happened to the attorney of old, who often carried his papers and briefs in a paperboard expanding wallet-type file, because he could ill afford a fancy briefcase? He was willing to help anyone in honest trouble who had been victimized by the system. Often he did not even get fully paid for his services.

What happened to the judges, who were not swayed by financial gain in rendering their decision? Often they were swayed by other thoughts of prejudice, but more often than not, the money element didn't enter the picture. Their integrity meant more than money, even though their integrity often sided with racial or other injustices that they may have believed were right.

What happened to the community leaders, who had the interests of those they represented at heart? They served for the betterment of those they represented. It wasn't their interest that mattered, but the interest of those who chose them to speak and function on their behalf.

What happened to the corporate president, who worked his way up from the mailroom to the boardroom and to the position of CEO? He then went on to retire with a watch and a pen, a modest pension, sufficient to live out the remainder of his life in reasonable comfort with the love of his employees and the love and respect of his family, friends and community. This type of CEO was never tainted by greed. He never earned in a lifetime what some present-day CEOs earn in one year. Many of the CEOs of today draw annual pensions that far exceed the lifetime earnings of most of the CEOs of old. Yet, those CEOs of times past built the successful corporations that were inherited by the modern-day CEO. Where is the justification for annual salaries in the hundreds of millions?

What happened to the government statesmen and officials of old, who served without pay and considered it an honor and a privilege to represent the people? Of course, you had corrupt politicians in the old days too, but today those that are corrupt are that way even in light of being well paid by the system. For those who fit this mold, enough seems not to be enough. Where does the greed stop? I guess it only stops at the jail cell.

What happened to that brand of policeman of old, who considered it an honor and privilege just to be able to wear the uniform? He made certain his uniform was clean, his shirt was starched, his shoes were shined, and his metal was polished. Sure, you had corruption in the old days, but not nearly on the scale as is witnessed today. The policeman of old was too afraid of being caught, and often those exhibiting bad behavior got their direction from the boss. Today, much of the corruption and bad ethics is an individual thing.

What happened to the salesman of old, who represented the likes of the character in the book entitled *Death of a Salesman*? What happened to the salesman whose honesty and integrity was his bond? He wouldn't lie to you or fool you, because he wanted repeat business from you and business from your friends and relatives. He wouldn't sell a product or service he didn't believe in, because what he told his prospective customer had to be the absolute truth.

What happened to the writers who produced the likes of *Ivanhoe, Anna Karenina, The Scarlet Letter, Pride and Prejudice, David Copperfield, Treasure Island, Gulliver's Travels, The Wealth of Nations, The Decline of the West, The Intellectual Love of God, Little Women, Death of a Salesman, Moby Dick, Roots* and *In Search of History*? The list could go on and on, and the time span for their place in history could go on and on. Those books were written by individuals who had something to say that was considered important, something they felt society needed to hear and could benefit from. It was evident that many were not motivated by the desire to make money, as much as by the desire to make a positive and definitive statement. Some never greatly benefited from their writing until well up in age, and others never lived to reap the benefits. They were writers who set good examples in their writings, and posterity remembers them with respect. Over time their children's children and other posterity will remember them with pride.

What happened to the sports figures of old, whose victory depended on their determination to prepare themselves to defeat their opponent by exercising rigorous acts of discipline in their training, eating, abstinence and study of who they would be facing in pursuit of victory? They had too much good sportsmanship in them to do anything that would give them an undue, unnatural or unfair advantage over their prospective opponent. The thought of cheating and being found out in that behavior was the last thing they wanted to happen. I'm sure most of them would not have wanted to risk corrupting their body with drug enhancers to gain an unfair advantage. Being gracious losers came easier in those days than it does today.

What happened to the teachers who wanted their students to think they were beyond reproach in their behavior? They wouldn't have dared to do anything to compromise their morality in the eyes of students. Their greatest desire was to teach and mentor. The last thing they would have done would have been to compromise the moral well-being of a student. They cared about what the students thought about them, they cared about what the parents thought about them, and above all, they cared about what their colleagues thought about them. They had integrity, and they were capable of feeling shame. Most of their students were young enough to be their children, and they cared about children. These later generations seem only to really care about self and what makes self happy. The consequences of their behavior are rarely considered.

What happened to the taxi drivers of old who addressed you politely, were eager to lift your bags for you, and would sometimes give you a tour of the city with their meter off, pointing out the city's landmarks and history and taking great pride in their knowledge of the city's highlights? They were especially courteous to out-of-towners, because they wanted them to think and speak well of their city. They felt comfortable in the thought that they would receive a nice tip, because they had served you with graciousness and the dignity that their profession demanded. They felt no need to shake you down, to earn a fare they didn't deserve.

Those taxi drivers were unlike the sour-tempered hustlers of today, who will leave your bags on the street for you to load, take you to your destination in the most roundabout way, and curse you out if your tip isn't what they expected it to be. Those who fit this mold are merely additional examples of improperly-parented children. They also represent the signs of the times and bad parental examples not to follow. Parents can't brag about their bad behavior. The father of an old friend of mine drove a New York taxi for years and often talked about his profession in glowing detail. She greatly admired him and how he handled his profession. But he was parented prior to the 1960s generation. He had set an example for his children, and he could certainly demand more of them.

In addition to the above that represented the setting of bad examples for children not to follow, there is a host of other individuals functioning in a wide range of other professions which have set similarly poor examples. They couldn't demand much of their children, because they didn't lead by example. It doesn't matter what your position may be in life, there always exists the possibility of making a mistake or misjudgment and causing shame to your children. Many such mistakes could have been avoided because the path leading to the shameful act is usually slow and winding, with landmarks along the way, that alert one to the direction toward which he is headed. Without the grace of God, many of us could be victimized by the negative temptations of life, but as the saying goes, "If you don't want to cook, stay out of the kitchen." Red flags are usually visible, giving adequate warning of what might be coming. Heed them for your child's sake.

The indication now is that parents don't care about embarrassing their children, and children have come to not care about embarrassing their parents. It has become a "what's-good-for-me" mode of behavior. Even some government officials have come to care only about what's good for them and no longer care about what is good for the citizenry. Those put in charge of upholding the law are breaking the law, so citizens feel justified in their own lawless behavior. Businessmen have come to not care about workers, and so workers have come not to care about businesses.

These behavior patterns are all borne out of what children have been taught as children. The mothers didn't properly parent the children, the grandmothers didn't properly parent the mothers, and the great-grandmothers didn't properly parent the grandmothers. It all goes back to the generations that came of age subsequent to the 1960s. There was once a time when grandmothers were seen as sweet, innocent, caring and vulnerable little old ladies. Grandchildren loved them, adored them and respected them for the life they led and the examples they set. The above is no longer the description of a typical grandmother.

In today's society, some grandmothers have come to symbolize law-breaking behavior typical of the times we live in. Some have been pulled over on the highway for speeding; others have been arrested for fraud, selling illegal drugs and taking illegal gambling bets. Buses headed for the gaming dens of America are often filled with gambling grandmothers, many on canes and walkers. It's an everyday scene to see a grandmother hobble up to the bank teller's window to get rolls of quarters to take to the casino for playing the slot machines. Some other grandmothers are characterized by drunkenness, swearing and brawling. Children, as well as grandchildren, have lost a great deal of respect for this new breed of their family lineage.

Grandmothers are wondering what's wrong with their grandchildren, and I'm sure a lot of grandchildren are shaking their heads and wondering what's wrong with their grandparents. Society is constantly posing the question, "What's wrong with the children these days?" But society shouldn't be perplexed, wondering what's wrong with children. Society should be wondering what's wrong with parents. There is nothing wrong with the child that's not wrong with the parents. Children stopped acting like children when parents stopped acting like parents. When children started acting up, they started acting like their mothers and fathers. Bad parents were breaking the law before their children came into the world.

Those parents were abusing drugs and alcohol before the child was born. They weren't good examples for them, so they couldn't demand much of them. It's not enough just to say to a child, "Don't do it." If a child thinks it was all right for you to do, she or he may think it is all right for her or him to do too.

A mother had her first child, and had no husband. The second child arrived, and she still had no husband. Can she tell her daughter to get married first and expect her daughter to listen to her advice? The daughter may find it convenient to do just what the mother did and not do what the mother says.

A father got indicted for theft and for running an illegal business scam.

The child may not want to follow in his father's footsteps and follow him to jail, but he also may not want to listen to his father and obey the law. Some of the parents speeding on the highway have children in the car. Do you think that when that child comes of age and gets behind the wheel he won't speed? He or she may just want to do what his father did.

Society needs to come to realize that it's less about what's wrong with children than what's wrong with parents. Two or three generations ago many of society's parents stopped parenting properly. This began in the 1960s, when all of the other positive social norms were being thrown to the wind. Now we see the fallout from it in the behavior of our children. Society may not be able to turn these children around, but if the coming generations begin parenting again, we may be able to save our society for future generations. Even if we begin today and get back to the old-fashioned parenting methods of yesterday, and if most of today's parents do it properly, it would probably take at least two generations of time to get back to a society which speaks of some of the civility of yesterday. That would take some thirty to forty years. It will take longer to fix the problem than it took to undo everything. We need to just stop telling children what to do, and start showing them, by example, what they should be doing.

3. You Can Set Positive Examples

Like many other parents, we were parents whose aim it was to live our life in such a way that our child would be able to say with pride, "That's my mother" or "That's my father." It was also our intention to raise the child in such a way as to be able to say with pride, "That's my daughter." For us to live this type of life as parents was not a challenging feat. We had come from backgrounds that shaped us in becoming what we became. We had no trouble staying on track, avoiding glaring off-track behavior. I had a terrible temper, which could have landed me in jail, but by God's grace I was able to avoid a complete temper collapse.

As children, we were raised with basic, acceptable moral values, social values, work ethics and the fear of God. Did all of us siblings adhere to the moral values we were taught? Indeed, we did not. Some went astray from those teachings and paid the cost of doing so. Was there a failure in the parenting style? I suggest not, but I do suggest that my parent had grown weary of the effort to keep up the hard parenting pressure required to keep children on course. The one or two siblings who went astray were a part of the youngest set of siblings who were carried by my mother in the later stages of her life. In addition, the illness she was coping with probably rendered her not strong enough to keep up the required parenting pressure, and those who did go astray may have taken advantage of her weakness.

As a sibling group, we didn't know out-of-control behavior in any of the above areas, so we basically lived our life as we knew or as we had been taught. We were taught to work honestly for our bread and to attend church for our spiritual direction and enlightenment. We were taught that sexual promiscuity was troublesome, and drunkenness was shameful. We were taught that the acquisition of knowledge was not only helpful, but basic and necessary for life's accomplishments. We were made to understand that required knowledge could be obtained in school, and that we should obtain as much knowledge as we could acquire, under any given circumstance—even through difficulty. We were made to understand that advancement in life came from a job well done, through know-how and perseverance. We were also taught that cleanliness and neatness would go far to make us feel good about ourselves, as well as present us in a positive light to others. We learned from our parents that it is better to own than to rent, but the decision of whether to own or rent is strictly an individual one. Each choice has its pros and cons. Last, but not the least, we were shown by example that we are (as parents) responsible for helping to shape the direction of our children.

Because we came equipped with these values, handed down by our parents, we went about our life functioning within the parameters of what we knew to do and the way we knew it should be done. The life we knew and endeavored to live was, most often, the example of how it should have been done, and our life, as parents, embodied some basic values that were good and right to pursue. However, if you could thumb through the pages of the lives of my siblings' offspring, you would not find all of the offspring fitting the mold of being on track. That is because some of my siblings "dropped the ball." They may not think so, but they did. They may know they did, but may not admit it. When those that did drop the ball look at the direction their children took, they must muse at the fact that something was not quite right. If they delve deep enough into their parenting experience, they might be able to admit to themselves that they should not have done "this or that" or that they should have done "this or that." Your children will often voice their opinion of what you may have done wrong as a parent. Their opinion may not always be truthful and objective but may give some food for thought.

My daughter's mother and I were married approximately eight years before she was born. This isn't in any way suggesting that a married couple should delay (for even a day) starting its family. We, as parents, were attempting to have some plans in place before starting our family. It was an individual thing. We spent the greater part of those years, before our daughter was born, thinking about and endeavoring to make economic preparation for the time she would be arriving. Of course, we didn't know we would be having a girl child in our future whose name would be Celeste. But before she came, we spent the time working our respective jobs and functioning as a family unit.

We attended church on a regular basis and were generally given to sober-minded behavior. We believed in the benefits of education, and I was busy completing my college education at the time Celeste was born. We worked hard on our jobs, with me putting in as much overtime as I could handle, and my wife availing herself of every opportunity to work overtime on her job. Our earnings afforded us sufficient wardrobes that allowed us to be neat and clean. We wanted our own space and wanted enough of it for ourselves and the potential child or children we expected would be coming, so we sought out a home to purchase.

Prior to purchasing our own home, we had been renting an attic apartment in one of the two houses owned by my wife's aunt and uncle, whom she had come to live with. We felt that if her aunt and uncle could own two houses, we should be able to own one. What's more, my parents owned their own home. It wasn't a *Wuthering Heights* mansion, but they owned it. My father was a contractor-type, so he was able to keep the home in good repair. Later on, he even added additional bedrooms. We all grew up in that modest house. We were unlike children who had moved four or five times before they became adults. By the time we had moved out of our parents' home, we were either married or grown enough to be on our own anyway.

When my daughter came into the world, we had been in our own home for two years. We were establishing guidelines all along the way and establishing the patterns of life we deemed positive. Were we perfect parents? No, we were not. Life doesn't require perfection in parents, any more than it requires perfection in children. If it did, none of us would measure up to the task of living. However, we were not carrying any of those heavy pieces of noticeable "baggage" that makes one fall down. Nor did we come into a marriage with negative baggage that would impact on the demands we would be making on our child.

Neither my wife nor I had a premarital family, so we could demand that our daughter think about delaying the start of her family, until she had found a suitable mate for a spouse. Neither of us came from a background of drug use or alcohol abuse, and neither of us had a desire to do it. There were no stories or scenes of her parents abusing drugs or falling down in a drunken stupor. Our daughter never saw us acting under the influence of alcohol, nor did she ever witness either of us smoking a cigarette. Her mother never smoked, and I had quit smoking ten years prior to her birth, after having smoked for about two years or less. I stopped and never took up the habit again.

When she entered the world, neither of us was a smoker, so we could demand that she didn't smoke either, especially since we weren't going to provide enough money for her to purchase cigarettes. We could demand that she refrain from the use of illegal drugs and nicotine altogether and delay the use of alcoholic beverages until such time as she reached adulthood and learned whether or not it was in her best interest and taste to indulge in a glass of dinner wine before and/or after her dinner. As an adult, that or more potent alcoholic beverages would be strictly to her desire and choice.

There was no gossip going around the neighborhood about either of us being involved in an outside relationship, so she couldn't look at us in a light of marriage infidelity. Based on what she knew, she could conclude that a monogamous relationship was the ideal way to go. If she did see infidelity in her parents' relationship while they were together and it presented an ugly picture to her, she could have also decided it would not be the way she wanted to go. However, it is best to not present this type of choice to a child.

When my daughter was born, I was in college, studying to complete my bachelor's degree. She was exposed to an atmosphere of schooling and studying, so that was an example that indicated the necessity of continuing her studies. Parents need not be in college to stress the importance of education. However, seeing a parent study can certainly help encourage a child to study and could give the parents more of an incentive to demand academic excellence in the child.

BE AN EXAMPLE ... AND YOU CAN DEMAND MORE OF THEM

Her mother and I always adopted business attire when we were going off to our place of work or business. Her mother always worked a nine-to-five job. I either worked a job or ran a legitimate business. From that example, we could demand that she exercise an attitude of industriousness and ambition. Her mother often took her to the office where she worked— even as a little girl—so she was able to witness an example in action. I often took her to my place of business and sat her at my desk, so she could get a feel of what it was like sitting in the boss' seat.

One of the businesses I ran had a complete office atmosphere, with secretary included. This may have been good exposure for Celeste, if she understood the nature of being in charge. She was rather young at the time. Another business I ran was operational, with merchandise purchasing and marketing. She was old enough to understand and relate to what was happening there. It was an example, as well as a motivation. We didn't want to demand that our daughter run her own business (her mother loathed the idea of me running my own business), but the exposure Celeste received gave her a basis on which to make choices for herself when and if the time came. She may also have seen examples of some of the struggles encountered in running your own business, and came to the conclusion that it would not be something for her to do.

The idea of demanding things of your child comes into play when the child veers off track. All parents need do to get the child going and to keep her or him going is strive to set an example for her or him to live by. Positive examples are often sufficient to keep a child moving in a positive direction. When a child begins to veer off track, we can point her to our example to give her or him a point of reference. A child may be inclined to follow the path of her or his parent, especially if it brought joy, pleasure and financial rewards, or if it is the easier path of the choices available at a given time. If you took the easier road and your child decides to take that road also—even against your wishes—then he or she can always say, "Dad, you did it" or "Mom, you did it." So when we start demanding that children do the difficult things in life or travel the road less traveled, we should have a good reason and an example to offer them to support our demand.

I remember the words uttered by Les Brown, a motivational speaker, when he was speaking to a crowd of some seven to ten thousand people at a convention: "You can't lead where you don't go, and you can't teach what you don't know." Truer words were never spoken. Children are people too, and they are more likely to follow where you lead than to go where you say.

Many parents have spent the better part of their life doing everything they felt big and bad enough to do, and all of a sudden they begin to demand a stellar life's performance from the child. In many instances, what they are demanding from the child may be correct and even in the child's best interest, but if the parent did not chart a good course for the child to follow, the child may be less inclined to wholeheartedly adhere to the demands of the parent. The best way to lead is by example.

Some individuals, prior to settling down to raise a child, were alcohol abusers, drug abusers and unwed mothers. Others were disobedient to their parents, ran the streets, gambled, stole and murdered. Others were drug dealers, rapists, loan sharks and prostitutes. The paths of some of these individuals became known to the child, either by their actions or revelation by the parent or someone else. If they have a child, I'm certain (at least in most cases) they would not want the child to engage in any of this antisocial behavior. A parent can demand, and it may be best for the child to do what the parent says, rather than what the parent did, but it is easy for a child to get off track and gravitate into any one or more of these habits. When you ask why, the child can be quick to point a finger at your past or even your present behavior.

People like crutches, because crutches are supports they can lean on. It is much more comfortable to lean than it is to stand upright. A child is no different from people in general, except in the sense that, she is being steered by the guidance of a guardian, who tells her what and what not to do and where and where not to go. That is why it is so important to set a good example, so the child will have a good point of reference.

The house we lived in was our own. Celeste helped me plant the flowers and sometimes shovel the snow in her own little way. She knew that no landlord came to collect the rent, and so we could turn the heat up and down as we desired. She had her own room, and we fixed and decorated it, just as we did other parts of the home. I'm sure she understood the nature of beautifying what belongs to you. That's not to say that the demand (by example) was for her to own her own home, but it was, at the very least, an incentive—if the desire was there.

In our family, we hugged a lot, and Celeste and I still hug a lot. When she was small, she would squeeze between her mother and me when we hugged. That was probably an indication of a little child's jealousy or the feeling that says, "Don't leave me out." We went to church, and when we went, we took her with us. That was a good example and set a positive precedent for a child to live by. Faith and strength can always be found in God, especially during those times when the "chips may be down." We shopped as a family, we entertained as a family, in terms of family entertainment. We spent time at home together as a family. We didn't allow her to enter, nor did we thrust her into, an atmosphere of adult social functions. That was an example we did not want to set.

All of the above and more represent examples we set for our child to live by, and we demanded a lot from her in terms of positive behavior and ambition. She gave us a lot in return and has made us proud of what she became. Be an example for them, and you can demand more of them.

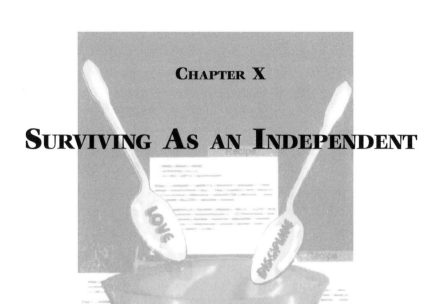

CHAPTER X

SURVIVING AS AN INDEPENDENT

We must raise our children to be independent,
Not to cling to us and need us for their very survival.
If we do not do this, that's selfish!

1. I'LL STAY, AS LONG AS I CAN HAVE MY WAY

The idea of twenty-five- and thirty- and forty-year-old children living in their parents' home is repulsive, unless the child lives there for some necessity of the parent or for some necessity of the child. Otherwise, it shows a lack of independence and a failure on the part of the parent or parents to raise the child or children with a sense of security and independence. It may also be an indication that the parental household rules that apply to the child or children are either very lax, or that the child is able to operate by her or his own set of rules. This tends to be so, because if the parent or parents had a strict set of behavior guidelines, most children would prefer being in their own space, operating according to the rules they prefer, rather than the rules their parents prefer.

One of the benefits of children becoming adults is the fact that they can make their own decisions about what they want and do not want to do. If you are sharing a space owned by someone else, she or he generally has guidelines concerning the utilization of the space you're using. Then why would a child want to live in a parent's space? She or he would only accept that, if the conditions are easier than living independently. Why would an independent parent want a grown child in her or his space? The parent would, only if she or he is insecure about herself or insecure about her child's ability to live independently on her own. Raising a child with this shortcoming is a negative. Regardless of the angle from which we observe the situation, we must notice that parents (in all instances) are different from their child or children. This is true, even from the mere fact that no two people are alike. There is probably never a situation where the parent or parents and child have all the same habits, likes, dislikes, enjoy the same music, have the same eating habits, the same cleaning habits, the same hygiene habits, the same phone habits or like the same type of people.

I can recall a case of a former co-worker whose forty-five-year-old son shared her living quarters. They were both normal and healthy, physically, mentally and financially, as far as I know. He was too dependent to move out on his own, and she didn't have the guts to ask him to move out. He didn't eat pork, and she did, but she wasn't allowed to cook pork in her own pots. There appears to be something wrong with this picture. These types of differences tend to create friction in the household, and because of this, an independent child should rather be in her or his own space.

Anytime a child is not independent enough and secure enough in attitude and character to go out on her own, the parent or parents have failed greatly. Most parents in this dilemma would probably be reluctant to admit the failure and even try to construe the situation as a normal process of existence. Wrong! There is something very negative about raising a child who lacks the ability to go out from the parent's household and function independently—especially if there is no disability or compelling reason that would preclude the child from being able to survive independently. The same could be said on behalf of the parent or parents concerning a compelling reason.

Functioning independently is one of the first laws of nature. Wild animals, and even the lowly birds, teach their young to go out from the nest and function and survive independently of the mother and father. If the lower forms of animals can teach this lesson, with their limited degree of intelligence (as compared to ours), what does that say about us? There are special circumstances or conditions, under which it is acceptable for adult children to be living in a household with a parent or other guardian, but barring any of these special circumstances, it is not normal independent behavior.

There appears to be a pattern or type of overall behavior in the ways of a parent or parents who raises a child that is too insecure to strike out on her or his own. In any case, this type of child is often the product of an insecure parenting style. Insecure parents have a tendency to cling to their child, just as they do to other things and, sometimes, other people. Even they seem to lack the ability to survive independently. This type of parent may have clung to her or his parent, or brother, sister or friend. Somehow, there seems to be a deep-seated fear of losing or being without the relationship that one thinks she needs. I have a personal philosophy that translates into a saying, and that saying is: "There is nothing in my life I can't do without, except God." That simply means that I am willing to let go of anything else—if it is in my best interest and well-being to do so.

Sometimes we may tend to cling to things in life that can be quite destructive to us or lead to our downfall, especially if the person or thing we can't let go of serves us no good. Having an independent or dependent type of attitude evidences a life thread that seems to run throughout the behavior pattern of an individual's life. Dependent attitudes seem to evidence addictive behavior. Being addictive simply implies the inability to free oneself from an entity.

For instance, suppose one is in a relationship that has turned sour, and one of the partners no longer has a desire to be involved in the life of the other. Suppose also that the other person is unable to come to grips with the desire of that person to be free of the relationship. The one who is unable to come to grips with the situation may continue to try to hold on to the relationship and to the other individual until it results in hurt. I'm reflecting on a line I remember from one of those Joan Crawford movies. It said in essence, "You've got to know when to hold on and when to let go."

Volumes have been written on the act of "letting go." How often have you heard the expression, "Let go and let God?" Letting go of your child or your child letting go of you, when the proper time comes is a good thing. It is, in fact, the most desirable thing to do. It is a normal mode of behavior. It's supposed to be that way.

When I reflect on the lives of my brothers and sisters, as well as myself,

I can recall that we could barely wait to finish school and reach the age when we could be on our own and in our own space. It wasn't that we didn't love our parents; it was the fact that our parents had rules of conduct and behavior, which may have been contrary to what we wanted to do at a particular time in a given circumstance.

Have you ever witnessed a parent or guardian pushing a five-year-old or six-year-old around in a stroller? I'm sure you've witnessed a four-year-old riding in a grocery cart, or a mother carrying a three- or four-year-old child in her arms, because the child frets whenever she or he is put down. In other instances, there is the six-year-old who refuses to be left at school the first day. The mother has to sit in the classroom for the entire day—if allowed. Another child cries when the mother prepares to leave her alone, and the parent sometimes cries too, because of the lack of the ability to free herself from the child's desire to have her continually by her side.

2. The Transition Is Taking Too Long

Some children are still sleeping in their parent's bed as teenagers, and some mothers are still buying underwear for their thirty-year-old married son. I have known of other children who could scarcely get married, because there was such a dependent influence between the child and the parent. The parent is always injecting his or her thoughts and desires into the life and behavior of the child or *vice versa*. The child is influenced by this, to the extent that she or he can hardly make a decision without consulting the wishes of the parent. On the other hand, I know parents who can scarcely have a normal social relationship, because of the influences of or interference from their adult children. Quite often the opinion or wishes of the adult child or adult children have ruined a parent's chance to be married or have a happy relationship.

How often have you heard the expression, "He's a mama's boy?" Well, that expression implies that practically every decision the man makes is influenced by the wishes of his mother or needs to have his mother's seal of approval. That man cannot even run his household without first getting the opinion of his mother. There are also daughters whose parent or parents have a similar influence over their lives. That represents dependent, destructive behavior. Ladies, you should steer clear of this type of man, and, mothers, steer clear of any attempt to leave this type of influence upon your son. It's neither healthy for him, nor for the family he may one day have. He will bring nothing but misery to the life of the woman he marries.

Men should also steer clear of the type of woman whose parent or parents have an overwhelming influence over her adult life. There are few things more frustrating than trying to come to a decision with your mate and having your mate put the decision on hold until he or she gets the opinion of the parent or guardian. Parents, don't raise your child in such a way as to be dependent on your help or opinion about her or his life. Don't raise your child to need you when she should be going about her life on her own. Don't live your life in such a way as to need your child or children to fill an emptiness or void in your life. When your child reaches the independent point in her or his life, let her or him be independent.

One point of reference concerning a state of independence is when a child is over eighteen and able to support herself or himself, independent of the parent. This doesn't imply that you refrain from speaking to negative behavior at any time. We need a point of reference here, because some seven-year-olds have been known to be able to support themselves independent of the parent. You certainly would not want to give a child that age unsupervised independence. On the other hand, some sixteen-year-olds may have joined the military or gotten married, and in every other way are self supporting. That child certainly should have achieved the rank of independence, especially if she or he is residing outside of your household.

Parents, get yourself a life of your own. Get a relationship, if not with a person, get one with God. Find a sensible pastime or a hobby to occupy yourself, so you will not always need to have your child or children around or have the need to always be around your child or children. I know of parents who cling to their children for fear of being alone, if they break off from the individual with whom they are having a relationship. The fear of being alone (in an adult) spells "insecurity." Don't take claim to that one.

We came into this world alone, and even if we are one of twins, only one of us could have come from the womb at a time. When we get ready to depart this life, we are going to be obligated to do it alone. Others may die at the same minute or second, but they won't do it with another. It's an individual thing. It's an act we must each perform alone—all by ourselves. Some come to the point of death and are frightened beyond belief, because of the inability to face it alone. I've seen many battlefield accounts of a dying soldier calling for his mother, thinking maybe she could get there and accompany him into that unknown realm, because at that instant, he lacked the ability to do that one thing that requires complete independence.

Your mother can be with you when you stump your toe or skin your knee. She can be with you on the first day of school, if she is around, or the first day of college. She can be with you when you leave for the military and when you throw your cap up into the air after graduation. She can be there when you're in labor (if you're having a child), but she cannot be with you in death. She can be by your side, but you will have to make the final journey completely independent of her.

Even individuals who form a suicide pact don't die together. One always goes before the other, even if only by a second or seconds, and one usually has to witness the death or unconsciousness of the other, unless, in an instant, all are rendered incapacitated. Parents, when you diligently teach your child to face life with a strong sense of independence, you, as well as the child, will have the ability and strength to face and stand up to whatever challenges may be encountered in life—as well as in death.

3. I'll Be Glad When I Get Grown

When I look back on my childhood and think about the attitudes of my sisters and brothers and those of other individuals in my surroundings, I can recall the frequent remark that said, "I'll be glad when I get grown." Some of us didn't know it at the time, but we didn't really want to hurry through our childhood. We thought we did, but little did we know what lie ahead. Getting grown required taking on the responsibilities of living—working to earn an existence, making the decisions that would impact our lives in a positive or negative way far into the future, and having to depend on and accept the sensibility of the decisions made. Sometimes, getting grown required taking on the responsibilities of raising or caring for a family member and making decisions that would impact those individuals' lives in a positive or negative way far into the future.

In contemplating thoughts of being grown, we often didn't deal with the above ramifications. The desire to be grown implied that we would be out from under the direction of our parents and their strict (if that was the case) rules. We felt we could free ourselves from having to adhere to their "dos and don'ts," that were part and parcel of parental guidance and direction. In those days, if the parent raised the child properly, the parent had a strict set of rules, coupled with a code of behavior that was equally burdensome to a child. When and if you broke one or more of those rules, it seemed almost certain that fire and brimstone would rain down upon your countenance.

Parents taught work ethics, moral ethics, respect for our elders, fear of God, parent's ethics, study ethics, accomplishing ethics, be-the-best-you-can ethics and on and on and on. It wasn't surprising that even a child of wealthy parents had a paper route, clerked in the local library, bookstore or grocery store or raked leaves for Mr. Winterleaf. They were being taught work ethics and "earning-an-extra-nickel" ethics.

It was no less surprising that we were sent off to Sunday school every Sunday, and some of us were altar boys, choir boys or rendered other services in the church. Parents were putting us in the church environment, so we could be exposed to moral and brotherhood ethics, as well as learn of the awesome power of God to bless us for good behavior or to suffer us to reap the wrath of Satan for bad behavior. Many of us read from the Bible at some time and encountered the passages that said, "Honor thy father and thy mother," or the one that talks of the destruction of the disobedient child. They were teaching us the fear of God and "love-thy-parents" ethics.

It goes without saying that we were taught to say, "Yes, sir" and "Yes ma'am" to our elders. They were teaching us "respect-for-our-elders" ethics. It was not unusual, when a child exhibited unacceptable behavior, to encounter the wrath of the almighty strap. That punishment was brought to your remembrance anytime you were tempted to unacceptable behavior in the future. That was part of the discipline ethics. Some children got scolded or punished when they brought home poor grades from school, or when they didn't do as well as a sister or brother did. They were admonished to study harder. Those parents were teaching the "Be-the-best-you-can" ethics.

All of these and more are part and parcel of the very basic requirements involved in properly raising a child and preparing her to go out into the arena of life and function successfully and independently. The lack of any of these, as well as others that may not have been mentioned here, could result in a breakdown in an important aspect of human development required in properly shaping the individual. How an individual shapes up as a child will determine how she shapes up as an adult and, subsequently, how she or he will go through life and out of life.

The most basic and necessary requirements in shaping a positive future for a child are good work ethics, good moral ethics, respect for elders, fear of God and parents and striving to do your best—not necessarily in that order. Many other values and ethics are needed and may be added to these, but omission of any of the above can lead to serious deficiencies in a child's ability to cope with life's challenges and survive as an independent. In raising our child, we used all of the above and invented others, as needed and required. We borrowed others from neighbors, friends, my parents, my wife's parents, elders, co-workers, relatives, the postman, ministers, the school teachers, the Sunday school teachers and even from the child herself. Sometimes a little child can drop an innocent gem of wisdom that you can use in effecting her proper upbringing.

We endeavored to enhance our child's life by giving her supportive educational props. We bought the child the button up, zip up, lace up and snap up book that taught her how to button her clothes, lace her shoes, zip her zippers and snap those things that had snaps. Early on, and before she started school, she was taught to hang up her clothing, straighten her bed, put books back on the shelf and put other things back in their proper place. She was given other chores to get her accustomed to helping around the house. She was given instructions on caring for and keeping up with items of clothing, such as gloves, hats, scarves and coats. She was instructed in matters of neatness in appearance, schoolwork and other chores.

Some parents don't let their child do anything for herself—not even wipe her own nose. That's a terrible mistake, because you may not always be there to tie the shoes and wipe the nose. From the time she was born, we took turns caring for Celeste, as the circumstance required, and teaching her how to be independent in little things that required "going it alone." These were things such as leaving (so-called) little friends alone, if they mistreated her. We taught her, as best as she could understand it, how to be kind and giving, while not letting others take advantage of her. She was an only child, so we gave a lot of love, but we also taught her how to be alone and be contented in her state of being by herself.

When she got an opportunity to play with other quality children, we allowed her to do so, but we also taught her to be able to adjust, when play time was over. We bought her books, puzzles, games and other intellectual items to entertain her, motivate her and to stimulate her intellectually. And we made sure that one of the two of us was always there for her.

4. HER PARENTS PARTED WAYS

At about the age of nine years, Celeste's mother and I reached an impasse, and we came to a parting of our ways. It was unfortunate for the child's sake, but since this isn't a book about us, as spouses or about perfect marriages, I see no need to elaborate on our breakup.

When I decided to move out of the house, I decided that I would leave everything intact to best serve the survival of my spouse and child. The year was 1977. I don't quite remember the time of the year, but my reflections tell me it was late spring or early summer. Whatever the date was, I had decided I had to leave that day. I left my wife with the three-bedroom house we had recently refurbished and remodeled. I left her the car to get around in, to aid her in fulfilling the needs of herself and the child. I left all the furniture and furnishings intact. I left her a note, telling her how I would lend support for the child. I took only my books, my records, my clothes and other items that belonged to me personally. Everything else was left for my wife and child.

They stayed on in that house for a year or two. Then, after the house was robbed for the second time, my wife decided that it was too much to cope with. The neighborhood had begun to undergo a drastic change. By this time, the drug epidemic had gotten a strong foothold in suburbia, and the wave of robberies was well entrenched. The house had been robbed once during the time I lived there. This new wave of crime was the aftermath of the whirlwind of the 1960s and the "new drug thing." The break-ins were a part of the effort to support the habits of the new up-and-coming drug addicts, and I was afraid for my wife and child. Since I was not there with them, I empathized with my wife, when she expressed her desire to sell the house and move to some other location.

One day, prior to her coming to this conclusion, she had called me on the phone complaining and saying how my little daughter had to help her by dragging the garbage can out to the street for garbage collection. The thought of it, at the time, virtually broke my heart. When I look back on yesterday and look at what Celeste has become (despite all of the challenges of life), I can't help but thank God for the wonderful partnership that was forged between Him, her mother and me in raising her.

That "garbage can" incident smacked of the independence, strength and courage we had tried to forge in our child early, and through many other future challenges, she would again (with God's help) emerge victoriously. This child represents a true sense of independence and survival instincts, as I enumerate in other chapters, and as her father, I can say I am truly impressed with her perseverance. We taught her, and she learned well, the tactics of independence and survival.

No, she did not have to overcome polio, MS or any other major illness— so far at least. Thank God, she only missed one or two days of school, beginning with her preschool period and extending through the completion of her high school. However, she may have faced many other challenges that I wasn't aware of at the time, because she seldom (if ever) complained. She just did what she had to do. On many occasions, the look on her face or the tone of her voice said, "Dad, I can do it."

The breakup between her mother and me affected her, I'm sure, but how much it affected her I will probably never know. Some things children just keep to themselves. Celeste had a way of tuning out unpleasant things, reacting to them and handling them in such a way that was most comfortable for her, but never mentioning the unpleasant experience again. Looking back in retrospect, I can think of several such experiences. One of them was the death of her grandmother, and she must have found it to be very unpleasant, although she was quite young at the time, but she never mentioned it from then until today. I also remember a very unpleasant argument between her uncle and me that she witnessed. She never asked me about that uncle (my brother) or mentioned his name again until she saw him at her aunt's funeral services.

Not too long after my wife and I separated, I got a call from my wife indicating that our daughter's grades were slipping, and she was becoming a bit restless in school. This was obviously a subtle reaction to our separation. Celeste never said anything; she just unconsciously reacted to what she probably thought would be the loss of her father. After all, we had done almost everything together and gone almost everywhere together.

When parents break up, it is only natural for a child to think that the other parent may be going away forever, and some parents do. But little did she know that I had no intention of going anywhere out of the reach of her voice and her needs. It was a foregone determination that whatever happened between her mother and me would have absolutely little or no effect on Celeste. When her mother called me with that piece of behavior news, I immediately got on the phone with Celeste, and the conversation went like this:

Me: Celeste, what's your problem?
Reply: Nothing, Dad.
Me: Do you have a mother and father?
Reply: Yes, Dad.
Me: Do you think your mother loves you?
Reply: Yes, Dad.
Me: Do you think your father loves you?
Reply: Yes, Dad.
Me: Do you have a clean bed, clothes, food and a nice place to live?
Reply: Yes, Dad.
Me: Well, whatever happened between your mother and me has nothing to do with you. Your job is to go to school, study and do as you are instructed to do by your parents and teachers, so get yourself together. I don't want to hear anything else about attitude and grade problems. Do you understand?
Reply: Yes, Dad.

And from that day forward, she went about her business of studying and achieving good grades. She did so well that she was allowed to skip two grades before high school. She entered the seventh grade at ten years of age and entered college at fifteen. She started in first grade in the fall of her fifth year of life and still, having been skipped twice, she seemed three years ahead of her classmates.

After the time of the separation between her mother and me, and prior to the time of selling the house, I had opened a ladies' and men's boutique on a main thoroughfare in the borough of Queens in New York. Subsequent to the sale of the house, my daughter and her mother moved into an apartment around the corner from where I operated the boutique. I don't know if this was plan or coincidence, but it sure worked out to be a blessing in disguise, because Celeste was close enough for me to see her daily, and most often, I saw her at least twice a day. I was overjoyed with their new place of residence, because it put me in virtual shouting distance. Celeste, somewhat of a "daddy's girl," enjoyed the fact that her dad was close by. She was about ten years of age when they moved around the corner.

From the time she was old enough, Celeste had been guided in using sensible reasoning to make sensible decisions. We never had a problem or worry about her playing with matches or fire or doing other immature

247

things, because we taught her that fire belonged in contained areas made for it, and that the use thereof should be by those qualified to do so. So there was no fear of her burning down the house when she was alone. She had been taught the tactics of surviving alone in her own space, so there was no need for her to have unwanted company in the home while her parents were away.

Another thing she was taught early was to be a leader, not a follower. Being a leader implies independence, because leaders are out front; they're first. They take the initiative. They are in charge and start the action. I taught her not to follow the ideas of her peers, because their ideas were not necessarily any smarter than her own, just maybe different. What's more, some of the worst of life's experiences borne by children have come about as a result of children following the behavior or suggestion of other children or adults who led them astray.

Many children are being taught at home concerning the avoidance of negative habits and behavior, but are not given a sense of independence and self-esteem. This puts them in a quandary as to whom they should be listening to or following. I stressed to my daughter that she must be a leader, and the point was brought home by these words, "If I ever happen to come upon a scene where something dumb or stupid is going on with you involved, you had better be leading the crowd. I dare you to follow someone else's stupid or dumb behavior." She received this well, because as far back as I can remember, Celeste has been a "take-charge" person. She took charge of everything she was allowed to control and organized everything she was allowed to organize.

5. She Was Alone and in Charge of Her Studies

By the time Celeste and her mother had moved around the corner from where I ran my business (which was also three blocks from where I lived), she had begun to take charge of her study habits independently, because her mother was going to work, and I was running a business. By this time, she was also well versed and conditioned in the norms of putting things in their proper order, things such as showing up and showing up on time, finishing what was started, doing her best and presenting herself in the best light.

I had taken on the habit of getting up every morning in time to go to her house, wait for her out front and then walk her down the hill to the bus that took her to school. I lived a few blocks from where she lived, and my place of business was between where she lived and where I lived. I would make the trek to her house every morning, rain, shine, sleet or snow, and she would come out of her house every morning at approximately the same time, looking for her father. I would engage in small talk, asking her what she expected her day to be like and other things, as time allowed, between her house and the bus. When the bus arrived, I would help her onto the bus and go back to my house to begin preparing myself to go and open my place of business.

Her mother may have been in one of those periods of spitefulness and decided to put a stumbling block in the path of my efforts to be there to nurture the child. One day she called me and said, "Celeste doesn't want you to meet her anymore. She can walk to the bus by herself." I knew she could, but I thought she enjoyed this little time we spent together at the beginning of her day. I felt a bit hurt when her mother gave that piece of information, because I also enjoyed the camaraderie we experienced on our little morning walks. However, I thought that if she felt she no longer needed me by her side at this juncture, it was okay. After all, I was raising her with a sense of independence.

The next morning I stayed home and didn't go to meet her to walk her to the bus. I was able to put the matter out of my mind and to go about my day taking the situation as it was presented, but little did I know that the situation, as presented, wasn't the way it really was. That very morning Celeste had come out expecting to see her father there as usual, and I wasn't there. Later, I was told that she had come back into the house in tears, very disappointed, because I was not there. As it turned out, she wasn't the one who had said she didn't need me to walk her to the bus; her mother had created that scenario. Perhaps her mother meant well and didn't quite realize what she was doing to the child. She wasn't just hurting the child's father; she was also hurting the child. The harm coming from that type of behavior was discussed in a previous chapter. Avoid it at all cost, for the sake of the child in the middle. Eventually, her mother felt bad for causing the child the unnecessary hurt, and she reversed her position.

At ten years of age, Celeste was very responsible and had her keys to the house. In addition to her being a responsible child, it was more the protection of God upon her life that some child molester wasn't hanging around watching her to seize upon an opportunity to push his way in behind her to do her harm. However, in those days, most of the child molesters were still in the closet. Drugs and free adult sex was the current craze. What's more, society wasn't the liberal bastion that it is today, accepting everything, excusing everything, permitting everything and condemning nothing. We simply went from bad to worse—from the frying pan into the fire with liberalism and the so-called freedoms.

At that time, Celeste would safely come home from school, use her key to let herself into the house and then lock the door. She would call both me and her mother on the phone, to let us know she had arrived home safely and that everything was okay. She would then fix herself a snack and settle down to do her homework.

She usually studied alone, never having a need to invite any classmates over to help her study or to help them study. She was independent and focused. I or her mother would check her homework, give her whatever instructions we felt were needed, and direct her in solving any problems at hand that may have caused difficulty. If any unusual academic problems came up, I was usually the one to interact on that level, because I was nearby to aid her during the course of her homework, and her mother didn't usually arrive until later in the evening. It was also thought that my college education rendered me more adept at negotiating difficult problems.

Sometimes, in the evening, after Celeste had finished all of her homework, she would walk around to my place of business, and I would give her little chores to do that she enjoyed doing. Gradually, as she got older, I would give her chores that required a greater degree of responsibility. I would explain how to perform a given chore and why it should be done in a certain way. She caught on fast, because she was a reasonably bright child. She loved interacting with customers and was very good with numbers. I taught her how to prove the day's receipts to the register and how to perform the closeout for the day. I also taught her how to prepare the deposit for the bank. It was a very good business experience for her and went a long way toward helping to sharpen her business acumen.

On days when she was off from school, I would often take her with me on trips to the designer showrooms, where I would be making purchases for the store. On occasion, when I would be buying for the store, I would buy things for Celeste. Sometimes, when salesmen from various designer houses would bring their designs into the store to show their samples, I would ask her what she would pick. I taught her the ins and outs of fashion selecting, marketing and banking. And she learned well.

6. She Had Responsible Summer Work

What Celeste learned around me in my business often proved helpful in other areas of her work experience. Before she settled down in her present engineering profession, she once worked for a designer fashion and accessory house and was offered a very responsible management position before she left it.

In the summer after school let out, she usually had a summer job waiting. She was fortunate in that she got a summer job at her mother's place of business and earned a very respectable salary at the age of thirteen or fourteen. She did filing and related clerical chores. She got working papers at the age of thirteen and spent the summer as a showroom salesperson in a very upscale designer furniture showroom that catered to the likes of stars and celebrities. She sold as much furniture as the regular showroom salesman, and this was no inexpensive furniture. Some of the sofas sold for upwards of $8,000.00, and the wall units were equally expensive. This was in the early 1980s.

Celeste learned the various styles and prices, was able to present the furniture in a positive light and earned a respectable salary plus commission and bonuses. In showrooms such as this, the furniture virtually sold itself to those who could afford to pay for it. People in that niche didn't shop price; they shopped desire. I'm sure some of the clientele bought from her because they were impressed that such an obviously young person could be so knowledgeable about the business. After all, she was only thirteen. She learned much from her mother, who was very experienced in the exclusive upscale furniture trade, because her mother had spent most of her adult working life in that business. Celeste often ran the showroom alone, with her mother occasionally looking in on her.

By this time and at this age Celeste had learned to be financially responsible. She was very prudent with money and not the least bit interested in the "baubles, bangles and beads," that often attracted the attention and desires of the average young person. She wasn't raised to spend her money on unnecessary frills. Neither did we buy those things for her. We bought her quality, "concrete" things, things of substance. We didn't go for the overpriced, designer sneakers and leather jackets. When I wanted leather slacks for her, I had them tailored by a leather tailor in the business.

I remember Celeste's husband making the remark, "My wife doesn't spend any money; she should go out and spend some money." She would always reply, "I have what I need." He earned a good living for her and his child and believed in them having what made them happy. When Celeste was young, I was in the habit of requiring her to give an estimate of her projected needs for the school year and the reason she thought she needed them. If the reason was justifiable by our standards, she got it. We weren't tight-fisted when it came to her needs, but neither were we spendthrifts. We couldn't afford to be.

Celeste was an only child, but she required a lot to keep going. After all, I was a business major with an emphasis on accounting and was in the habit of counting dollars and cents. I was also in the habit of reducing everything to numbers. That's all I knew. When it came to Celeste's school clothes and allowance, she justified the amount of clothing and the allowance she thought she needed, and if the logic made sense, she got it. She supplied a laundry list of how many skirts, slacks, jeans, blouses, shoes, coats, etc. she would be needing for the coming school year. Of course, I had the freedom to alter that list, and I usually did, at my discretion. Her allowance was always adequate, and she was thrifty enough to save out of it.

She was shrewd with money. Sometimes, instead of taking the bus from the train, she would walk and save the money. I didn't mind that. I admired it. My philosophy was, "Don't ask for the obvious. If you need it, and we can afford it, you will have it. For those items and monies you may need that we don't know about, you can tell us." I came to this position by witnessing children "getting attitudes" toward parents, when they refused to buy them something they could not afford to buy. I was so fed up with seeing them come into my store, asking parents to buy items they could hardly afford, and the children often getting angry if the parent didn't purchase them. I vowed I would not be held hostage to that type of attitude or behavior. I refused to be put against the wall to purchase unnecessary things or things I might not be able to afford. The modern-day generations nurtured those types of demands, and the modern-day parents yielded to them, because often the child was in charge—not the parent.

Celeste itemized the cost of her school transportation, lunch and all other everyday necessities, except for those unexpected things that sometimes came up. If I felt what she requested wasn't adequate for her to go about her life comfortably, I would often add to it. When she was thrifty, she was welcome to keep what was left over. I always admired ambition, and when she walked about a half mile from the train with a heavy book bag to save her money, she deserved to keep it.

Her book bag was always heavy, because in her school, the teachers gave homework every day. We didn't require her to, but we allowed her to do whatever she thought she could do—as long as it was positive. We permitted her to exercise ingenuity on her own behalf and reap the benefits of being creative and ambitious. She worked part-time jobs at her mother's place of business and in my place of business from time to time and earned extra money doing both. She manipulated her allowance and saved the spoils from this and all of the other endeavors.

7. WHEN THE GOING GOT TOUGH

Celeste worked a temporary job outside of her field of study for a time while waiting to get settled into work which she was trained for. After all, she had turned down a position in the packaging engineering field, because she wasn't happy in that particular type of packaging. She was constantly interviewing and seeking the position that would fit her desire for her field of endeavor. On one occasion, she had to leave home before daylight to keep an appointment, but she was bent on doing whatever it took. That's how she was raised, and that's how she was made. On one occasion, I went over to accompany her, because I didn't want her out on the street alone at an early hour. I took her to where she would be boarding the transportation to take her to the place of the job interview, and she took it from there, did what she had to do, and returned home safely.

One day her mother called me and said, "Did you know Celeste rented a car and drove to someplace in New Jersey?" I said "No, I did not, but what's the problem?" She said "I'm afraid for her." I said, "Why are you afraid? If she thinks she can handle it, she can handle it." She did handle it, just as she did all of the other challenges she faced in her life. She was a take-charge child, and her independent attitude didn't wait for anyone else to solve a problem she could solve herself. When something had to get done and she had some responsibility for getting it done, she stepped up to the plate to make it happen. She didn't need anyone to hold her hand. She continued to go about as circumstances dictated. However difficult the circumstance may have been, she just kept on going. When the going got tough, she got going.

When an individual accomplishes the unexpected and does it without the need to call on anyone to help her do it, this is the true essence of going when the going gets tough and surviving as an independent. Celeste has demonstrated this again and again in how she pushed through and pushed aside challenging circumstances to accomplish what was before her that needed to be done. The things enumerated in this book aren't about survival against all odds, nor are they about the triumphs of a child who had little to work with. They are simply about a child who was properly parented and in so being, showed herself to use what her parents taught and came forth with the values that herald a successful transition from childhood to adulthood.

The efforts of these parents and this child are intended to point out what can be accomplished in a child, if both the parents do their part properly to be good parents. There are lessons here, and they simply speak to a parent-child relationship forged in the endeavor to successfully raise a child. The way the child responded to how she was parented demonstrates how well the lessons may have been taught and how well the child learned them. The examples given support the instructions and the learning.

There were many instances when Celeste demonstrated the need to get a job done and the independence to perform the task, and the following is no exception. This particular year, Christmas came during the time when Celeste was transitioning between the job she was performing for economic stability and the job she was educated to do. She was working a temporary position which was somewhat out of the field she was trained in. However, being as flexible as she showed herself to be throughout her life, she had settled into the position and proceeded to make the most of it. She wasn't earning the salary that she would be earning later in life, but she didn't let it prevent her from accomplishing what she deemed proper to do—in spite of the odds.

She was always thoughtful about getting things she thought her parents wanted or needed. Her mother wanted another stereo system, and she thought her father needed a microwave oven. I didn't have a microwave oven and was not very excited about getting one, because the idea of cooking my lunch or dinner that way turned me off a bit. I always deemed it a "lazy housekeeper's" gadget. However, my daughter always felt she had to push me into the next century. She had not quite realized, at her age, that I had a mind of my own, and if I had not bought a microwave, it was probably because I didn't want to.

I had all types of other appliances and gadgets, but the idea of microwave cooking had not, as yet, become one of my desires. Microwave ovens had not been around long enough for me to feel comfortable about their use. I was reluctant to acquire one, until they had been on the market longer, and the safety of their use had been fully established. I didn't know until Christmas arrived that she was getting me one for my Christmas present.

When Christmas Day arrived, I went over to her mother's home, where we traditionally got together with our daughter to celebrate the occasion. I don't think the three of us missed spending one Christmas together in all of the years, from the time our daughter was born, until she got married. That was all a part of that "being there" requirement. Wherever we were and whatever we were doing, we always put it on hold until after we (Celeste, her mother and I) had assembled for the Christmas morning get-together. There were certainly other places either of us parents could have been, but the place to be was with our child.

I was sitting there this Christmas morning looking around and spotted three or four large packages wrapped and underneath the tree. I couldn't imagine what could have been in them. After Celeste gave them out and they were opened, mine contained a microwave oven, and her mother's contained a stereo system, with two stand-alone speakers. I was perplexed, because I didn't even understand how she got home with such large, heavy packages. I asked her how she had gotten them home, and she said she had taken a cab. She bought them from the store, someone got them out to the curb, hailed a taxi and brought them home. Then she got them into the house and wrapped them before her mother arrived, thereby keeping the contents a secret until Christmas. That was really "doing it." That was an example of functioning independently. This child was an independent survivor when she had to be—even as a young adult. In later years, she would come to have a group of loyal friends who would not hesitate to be there when she needed them.

It is desirable and admirable to see your child take charge of her or his life and make those independent moves required to take her or him through the matters at hand that need attending to. It is also desirable that you not allow the child to make decisions bigger than her ability to make before it's time. More often than not, good and right decisions are better made if they are made with some solid experience backing them up. Also, we should not overestimate our child's ability to make a right decision, even though she may often attempt to convince her parent that she can handle the situation. Often there can be subtleties lurking in the background that are only known to a parent who has experience yet to be acquired by a child.

The decision Celeste made to turn down the management-type position in the job outside of her field was a good decision and one which bore no long-term negative ramifications. It was the kind of decision a seasoned parent would likely have made. However, the decision she made, turning down the position in her field, which grew out of her summer's intern program, was one that a more mature mind might not have made. There were more negatives following this decision than were positives. The only positive surrounding this decision was the fact that she didn't like this type of packaging engineering. She could have garnered something good out of it, if she had made an opposing decision. She would have had the uninterrupted cash flow from a very well-paying position in her field, and she would have had the experience in her field to add to her resume.

This brings to mind another incident that came about sometime during her second or third year in college, and whenever I think about it, I get a bit annoyed. On the occasion of this incident, she made a decision that may have been larger than her ability to make, because the ramifications emerging out of the possibilities of what could have happened were probably not understood by her. It wasn't that it was such a terrible decision, and, thank God, nothing disastrous resulted from the decision. But I got annoyed, because I felt she took more liberty than she should have taken.

Both I and her mother had been calling her for two or three days. We called frequently to check to see if all was well, and she would call us from time to time to let us know she was okay. Sometimes I would call her mother to ask if she had heard from the child, and sometime her mother would call me and ask the same. On this particular weekend, both of us had been calling, and neither of us had been able to reach Celeste. On my last call, I left a message with her roommate, to tell her to give me a call when she came in. We were both worried, because she had never been unreachable like that in the past—nor in her entire life. She had always been conscientious enough to made the effort to check in and let us know of her whereabouts. This time we had no idea where she was.

For all we knew, Celeste could have been injured or dead, or anything else. Parents can experience a lot of anxiety over not knowing the whereabouts of their child, especially in the type of world we live in today. I can vividly recall how my mother couldn't fall asleep until she knew all the children still living in the household were safely inside.

Sometime around 10:30 to 11:00 P.M. on Sunday night the phone rang, and Celeste was on the other end with the usual, "Hi, Dad." But I was so annoyed that I couldn't even greet her. My immediate quip was, "Where were you?" She said, "I went to Niagara Falls." I said, "Niagara Falls? Who told you to go there?" She said, "Nobody, I thought I was grown up enough to make that decision." This left me speechless, because it was so unlike her and so "off the wall." I felt like immediately hanging up the phone and going to Rochester for a very urgent and personal meeting with her. I said, "You're not grown enough to make any decision that leaves your mother and me sitting here wondering if you're alive or dead."

Children just don't get it sometimes. That's why it shouldn't be put upon them to make adult decisions until they have the experience to do so. I said, "You could have been in Niagara Falls dead, and when the authorities called us, we would have disputed them up and down that the body being investigated was not that of our daughter ... because our daughter was not in Niagara Falls." She listened to me in silence, and I still wonder today if she understood where I was coming from.

8. Leaving Childhood and Entering Adulthood

Celeste was preparing to embark on a new journey. She was on the verge of doing work in the area of her training. She was starting a job as a packaging engineer with a pharmaceutical company in the business of making medical supplies related to procedures that transported various medications throughout the body. The work location was some distance from her home and required her leaving home at a very early hour. For her, that was not at all unusual, because she had been required to do this on other occasions. This was only "par for the course." She traveled the distance and went about the effort of establishing herself on a job in her field. She was contented. After she settled into the job, she decided to get a little car to help her get back and forth from the job in a more convenient and timely manner.

A TABLESPOON OF LOVE, A TABLESPOON OF DISCIPLINE

After the job fell into place, she felt that it was time for her to get her own space, to move out of her mother's home. She was also courting and anxious to accomplish this move. Her sense of independence, which was an outgrowth of successful parenting, dictated that she detach herself from her mother's "apron strings" and live independently in her own space. She was bent on doing this and began diligently to seek out an apartment. She searched in all of the locations where she thought she desired to live, but she wasn't successful at renting the desired space at an affordable or desired price.

In the course of her searching, she came upon the potential to sublet an apartment she had heard about through a mutual friend. She waited for that potential to materialize, but it did not. As a matter of fact, the possibility finally fell through. At this juncture, she was disappointed, frustrated and fed up, feeling that none of her efforts were proving to be very successful. She came over to where I lived, virtually in tears, lamenting that nothing ever seemed to work out for her.

I'm sure that, at various time in all of our lives, we have felt this same way. However, I couldn't cry with Celeste. That would not have shown a sense of strength, and strength was what she needed at that moment. It was needed on my part to give her a sense of direction and resolve to pick up the pieces and go forward. So I did what seemed most natural for me to do in that circumstance and what I had always done in similar times of challenge in her life; that was to tell her she could not give up on the goal she was seeking. I admitted the going may have been tough, but I also brought her back to the reality of life, and that reality asks the question, "Who said life was going to be easy?" Reality also states that, for those who will win, they must be motivated by the statement that says, "When the going gets tough, the tough get going."

So I said to her, "What's your problem? We have given you everything you need to survive in life. We clothed you, fed you, gave you a private school education and put you through college. We were always there for you. We loved you, nurtured you, encouraged you, supported you and gave you a sense of self-worth and belief in yourself. You can just dry your tears, get your act together and go about solving the problem at hand.

"Why don't you buy an apartment," I suggested. She said, "I don't have enough money." "Well, then, save some more," I said. "I'll tell you what I'll do: I'll put up half, and you put up half, and we'll buy an apartment together." She liked the idea, and we went about looking for an apartment to purchase, and she went about saving her money.

Over the coming weeks, we looked at several places and finally found one a lawyer gave us positive feedback about. It was a newly renovated apartment on the fifteenth floor of a building that had recently gone co-op and was located in one of the more desirable parts of town close to quality shopping, dining and movies. The lawyer said it was stable and had a positive cash flow. The building had twenty-four-hour doorman services with substantial security, and for Celeste, this was a definite plus, because the apartment she was moving from, where she had lived with her mother, had those features and more. We concluded that this would be the one to purchase. Only some thirty to sixty days had gone by since Celeste had seemed to be at a crossroad in her efforts to find an apartment, and now she was preparing to go into contract on the purchase of a very nice apartment.

I prepared her mentally to go into contract for the apartment. We had the money for the contractual obligation, but I wanted her to experience the contractual proceedings on her own—of course, with a lawyer looking on, but without my being there. This would be another part of the independence and survival training. She went to contract, performed all of the necessary signing (along with the lawyer's direction), and put another of life's learning experiences among her accomplishments. I'm sure she felt a deep sense of development, having done this for the first time, and having done it on her own.

After the signing of the contract, we both began preparing for the closing scenario. She obtained the mortgage commitment and was in touch with the parties involved on an ongoing basis. She apprised me of the progress from time to time and of the other requirements for the closing. I had a sum of money for her from part of the graduation present I had given her and had invested for her. It had earned some return. This was to be used as a part of her fifty percent required investment in the apartment, and in addition, I was to put up the other half of the total cost to acquire the apartment.

Time passed, as would be expected, and the closing date finally arrived. We went to closing. Celeste executed our side of the closing, with me looking over her shoulders and our lawyer assisting us. Everything was finalized. Soon after closing, she moved into the apartment. Now she was going about her life, functioning independently in all the various aspects of existence.

A TABLESPOON OF LOVE, A TABLESPOON OF DISCIPLINE

She had completed college, had a full-time job in her field and her own living space. In addition, she was taking care of all of her own financial needs. That's independence. She was ambitious and caring at the same time and came to my office once or twice a week to assist me with my work, from which she earned some extra money. This continued for two to three years.

During this time period, she got an offer to take a new position with another pharmaceutical company. She would be a packaging engineer for their larger subsidiary. This subsidiary was owned by an American company, which wanted to spin off some of the entities that weren't directly involved in their line of business. Some companies had come to realize that many of the entities purchased during the time of "takeover fever" didn't contribute positively to their income stream. Others were so diverse in what they did that it became difficult to manage them and make them profitable.

She accepted the offer, and her job location changed. By this time, she was also seriously involved in a relationship that kept her on the go most of the time, when she wasn't fulfilling the needs of her job. The times she worked with me grew to be less and less frequent. Eventually, her time schedule could only accommodate her job and her social existence. That was okay with me, because she had her independence and was happily involved in various activities with her friends. This direction continued until the time came when her company was to be sold by its present owner to a large pharmaceutical company that came to be its present-day parent. The subsidiary eventually moved to Princeton, New Jersey, and, for a period of time, she was commuting from her home in New York City to the office location in New Jersey.

One evening shortly after this I was sitting home doing nothing in particular, as was often the case. I wasn't thinking about anything in particular either. My mind wasn't even on the children—Celeste and her constant companion, David. They were always on the move, so it was virtually impossible to imagine where they may have been headed at any particular time. However, while I was sitting there, the door buzzer sounded, and it was David downstairs. Usually, when he popped up alone, he was expecting Celeste to be there, or he thought she was coming there. This time, she wasn't there, and I wasn't expecting her.

David came up, sat down, and said he would like to talk to me. I said, "Okay, go ahead." His statement was, "I would like to marry Celeste and want to know what you think." I wasn't really prepared for that conversation and had not prepared an answer in advance. My response was probably what any typical father would have said in such a circumstance. I inquired about the feelings they have for each other, gave some input as to what I was about and what I expected him to be about. After all, I would be relinquishing my only daughter to the care and protection of someone else. It is only natural that I would want to give some input into how I expected him to behave toward her.

We had raised our daughter to be independent, but I was also a very peculiar dad when it came to her well-being. I wouldn't sit idly by and watch her being mistreated by any man. I had no reason to think that David was the type of young man who would mistreat his wife, but I wanted to start off by setting the record straight. I wanted there to be no misunderstanding along those lines. If a man ever wanted an invitation to clash with me, he could get one, when it came to the women who were a part of my life, and especially my child. I become an interfering father, when it comes to male abusive behavior. I think it's bad and consider it among the social ills that should be eliminated from modern-day society altogether. It should have no place in any civilized society.

Once we had the conversation, I left it to David to determine if we had come to a meeting of the minds, and he could make his decision accordingly. In a few brief moments after the conversation, he left. A few weeks subsequent to the time we had that conversation Celeste showed up with a sparkling engagement ring and informed me that they would be getting married on September 30, 1995. From that point forward, they went about independently making their wedding plans.

They were two of a kind, because David had a streak of independence as strong as that of Celeste's. They made their own decisions about who, how many, how much and where. She would give her mother and me input concerning their progress, but they were not very open to directions or suggestions from bystanders. They had their own independent agenda and ran their own show. That was perfectly fine with me, because my hands were full from running my own life. However, I believed that if we had some needed advice and offered it, they would have taken it under consideration. I had no such advice to offer. They were quite capable of making their own independent decisions. After all, they were paying the bulk of the expenses to pull off the type of wedding they desired to have.

A TABLESPOON OF LOVE, A TABLESPOON OF DISCIPLINE

I had always been of the opinion that I did not believe in paying for just any type or size wedding the children desired. Sometimes it doesn't make a lot of sense to do so. One reason is that often parents cannot afford to do it. Another reason is the fact that parents don't really know how grounded children are to each other. Parents could go to great expense, only to see the marriage fall apart after a very short time. Finally, if the wedding couple feel they want to do something outside of the norm, they would feel better knowing they did it at their own expense, not leaving the parents feeling any financial burden. I believed that the couple getting married should have any type and size wedding their heart desired—and that their pocketbook could afford.

I, along with Celeste's mother, agreed to contribute a sizable sum of money toward the occasion. The amount we contributed could have paid for a modest wedding in a modest setting. I have attended more than a few weddings that were pulled off at a cost even less than what we contributed. However, David and Celeste chose to have a more elaborate event and were in the position to afford it. They planned it, executed it and paid for it and did it virtually independent of their parent's input. In so doing, everything went off without a hitch, as far as we were able to observe.

They had gone into contract on their home prior to the wedding ceremony. The home was to be about a half hour from Celeste's job. David's office was back in New York City, but he was able to execute most of his work requirements from the bank of computers set up in his home. So location wasn't as important for him as it was for Celeste.

A few days after they returned from their honeymoon, they had a closing on the house. Celeste's company took over the responsibility of getting their things moved to the new location, so this phase went off seemingly without a hitch.

They settled into their new environment and began getting it set up as they desired, and when they desired—again, independent of any need of suggestions or opinions from the outside. If you suggested that a picture was hanging crooked, they were likely to ignore you, as if you had not said anything. In this, they, no doubt, were expressing a desire to exercise their independence, make their own decisions and do their own thing and subtly let you know by their responses.

They had crossed the final threshold. They had transcended the last barrier that allows children to pass from childhood to adulthood. They had broken the final ties that bound them to their parents. They had done, and were capable of doing, what well-parented children could and should be doing and, in so doing, had earned the right to be free and independent adults. They were both "only children," they were both products of split marriages, and they both had learned the art of independence, because neither had the benefit of a sibling to lean on.

They had much in common—similar educational backgrounds, having attended some of the same schools and graduated from the same college. They both had parents and guardians who loved them and who were always there for them, but in their circumstances, they both learned what it meant to function independently and to stand independently in their decisions. They also learned how to independently take charge of their lives. With them bound together, they constituted a strong pillar, supporting each other in a bond twice as strong together as they had been separately and surviving as independents. That's what life requires of us all.

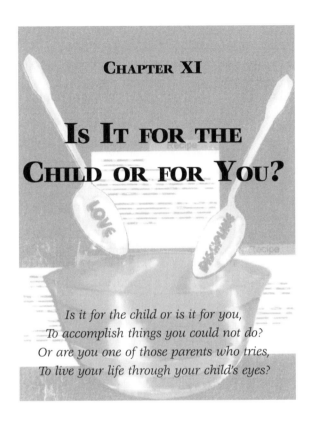

CHAPTER XI

IS IT FOR THE CHILD OR FOR YOU?

Is it for the child or is it for you,
To accomplish things you could not do?
Or are you one of those parents who tries,
To live your life through your child's eyes?

1. YOUR DREAMS AND GOALS

Was it your ambition to grow up, finish high school, go on to college and acquire your degree, then go out in life and earn your living as a professional woman or man? Was it your intention that the children could come later and could fit into your established career? Was it also your intentions to strategize your plans for marriage and, when the time was right, your plan was to have an elaborate church wedding with twelve bride's maids, two flower girls, four limousines, a twelve-piece orchestra, three hundred invited guests, an elaborate cocktail hour and a main course meal that could rival a full-course meal at any posh restaurant establishment?

The man you will be marrying will, of course, give you a three-carat, pear-shaped, blue-white engagement ring, because he will be able to afford it. After all, you will meet him in college, and you're only going to settle for a man who can afford to give you the best. You're going to have your MS in nursing, with further course study in business, to qualify you to be a nursing director and instructor. After you get that nailed down, you want to start your family. You want a boy and a girl, and they will both attend private school. You will have your career in hand and will be living your dream. You have concluded that whatever your children want to be when they grow up will be yours and your children's choice to become.

But you didn't accomplish any of these things. Instead, you met a handsome, smooth-talking guy, who told you all about his dreams. You got caught up in his dreams and ambitions and forgot about your own. He convinced you to marry him, and you consented, because all you could see was being married to this man, who seemed to have all of the right ingredients for putting together a successful life for himself and a family. He didn't have enough money for the big wedding you dreamed of, nor did your parents, so you ended up not even having a wedding. You just got married. The three-carat diamond turned out to be a plain gold band, but it didn't even matter to you, because you felt you had to capture this dream before it got away.

College was still possible for you, but you got sidetracked in that ambition also. Much to your surprise, you were pregnant with your first child. Maybe you could go to college in between raising the child. However, that was not to be, because the pregnancy was repeated over and over, almost every eighteen months, until you had six children. One child was hardly out of the crib before another was poised to occupy it. Instead of going to college in between raising the children, you had to go to work, because there was hardly enough money from your husband's work to support the family and make ends meet. Your husband, the man who had turned your head with stories of becoming an architectural engineer, never even finished college. He attended one year and had to drop out and get a regular job to support himself and his wife, who was expecting their first child just ten months after he married her.

The closest he got to becoming an architectural engineer was a job in a construction firm. He worked his way up to foreman, was a member of the union and made a decent salary, but every winter he was laid off for two to three months. So the family couldn't really get ahead. Every time you created a little nest egg, the circumstance of his layoff would eat away at it.

The home was middle-class and took all of the money coming in from both salaries to meet the mortgage and other bills, to keep food on the table and clothes on the backs of the children, a wife and a husband. In addition to these things, there were the other ordinary and necessary expenses of raising children and maintaining a family. Life wasn't bad, but it was one continuous struggle to remain afloat. There were no longer dreams of getting ahead. The only thing you could look forward to would be a quiet retirement that would hopefully afford a modest pension and a modest retirement home in the country, after the children were grown and on their own.

Consequently, you felt that maybe the children would be able to accomplish what you were unable to accomplish. You had four sons and two daughters and put aside some funds for the daughters' weddings, and you both refused to touch it under any circumstances. The thinking was to maybe take a second mortgage on the house to pay the balance needed for the daughters' weddings.

Or you are the man who wanted to become a doctor and had all of the skills and potential to make it happen, but you got distracted by a social life that got out of control. You were excited about the girls around you and only discovered later that your interest in girls was controlling you, after your grades slipped to a level that prevented you from being accepted into medical school. Subsequently, you did enroll in college, but ended up majoring in computer programming, with a minor in sales. You continued on the dating circuit, but based on your academic ability, you were able to handle your grades and your social life, because your major concentration wasn't as demanding as pre-med school would have been.

You got your degree and started out in life as a computer salesman, while working part time as a computer programmer. You decided to marry your childhood sweetheart, and by now, you have two sons. Your wife believes a woman should not work but should stay home and take care of the family. After all, her mother never worked. Her father made a good living for her mother, for her and for her other sister. You agree, because your childhood sweetheart is bright and attractive. Being somewhat insecure as you are, you don't want her out there in the workplace, while you spend your days worrying about who is making a pass at her, and if he has more going for him than you have going for you.

You know she loves you, but she is so attractive it keeps you worried all of the time. So you work hard, while she stays home to mind your two sons. You think to yourself, "Maybe one or both of my sons will be more focused than I was and not be distracted by girls. Maybe one or both will go on to become the doctor I never became, simply because I didn't have the discipline to go all the way. I'll make my son William a doctor. I didn't become the doctor I had dreamed of becoming, but I'll make a doctor out of my son."

These are two likely scenarios that could possibly fit the lives of many mothers or fathers throughout the country and the world. I'm sure you could fit any individual into a mold of this fashion. The ambition could be different, and the goals could be different. However, the idea of not becoming what he or she aspired to become and of endeavoring to make the child do what he or she could not do and be what he or she could not be is very real in many families. It is a thing that most mothers and fathers would probably not admit. It could also be an unconscious endeavor, with the parent not realizing he or she is trying to accomplish something through the child that he could not accomplish through his own efforts. He or she is trying to live his life through his child.

Children are living their parents' dreams everyday. Some are living them unknowingly, and some are living them subconsciously. Others know they are doing that very thing the father or mother wanted to accomplish but could not. The above examples are all about shattered dreams, unfulfilled goals and unfinished projects. When children live our dreams, reach the goals we couldn't reach, or finish the projects we couldn't finish, it should not be by our choice, but by theirs. Children may have their own dreams they want to make into realities, they may have their own goals they want to reach and their own projects they have to complete.

Sometimes their dreams are the dreams we had, sometimes their goals are the goals we wanted to reach, and sometimes their projects are the projects we wanted to finish. If that is so, it is good. If that is not the case, we, as parents, should move on and maybe find other dreams to chase, other goals to set and other projects to take on that we may be able to complete. We should not try to live our life through our child's eyes. Living our life through our child's eyes often boils down to a parent endeavoring to shape the life of the child in a fashion he or she desired his life to be, but never made it happen.

Many of the things a parent will come to do for his or her child will not really be for the child at all, but for himself. Many of the things he may push the child to do or be may be related to his own failures as a parent. Not all parents try to live their life through their child, but some do, and it is unfair to the child, who may be pushed to do something he or she may not really desire to do. There is nothing about this that is out of the ordinary, except that it may sometimes cause a parent to go beyond his means, in an effort to do something for his child he cannot quite afford and something the child may not want.

In another vein, the parent is often found pushing the child beyond the limits of the child's ability, by trying to make the child succeed at something he or she doesn't want to do and, in some instances, cannot do—even if the desire is there. These two scenarios embrace a broad spectrum of parental motives, as they relate to children. Everything that parents do for children and everything parents want children to do can be addressed by the question, "Is it for the child or for you?" There are many different reasons why parents do what they do for their child or children. Some are strictly out of love and a sincere desire to be "on target" in right parenting. Other things done have a different relationship to what a parent desires, as opposed to what a child needs or wants.

On the other hand, there are just as many reasons why a parent may want a child to pursue a particular course of endeavor. One reason can be purely objective, while the other can and may have a distinct connection to some failed attempt on the parents' part. As a parent, you should be aware of your child's needs. When you provide things that go beyond the child's needs, it would be better if it satisfies the child's desire, rather than yours. When you try to live your failures or your dreams through your child, it should only be a focus, if the child has both the desire and the ability to live and successfully execute your dream or your goal.

A parent was once a child, just as the child is, who is now being raised and nurtured. There may have been things the parent wanted in life, as a child, that his parents or guardians neither desired to give him, nor could afford to give him. That aspect of his life may have made him unhappy, as well as uncomfortable. He carried this feeling into his adulthood and made a silent promise that he would make things different for his child. After the child came into the world, the parent began to envision the joy the child may get from having the things he couldn't have, because this parent is relating the child's wants and feelings to the ones he harbored as a child. So, this parent buys everything for the child that he thinks the child wants, regardless of whether the child actually needs it or wants it, or whether or not he can afford to get it for the child.

Some parents, as children, had dreams that included graduating from a prestigious college, going to work on an important job, marrying the high school beauty, moving to a stately home in suburbia and traveling about the world, seeing things and meeting people. As a young adult, the parent may have started in a college that didn't satisfy his dreams, or he may have enrolled in a trade school that, when completed, would have put him on a job track that would take him to a desired level of success. That may have given him the important job, the home in suburbia and the travels, but I'm not sure it would have given him what the high school beauty may have been seeking in a man. However, this didn't happen, so dreams were unfulfilled, and goals were not reached.

Looking at children today in your own family, in the neighborhood, on TV shows and those we read about in various newspapers and books, we must sometimes wonder if they're going about their own business or the business of their parents. Sometimes a child may meet and talk to other children who may not have wanted to attend that particular school. It was the school the mother or father wanted him to attend. He didn't even want to major in that particular profession or subject. She didn't want to marry that particular guy; her mother liked him. She didn't want a big wedding; her mother wanted it. Her parents kept sending her money she didn't need or ask for. She could use it, and my, how it comes in handy for something, but she would rather her parents just let her do it herself.

As a parent, are you giving due consideration to the needs and wants of your child, as they relate to what's good for your child, or are you subconsciously striving to make those things happen for the child that didn't happen for you? Are you trying to persuade your child to pursue the profession you couldn't pursue, because of various reasons beyond your control? If you are consciously or subconsciously doing any of these things, you should stop and reckon with your path of pursuit, because if the child doesn't want it or need it, it's not for the child; it's for you. It may not be a bad idea to sit down with the child, prior to your buying something unnecessary, and ask her if she wants it. As a parent, you should also be mindful of the direction in which you may be steering your child. If it is not where the child needs to go or wants to go, then, it is not for the child, but for you.

It can often be harmful for a child and her or his future, when you, as a parent, do things for her she doesn't need or want or attempt to steer her to become something she neither needs to become nor wants to become. In addition to the harm you may cause the child, you may also bring harm to yourself, because sometime you may not be prepared to bear the burden of giving that child what you desire her to have or straining to help her become what you may want her to become.

2. Through the Years

Let us walk your child through her or his formative years, up to the point where she or he has had the wedding ceremony and is moving on to live independently with her or his spouse. The basic things you do, as a parent for your child, during conception, are definitely for the child, as well as for the mother of the child, because a healthy mother aids in a healthy birth delivery and healthy newborn child. Conceivably, there is nothing that can be done, as parents, to insure a healthy baby that could be considered excessive or unnecessary. The failure to do anything or the failure not to do anything that would enhance the health of the expected child and the expectant mother can be considered neglect, if it is within the power of the mother to do it or to refrain from doing it.

Seeking out the best doctor you can afford or the best doctor you cannot afford serves only a good purpose. There is no such thing as too much good information. It usually stands to reason that the better qualified a doctor is, the better the information tends to be. Your responsibility, as a parent, is to follow the good advice of your doctor on this matter. If the child is born healthy, you didn't just make it happen for the child, you made it happen for you, as well as the child's father. What's more, a parent has the obligation and responsibility to do everything, within the scope of her or his knowledge and ability, to make certain the child enters the world healthy.

The newborn infant preparation that the parent or parents undertake depends on how elaborate they want to get. The basic things prescribed for newborn care are a must. Newborn formula and other foods are "good and better." There are certain basics the FDA requires of those producing infant foods. Thank God we have some regulations in place in this area, in this country. Whatever is put on the market for newborn feeding must meet the standards of being good enough for your child, good enough to insure your child's positive development (barring any allergies), as opposed to things that would be unhealthy for your child. Whether you buy Heinz baby food or Gerber is of no great consequence, or whether you buy Enfamil or another brand of baby formula is of no great consequence. The difference in cost and how the ingredients integrate into your child's digestive system should be the determining factor concerning which one you buy. No definitive studies have been conclusive as to Heinz being healthier than Gerber or *vice versa*.

The other supplies you use in the care of your baby can be either a well known and established brand, such as Johnson & Johnson, or maybe an off-brand with a store or generic name. Often the store brand is produced by the same high quality company; it just lacks the advertising costs paid to keep the brand names out front. The off-brand or generic brand will probably not harm your baby, except for the possibility of your baby's skin being sensitive to one or the other of these products.

We all know that better quality products are usually prepared with better quality ingredients. My mother preferred the old standard: Johnson & Johnson baby oil, baby powder, swabs, cotton and anything else needed, if Johnson & Johnson produced it. My wife and I also preferred the same. The products cost a bit more, and may have been for us, rather than for the child. However, the extra cost didn't compromise our life in a negative way, nor serve to compromise the child or her future in a negative way.

The baby carriage or stroller you may buy for your child, if you choose to buy one, can be okay, better or best. The idea in buying any stroller or carriage at all is to avoid having to carry the infant in your arms continuously. An "okay" stroller is a necessary convenience for a mother. Anything better may provide a more comfortable resting position or smoother ride for the baby, and that has some validity. The parents who buy the best are buying it for themselves, not for the child.

For some parents it's a show of status the parents have or wish to have. The child neither needed it, nor asked for it. Maybe your mother used a hand-me-down stroller or carriage for you, maybe she used none at all, or maybe you don't even remember. My mother probably used a carriage or stroller which had been used prior for other brothers and sisters, because I had lots of siblings. I don't remember. She may not have used one at all. Maybe she couldn't afford one, and if that was the case, it didn't, in the least, detract from my well-being, because I grew up just as well and physically intact.

We passed Celeste's carriage on to someone else, my niece, I think. It was a beauty, with white-walled tires and chrome fenders. The interior was adorned with all of the frills and ruffles and accompanying satin lining. For us, it was a "head thing." It was probably one of the best available at the time, and it was a show of the status we wished to have. The child didn't need it, and I am sure it didn't impact her life one way or another. For it was not for her, but for us.

The clothes you buy for your new baby (those darling little ruffles and frills if she's a girl and velvet collars and all that stuff if he's a boy) can overwhelm the need of the child, as well as your budget. Most of the non-basic things you buy, at this stage, are for you, definitely not for the child. Can it be harmful? Possibly. You may be setting the stage for establishing the wrong priorities. Don't get locked into that kind of thinking, because it isn't the most positive way to go.

Some parents don't handle this direction very well, and most tend to go overboard, in an effort to provide for their darling little child. Don't be that type of parent. Parents who travel down this road are often traveling a road that never ends, because the child often takes the torch and endeavors to continue where the parents left off. Some may be able to do it successfully, and just as many others may not. That's where the trouble begins. After a while, what you, as a parent, may consider basic becomes toys. These types of children's "toys" are for parents. They aren't necessary and are not for the child, and you, as a parent, are not able to play with them.

The type of school your child attends can either be for you or for the child. A child's "gift" or lack of a "gift" sometimes requires a specialized learning environment or attendance in a specialized school that has a pro-gram geared to meet the needs of the child. It is sometimes geared to bring out the best of a child's gifted abilities or enhance a child's lack of abilities. When this education has to be paid for, it becomes a parental responsibility. It also becomes a matter of whether a parent or parents can afford it and whether the child's abilities and potentials are enhanced by him or her having attended a private, specialized school.

Any education that develops and positively enhances a child's basic abilities, unique skills or adverse disabilities is an absolute must, and the expense of providing the same must be borne—if at all possible. My reason for sending Celeste to a private learning institution encompassed some of the above, as well as a desire to keep her out of the public education arena that had already gone bad—discipline wise. I felt I lacked the ability to cope with the child behavior that took other children's lunch money and beat them up. So, rather than my getting into a hassle for putting someone's out-of-control child straight, I opted for a more sane learning environment for our child.

Providing funds for this type of needed education is worthy of parents rearranging their priorities and making those priorities of lesser importance, subordinate to the necessity of that type of education for their child. Doing this is neither for the child, nor for you. It can be beneficial to the child, as well as to the parent. It can be construed as one of those basic and necessary obligations of preparing your child for survival and success in life. It will support and enhance her or his chance to make a successful transition from childhood to adulthood.

However, if you are paying the cost of a private or specialized school for your child, and the child is demonstrating progress and ability only equivalent to what would be expected of a free education, keeping your child in that type of educational setting is strictly for you, and could possibly be squandering valuable resources. If having a child in that type of setting is something for "your head" or something for you to beat your chest about, you're probably missing the point. In addition, maybe you should speak to the child. Quite often children prefer being in a public or free school setting. They sometime want the opportunity to know and interact with children of varied cultures and with those of various ethnic and economic backgrounds. There is something to be learned from all.

Parents sometime have other reasons for putting a child in a private school setting, and they may not be for the parent's head or for the need or enhancement of the child's abilities—although the reasons may serve both purposes. A parent may desire to put the child in a religious school, because the discipline there may be more rigid (which is positive), and the discipline technique in the religious school may be more in line with the child's upbringing. There are positive benefits in doing this, if a parent is willing to pay the cost.

We sent our child to private school for reasons different than many of these, although we may have gained some of the benefits that represent offshoots of that type of education. My reason for wanting her in private school was strictly from the viewpoint of keeping my sanity and staying out of trouble. Our daughter was growing up during the turbulent late 1960s and 70s, when everything seemed out of control—especially children. It was the beginning of the period when young children were packing guns in school, as a rule, rather than an exception. Other children were being picked on and beat up at random. Often a child's money was taken, and he or she was stripped of his or her leather jacket and hijacked for his or her jewelry. He or she was left helpless at the hands of public school bullies. And the school system and the law were doing little more than making excuses. I was not geared to deal with that type of behavior, especially if my daughter was the victim. I loathed the thought of any kid beating up on my child, for no reason she was responsible for.

During that period in my life, my hands and body were likely to go into gear before my brain got engaged. Based on that, I would have been likely to get into a confrontation with one of those school bullies, because our daughter wasn't raised to be a "toughie" and would probably have been a likely subject for tough kids seeking an easy target. We enjoyed the benefits of the private school education afforded our child, and I would say (looking back in retrospect) that it was well worth the effort and the sacrifice. But it was for our direct benefit, not for the child's.

It was inspirational to me that Celeste had enjoyed her school career, and we were happy about it. She and I both came through unscathed, and neither of us had to undergo a physical confrontation, as far as I know. If she did, she never told me about it. Of course, children sometimes keep things from the parents to avoid conflict. Sometimes they don't want the confrontational kid to think they can't handle themselves.

3. Do You Want to Do It for Your Parents?

Parents, almost from the time a child begins to walk and talk, decide in their own mind what they want the child to be. Sometimes the vision or desire is leftover from the parent or parents' life as failed ambitions. Quite often the mother or father had aspired to a certain profession and never got there for reasons of lack of opportunity, lack of finance or lack of ability. Whatever the reasons, the failure to reach a desired goal became a dream that didn't come true. Parents often carried that thought or failed aspiration into adulthood. Sometimes it may have become an obsession transferred to the child or children.

The ritual may start by telling the child what she or he is going to be or do, even prior to the time the child is old enough to have any say in the matter. Sometimes the parent buys toys, books or other props for the child that may have some relationship to what the parent wants the child to be or do. For example, the father may have been a frustrated football, baseball or basketball player, who never made the team. So he thinks, in his head, that his son can take up the mantle and fulfill his unfulfilled dreams. When you see a father purchasing expensive sports equipment for his son, religiously taking him to every little league practice and pushing him with all of his might, then it's probably not for the son. It is probably for the father.

The child may have only gotten caught up in the fray, not even realizing why he was working so hard at that endeavor or even why he likes the sport or wants to do it. However, if he likes it and wants to do it, it doesn't matter that it is his father's dream rather than his own. Even a parent's dream is okay for a child to pursue—if the child likes what she or he is pursuing, is capable of pursuing it and has the desire to make that dream her or his own. When a parent is grooming or shaping a child from a young age, to prepare the child to possibly accomplish something he or she couldn't, he should allow time and circumstance to dictate whether or not the child should be pushed in a given direction.

When your child reaches the point of choosing an option for her or his professional career, your input should only extend to assisting the child in making a sensible and realistic appraisal of her goals and her capabilities of achieving them. Preparations should have been made in the process of coming through school, even from the earliest beginning in education. In that process, there were some basics to be learned that would be required, whatever the intended profession would be. The basics are required merely to get through life successfully. Those include the ability to read, to express oneself in the written word and to have solid basic math skills, which would include proficiency in adding, subtracting, multiplying and dividing numbers. In addition, math skills should include a basic level of proficiency in handling fractions, decimals, percentages and verbal problems. Without those basic skills, a child can't expect to rise very high in any profession, even on the most basic level.

After a child has mastered these skills and gone beyond them to the higher forms of math, such as algebra, geometry and trigonometry, she or he is prepared to take on the other sciences—biology, chemistry, physics, etc. With this type of academic preparation and aptitude, a child can have choices, when she or he eventually reaches the point of choosing a profession. It is necessary and beneficial for a parent or parents to help and encourage the child to excel in as many of these areas of reading, writing and arithmetic as possible. That's basic, depending on the child's aptitude and ability.

When a child has shown herself to be proficient in these advanced disciplines, there can be broad choices as to what a child may want to become and is capable of becoming. A parent should not choose a profession for a child, simply because he or she has another motive for wanting the child to be or become a particular professional. Advice should be given, and what the child aspires to should be worked out between parent and child, giving overwhelming consideration to what the child wants and is capable of achieving.

Most parents would like for the child to become a doctor, lawyer, engineer or some other glorious professional. Above all of that, the main concern of the parent should be the child's happiness and comfort in the chosen discipline. Sometimes, heavy-handedly persuading your child to go into a profession not desired by her or him may be setting the stage for unhappiness—for you, the parent, as well as for the child. Children have been known to be coerced into undertaking professional disciplines to please parents and ending up failing miserably. Some children have even suffered nervous breakdowns and resorted to attempted suicide over failure in things that weren't for them, but for the parent.

Before you attempt to coerce your child into a certain profession, you should stop and ask yourself, "Is it for the child, or for me?" If it is your dream and does not serve the child's desire or well-being, don't try to live it through your child. If your child has the desire to pursue your dream, cheer her or him on, encourage her or him and give all the support you can give. It is both wonderful and inspiring to see our children fulfill the dream we had to abandon, but it should be voluntary and desired by the child.

4. LET THE CHILD DO IT

When it comes to your daughter selecting a suitable husband or your son selecting a suitable wife, the selection should be in the eyes of the daughter or son. Sure, you should give your opinion of what you see in the one selected—even if your opinion is not solicited. There should be no ulterior motive behind your liking or disliking an individual your daughter or son selects for a spouse. Parents should not make a business out of the child's marriage. Yes, it is most desirable for your child to marry someone whose family is well-off or someone with a profession that gives him or her the ability to become well-off. That may be what we desire for a child, but may not be what the child desires for herself. Kings and queens have given up thrones to marry their heart's desire.

When a child selects a mate, it is her or his happiness that is at stake. It is better for your child to be happy with a construction worker, mailroom clerk, postal worker, ditch digger or any one of the various nonprofessional positions, than to be miserable with a doctor, lawyer or Native American Chief. What's more, you don't have to live with the person your child marries; the child does. When you try to push a mate on a child, just because you like that person, for whatever reason, and think him or her the best for your child, remember the saying, "If you like him or her so much, why don't you marry him?"

Sure, children often make mistakes in choosing a mate. We would be well advised to put our thoughts into the choice, to help them avoid getting into something they may not have been fully aware of. Our help should have the child's best interest in mind, not the parent's best interest. Parents have sometimes made gross misjudgments in their efforts at choosing a mate, and they're still making similar mistakes today. However, today's society has less tolerance for remaining in any unhappy situation that they find unfulfilling and negative.

When parents attempt to aid their child in choosing a mate, they may be trying to correct their own mistakes, through the child, by suggesting the child marry a particular type of individual. The idea and effort may be admirable, but others have a say-so in the matter too. Maybe you, as a child, wanted to marry the neighborhood beauty queen and ended up with the ugly duckling, because that was all your self esteem could do for you. Don't try to persuade your son to marry the girl who has the crush on him, just because she is beautiful and lives up to the desire you had and never fulfilled. That may or may not be what the son wants to do, and if he doesn't do it, he may not be any the worse off. That may not necessarily be his dream.

The same goes for a mother's daughter. Don't try to push her into marrying a man just because he is handsome. Sometimes handsome men only have looks going for them, and sometimes they have that and more, but remember, God didn't give anyone everything. That "hunk" you see for your daughter may be your own "head thing." Your daughter may just desire to have a hundred-twenty-pound weakling. What's more, the hunk may be missing some other things possessed by the less bulky weakling. God didn't make any one of us perfect, because if He had, we may not have been able to stand ourselves or Him. And remember, what you see isn't always what you get. Beauty may be the desire of some and nice to look upon for all, but it doesn't always go beneath the skin. One shouldn't hang her or his dreams on it. It is only in the eyes of the beholder and fades quickly in some.

I guess you may be able to recall what your husband or wife looked like when you first got married. Right? Well, look now. Give your child a chance to make her or his own choice, and attempt to aid her or him in doing so, but let your aid always be objective. Just hope and pray the choice will bring your child happiness—even if it makes you miserable. Children don't necessarily listen to parents anyway, when it comes to choosing a mate. As parents, we can talk until we're blue in the face, and the child still may not listen. What's more, the child's choice should be the child's dream (or nightmare), not the parent's.

Did you ever witness wedding plans unfolding with parents in charge, running all over the place, inviting whom they wanted to impress, calling the shots, renting the place, ordering the gown and flowers? Those parents wanted the wedding to come off in perfect form, and they orchestrated the entire affair. It wasn't for the child; it was for them. My daughter and her husband-to-be gave the wedding they wanted—the one which was for them. They called the shots and paid the cost. That's the way it should be, if it is for them, rather than for the parents. They said to us in so many ways, "Mother and Dad, step back. It's our wedding." That was fine with me, because it was not our wedding; it was theirs. We gave them a financial gift toward it and moved on. They did things as they wanted them to be done.

Here in this country it is a tradition for the parents of the bride to pay the cost of the child's wedding—to whatever extent they can or cannot afford. However, given the circumstance of today's society, parents are not always in the position to give the type of wedding a child may desire, and often the children getting married are in a much better financial position to give the type of wedding they desire to have, and to pay the costs. It may be foolish for a parent or parents to nurture the desire to sponsor a wedding of whatever size or scope a child may desire—especially if the financial means aren't in place to do so.

A TABLESPOON OF LOVE, A TABLESPOON OF DISCIPLINE

Must the parent or parents make provisions to afford any type of wedding the child may desire? I don't think so. If a child is willing to settle for the type of wedding a parent can afford, be it ever so humble, then let it be done. A child's wedding shouldn't strain parents, break parents or leave parents up to their chin in debt—unless parents want to give the child's wedding for themselves, the one they never had and are willing to pay any cost. The act of giving your daughter in marriage represents the last symbolic gesture of a parent or parents of putting his or her daughter in the hands of another man, to nurture her and see to her health, wealth and well-being. A father is actually handing over his burden to another man to bear, so the act of giving the wedding is, in essence, depicting the style and grace by which a father surrenders his responsibility to another, if he was indeed a responsible father.

Society has changed quite a bit in terms of wedding costs and in terms of who is paying for them. There is nothing wrong with paying the cost of your child's wedding—if you have the means to do it comfortably. However, children of today's society have their own mind about what, how and how much they want for their wedding. Since children today are better off financially than were children yesterday, they're in a much better position to make the wedding of their dream a reality. Therefore, children should be free to have whatever type of wedding they want and can afford.

Parents should give whatever size gift they can afford. The gift may be adequate to pay for the wedding, given the expense and scope of what is desired—and it may not. Do you recall the scenario of the girl who wanted twelve bride's maids, two flower girls, four limousines, a twelve-piece orchestra, an elaborate cocktail hour, the full course meal, etc.? Should the parents pay for all that? I don't think so, because that doesn't nearly border on basic, but is somewhat extraordinary. If the parent or parents want this type of wedding, the child wants it also, and the parents can afford it without any financial burden, then it is for both the parent and the child. If the parent wants it and has to go out on a financial limb to make it happen, then it is likely for the parent, because the difficulty of making it happen goes beyond what a reasonable child would probably ask of the parent or parents to do and maybe beyond what the child would have done for themselves.

Weddings are intended to initiate the beginning of a state of happiness between a couple that is meant to last a lifetime. The greater the scope, the greater should be the bliss, but that is not always what happens. Some marriages begun with great weddings last a very short time, and some marriages begun with simple weddings last a lifetime. When you invest greatly in your child's wedding, you're not always investing in her long-term happiness. Since we all, including parents, recognize that this is so, we should also question in our minds whether the wedding is for the child or for us, the parents. Some parents would do it at any cost because it fulfills the dream they didn't get the chance to fulfill in their own wedding. They couldn't even afford a wedding, so they go overboard in giving the wedding for the child. In this case, it is not for the child. It is for the parents.

It would be a very selfish and uncaring child who would watch a parent or parents exhaust their life's savings, borrow from their retirement or take a loan or mortgage on the home to get money for the child's wedding. Most properly-raised children would be caring enough to not require this of a parent or parents. If the parents insist, it would be for the parents' "head," for their friends, their relatives and their associates. In this case, the child should allow them to do it. Maybe the parents need it. It's their dream, and maybe they don't mind paying the cost to make it happen.

What you do for your child may not be what the child wants. What you may want your child to be may not be what the child wants to become, and who you want your child to marry may not be who she or he wants to share her or his life with. Don't try to make up for what you didn't have by giving your child what she doesn't need or want. Don't try to perfect in your child what you were unable to perfect in yourself. Don't try to live your unful-filled dreams, reach the goal you never reached or finish the project you never finished, if you have to do it through your child—especially if it is not the child's dream, intended goal or likeable project. Be certain that what you do for the child is for the child and not for you.

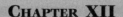

Chapter XII

Be Strong, but also Be Human

Your child thinks you're a Rock of Gibraltar.
She thinks you can't stumble, fall or falter.
She may not realize the things you cannot do.
You're only a person, and you're vulnerable too.
So, don't make her believe that you always can,
Because you're only human; you're not Superman.

1. Your Child Thinks You are a Rock

The Rock of Gibraltar is unmoving and dauntless. It just looms there in its place, unaffected by winds, rain, dust, sand, fog, man, beast or any of the other elements of nature. When an individual or entity is referred to as a Rock of Gibraltar, it implies that the individual is steadfast and unshakable. Much too often children tend to look at parents in that very same light, especially if the parent displays a strong countenance and is not often given to tears or to exposing a weak side.

This isn't a healthy way for parents to present themselves, and it is also not a healthy way for children to view their parents. When a parent is seen in this light, a child tends to think the parent is fine, regardless of what may be going on in the parent's life and regardless of what age the parent is. Maybe it is convenient for a child to dismiss a parent's circumstances as always being "fine," or maybe a child assumes that because a parent never expresses a need (not necessarily a financial need), everything is fine. Some parents may be broke, hungry, depressed, ill or worried or any one of a number of other things the child may not be aware of, and because the parent isn't given to crying or complaining to the child concerning her or his shortcomings, the child doesn't know. More often than not, parents may not want the child to know they have shortcomings, but some parents just don't know how to let a child know they are human and vulnerable. Others know how to do it very well. Children can't understand how to love a parent, if that parent never shows he or she needs love or help.

As parents, we know the strengths and weaknesses of our children, because we have been there for them from the time they had to depend on us to feed them, wash them, teach them, give them what they need, listen to them and support them in those times of need. When the child met the parent for the first time, the parent was already seeing after himself, as well as possessing the ability to see after the child. Therefore, the child hardly got an opportunity to witness the parent's weakness and exposed characteristics. A parent has to virtually be helpless like the child was, as a baby, before the child realizes the parent is vulnerable and also has needs.

There are times in between the periods when a child first gets to know the parent and the time when a parent reaches a helpless state (if it indeed happens), and in that period of time, the parent may have any number or manner of needs. Some parents are able to communicate their needs to the child or children. They're able to teach the child through their manner of communicating. There is help needed, for instance, when certain signs appear. Some of these signs may be silence, a frown, tears, an exhausted look or any number of other expressions or behavior. In the process of teaching the child to come to your rescue, you, as a parent, will exhibit the various necessary signs that will tell the child, "There is something wrong with Mother" or "There is something wrong with Dad."

A sensitive, loving and caring child will come to know a parent's challenge, when she or he sees a sign she can relate to. The child will begin to recognize what certain signs are indicating. The child will be able to say, "Mother is unhappy today" or "Dad has a financial challenge today." Next, the child will begin to wonder what she or he can do to rectify the parent's discomfort in whatever area. This is part of the process of teaching a child to love you, care about you and be concerned about your needs, as a parent. Depending on age and other factors, the child may not be in a position to address the need, but when she or he can, it will be addressed. This lesson of love will often spill over to how your child will relate to others on life's journey, with whom she may have formed a close attachment. That's all a part of teaching a child how to love and care.

A parent who fails to teach these lessons will often endeavor to mask every pain, every strain, every need, every hurt, every disappointment and every shortcoming. The child will go on to relate to that parent in a detached manner, in terms of their various vulnerabilities. It may not mean that the child doesn't care; it simply means that you haven't taught the child to be sensitive to and respond (in a loving, caring manner) to your needs and frailties. If you always display a side to your child that indicates you have no needs or frailties, how can the child know that there is a need for involvement in your condition?

My mother was a virtual expert at teaching her children to love her, and she gave so much love in return. Boy, could she make you love her, by exposing her vulnerable side. If my mother ever shed a tear, you would want to immediately move Heaven and Earth for her, and if someone hurt her, you would want to make Heaven and Earth fall down on the one who caused her hurt. She could exhibit a sad countenance that would make you want to cry. If she said, "My washing machine is broken, and I have to wring all these clothes out by hand" (this was before automatic dryers), some one of the siblings would immediately go and buy her a new washer—if at all possible.

I had another friend whose daughter was the same way. Her daughter was at her every beck and call, not because she demanded it, but because the daughter seemed to have found no greater joy than seeing her mother happy. Her mother frequently said, "I sent her to college on MasterCard and Visa." This let the daughter know that her mother hadn't had much money. The result was that if the mother cried, the daughter cried. If the mother didn't like you, the daughter didn't like you either. That child seemed to have had a special knack for sensing her mother's times of vulnerability, even before her mother told her of her hurts or needs.

We were the same way about our mother. We could sense her needs, and we did something about them. Celeste was also the same and still is to this day. If she sensed her mother's pain, she sought to address it in whatever manner necessary. If she thought I needed something, she got it for me, if it was within her sense of reason and power to do so. These later generations of children who have grown up don't seem to possess that type of sensitivity to the needs of their parents, as they should and as the older generations before them possessed. Maybe some of the parents of the later generations failed to teach them to recognize and sensitize themselves to the parents' weaknesses and needs.

You have to teach your child or children how to love you, and love is mostly about being sensitive, caring and being there. Maybe, if we, as parents, show our children only our strong side, if we only cry silently on our pillow and never reveal our needs except to God and our most trusted friend, our child may assume we never hurt or we never need. The child may take us to be like the Rock of Gibraltar.

2. Do Children Really Care?

There is much evidence to support the fact that some children don't care about their parents' needs. Maybe those children weren't taught to be sensitive to the parent's needs. Or maybe there could be some other underlying factor afoot. When you look around you and see little old ladies trying to navigate wide thoroughfares with grocery bags in hand, hardly able to distinguish the color of the traffic signal, you realize that their child (if there is one) lacks the kind of love that is sensitive to her needs. When you see mothers or fathers living in cramped, hot, dusty quarters in the summer heat or in cold, dusty quarters in the winter's chill, you realize their child isn't sensitive to the parent's needs. When you see a mother or father at the grocery checkout counter with what seems like barely enough food to make a meal, and the bulk of the items consisting of off-brand merchandise, you recognize that an uncaring child is in the picture. When you see mothers or fathers out of doors in inclement weather, wearing inadequate clothing for the conditions, or wearing clothing that has long outlived its serviceability, you realize their child isn't sensitive to the parent's needs.

It is a known and understood fact that some children are unable to speak to the negative plight of a parent, regardless of the parent's state of existence or condition, because those children can scarcely address their own plight. However, there are just as many other children who recline in the lap of luxury, as well-paid professionals, reside in the best of neighborhoods and drive top-of-the-line cars, while the parents go from store to store in order to save money and, after they finish the shopping, lug home bags much too heavy for them to be carrying. The child hasn't even picked up the phone to say, "Mother, I'm going to come and take you shopping for groceries." Sometimes the child is too busy on the golf course, playing bridge or hooting it up at the country club with big-shot friends.

Some parents don't even bother asking their children for anything or to do anything. They have too much pride. They think if children wanted to do these things they would volunteer to do them. However, the children were never taught how to love their parents. Should the parents have to ask? Concerned children would be asking their parents if they needed anything, if they had enough money or if they needed to be taken anywhere. What's more, a child can go to the parents' home and take a look in the cabinets and refrigerator. That should give a good indication of how the parents are getting along. If what the child sees in the cabinets and refrigerator doesn't make her or him happy, he or she should go out, buy some groceries for the parent or parents and stock the cabinets and refrigerator. It would be a very foolish parent who would reject needed help.

A child need not ask if the parent needs food, when it is obvious, from what the child observes, that the parent doesn't have enough. On the matter of clothing, a child should be able to tell by what a parent is wearing if the parent needs clothing. If the parent has clothing still in the wrapper, it may be for fear of wearing them and not having anything else decent to wear, when an occasion calls for something. Some other clothing may have been in the wrapper too long already and may be out of date. If a parent had assurance in mind that the child would be there in her or his time of need, she or he would probably have no qualms about taking the garment out of the wrapper and wearing it.

Parents aren't all stupid. Some were smart enough to raise children with the ability to accomplish smart things. The parents may not have been endowed with technical skills, but they were endowed with directional skills, which may have made all the difference. Some parents can't help their children with matrix algebra or economics, but they can teach them something else that will enable the children to go out and learn these things for themselves.

If a parent sends a child an envelope or parcel requiring $5.24 postage, and puts ten-cent, five-cent or one-cent stamps on it, a child could safely conclude that the parent could use some thirty-nine cent stamps or fifty-cent or twenty-four cent stamps. That child could go out and buy the parent a couple books of stamps and send them to them. I'm sure the parent would be grateful.

Unless a child knows for sure that her parent owns thousands of shares of stocks, owns bonds and has a mid-six-figure bank account, that child should not assume that the parent has adequate financial resources. It may not take that much for a parent to be financially stable, however, it would depict a position of certainty concerning the parent's present financial stability. I wonder where most children would have been, if their parents hadn't always recognized their needs and challenges and did something about them before the child had to ask? Parents studied their children with concern for their well-being. They could tell if a child was getting ill or hungry or sad or needed money or needed shoes or had a dispute with another child or was having challenges with school or other work. Wouldn't it be great if children knew how to be discerning like that when it comes to the parent, and stop conveniently assuming that parents always have things in hand?

Just as we should raise our children to be independent and to thrive in a way in which they will be able to take care of their own children, we should also give thought to teaching them to not only look to the generation ahead (their children) but also to the generation before (their parents). Each generation of children and parents seems to be a little better equipped financially, if it was done right. For those parents who tried to do it right and didn't quite make the grade, children should try to make the ultimate sacrifice and share their own resources with their parent—who didn't quite make the grade and who may need a little assistance from time to time.

I can recall a conversation with an acquaintance of mine, and we were reflecting on days gone by and her efforts in raising her children. She said, "I have spent the better part of my life as a single parent, raising my children and getting them to a quality state, and now I'm here with nothing for myself." Her children graduated from prestigious colleges of the likes of Brown University. One is an officer for a major financial institution, and yet it takes whatever he earns to support his wife and children in the style they expect. What happens to the mother doesn't seem to be a priority. Just as children pay off student loans and loans to purchase luxury automobiles, maybe it would be proper for them to take out a loan for an annuity for a parent who has inadequate retirement resources. Maybe successful children should not think only about what they can do for their own future, but also of their parents' past sacrifices.

Parents spend the better part of their life helping their children achieve success, and by that time, they may have only a few years left. It should behoove a child to explore the possibilities of doing something from time to time to make those years for the parent or parents a bit more comfortable and enjoyable. Children should avoid, at all cost, the possibility of being a burden to parents in the parents' senior years. Some things and circumstances are unavoidable for children, but that which can be avoided should be avoided—especially if it doesn't lend itself to what's good and right to do.

Parents sometimes get it wrong, and sometimes children get it wrong. If your parents get it wrong, try to help them, and maybe the next time they will get it right. That's what they would have done for you. Some children fall down over and over and over again, even after being taught better, and parents go on picking them up over and over and over again. Does a parent not deserve another chance to get it right?

3. Being Strong Is Our Role

Children need to grow up thinking their parents are strong enough to carry them, when they are too weak to carry themselves; strong enough to protect them, when they don't know how to protect themselves; strong enough to support them, when they can't stand alone; strong enough to face the sight of blood or injury, when they think they might be dying; strong enough to be strong for them when they face an uncertain future; strong enough to lift their burden, when it's crushing them down; and strong enough to encourage them and walk the last mile with them, when they feel like giving up.

We, as parents were fashioned from the beginning to have and exhibit this kind of strength. That's why God made us parents, and that strength is what we need to see our children through their period of nurturing. There is a period all children go through, when parents will need to carry them—figuratively and literally. Parents carry them in their arms, when they are babies, off and on until they begin to walk. Even after they begin to walk, parents sometimes carry them, because they tire easily during the early stages of their development. When the stroller isn't available to wheel them around, parents often carry them. Yes, we need to be strong enough to carry them, because during that period, they're too weak to carry themselves.

Parents need strength to protect children from all types of possible dangers that children are unable to protect themselves from. Sometimes a child may be in danger from a stray animal, sometimes from a wild animal, sometimes from other humans. In addition, there are many other unnamed dangers that children may encounter from the time of their birth to the time they die. The need to protect them can go on almost up to the time a child reaches adulthood. Some children become tough enough to protect themselves earlier than others, but they all need protection by parents, at some time, from the things they can't protect themselves from. Children have been snatched from the path of an oncoming car, shielded from onrushing animals, rescued from raging waters, burning fires, gunshots and child molesters.

Often children suffered illnesses during the period of growing up. The illnesses have ranged from the very minor to the very serious. During and through all of those times, parents needed strength to support the child, when they may have been too weak to even stand alone. Sometimes the strain of dealing with a child's illness drains strength from the parents. However, during these times, the parent has to summon whatever strength she has left to support the child, who will draw strength from the parent.

Most children suffer injury at some time in their life, and at the time of the injury, it may have appeared to be worse than it actually was. Quite often, the mere sight of blood issuing forth from the child's injury would be enough to make a parent "lose it," but the parent couldn't afford to "lose it," because she or he had to keep it together for the child's sake. I remember the time Celeste fell down and cut the inside of her lip. The manner in which blood was issuing forth made one think she was critically injured. Her mother didn't react well to the sight of blood, so I had to be there with strength. These are the times and circumstances that children remember and relate to a parent's strength.

Some children have had to deal with difficult challenges in their life, and some of those challenges have left them with an uncertain future. Sometimes it was an illness, sometimes an academic challenge and at other times it could have been a job or family challenge. During these times, the strength of parents has often been instrumental in helping the child to get through the difficult times. Children often get burdened down with the cares of their circumstances and of their life. Just as often, they may not know where to turn or what to do. During these times, some of them are unable to pray, because they don't know God in an intimate way, and more often than not, the parent becomes the only god they know. During those times, the child turns to the parent for encouragement and consolation. The parent's "being there" can help lift the burden that could otherwise crush the child.

Children need lots of encouragement. They're no different from adults, who also like to be encouraged. Encouragement is parallel to praise, and there are very few who aren't moved by praise. Many of us, including children, could not make it without the charge and boost that comes with encouragement and praise. Children must continuously be encouraged and praised, or they may give up on themselves. Often we must walk the last mile with them, encouraging them in their efforts, until they have successfully finished their course.

All of the periods that require parental strength may lead a child to think a parent is a pillar; undaunted and unmoved by anything. I always thought that about my father and still think that today, although his form lies reposing in the earth. Even today, I often say, "My father wasn't afraid of anything or anybody." I wonder how I could have thought him to be such a giant. One reason is because he was my father; he was strong and in charge. His voice said he was a giant. I felt I could go anywhere with my father and not be afraid, because I thought he was strong enough and tough enough to protect me from anything. I never remember my father showing fear, but I'm sure there were times when he was frightened by something, although I never witnessed those times.

Are all fathers that way? I think they all endeavor to be strong for their children, in order to teach them strength. Many fathers succeed at this. Functioning in the capacities of the strengths enumerated above is a natural and is expected of all parents. Some parents will experience all of the above times of needed strength, and all parents will experience some of the above times. Handling them becomes secondary. We can show, by our actions, that we are up to the task of handling everyday occurrences, but we should let the child know that we are vulnerable to all of the other challenges of life, which we may be subjected to at any time.

We may not be strong enough to fend off a raging bear or a hungry lion, nor are we likely to be strong enough to stop the waters of a raging river. Some of us will be strong enough to disarm a mad gunman, climb Mt. Everest or swim the English Channel. Most of us will not be—parent or not. Our weaknesses are exposed in the face of those things we cannot do. That means we are all vulnerable to some of the forces of life. We all have strengths, and we all have weaknesses that leave us exposed and needing protection for ourselves. We should let our children know that, even though we are strong, we are also human and subject to the more powerful forces of life that can overwhelm us, just as the less powerful forces of life overwhelm children. We may not cry during these challenges, and our faces may not depict the hurt, the pain, the sadness or the loneliness that we may feel, but they will still be there and still may hurt.

As parents, we should not always behave in such a way that would make our child think we don't ever feel hurt, or pain, or sadness or loneliness, or any of the emotions that comprise the human makeup. Some parents don't always do so, but it is acceptable to let our child know, if we're hurting because of a challenge, in pain because of an illness or other adverse occurrence, sad because of the loss of something or someone dear to us, lonely because of the absence of a person or connection that had been a part of our life. We're never going to be Superman. We are human first and parent second.

As human parents, we carry human frailties, and there is nothing wrong with our child or children knowing when we're exposed. Sometimes human emotions evoke caring responses. One may be eager to help when she senses a need. Sometimes parents need to vocalize their discomfort, and sometimes it doesn't hurt to shed a tear over them. At the least, it may open up an avenue to let our burdens fly out, making our heart lighter and our burdens brighter. Venting our emotions can also show the human side of us. As parents, the child may have thought we had no weaknesses or shortcomings that need and sometimes cry out for help.

4. PARENTS ALSO HAVE NEEDS

Don't make your child or children think you never need anything. There probably isn't a parent alive who never needs anything, and if there is such a parent, he or she will surely need something if he or she lives long enough. It may not be anything material. No parent has it all or is able to do everything for him- or herself that life demands. Some parents may not ask a child for help in any need, which may stem from a desire to mask her or his vulnerability. Sometimes a parent should open up and present him- or herself to the child in an unprotected state. It's human to need and "real" to admit your exposure.

BE STRONG, BUT ALSO BE HUMAN

Isn't it amazing how so many children grow up thinking their parents are wealthy, when in fact, many are not. Are you wealthy? Maybe you are, and then, maybe you're not? Even if you're not, your child may still think so. Why do children so often think the parent is wealthy? It seems children always think the parent or parents have more than they actually have. Maybe that's because parents always give close to all they may have and seem to always have resources to take care of the financial needs of the child. Parents are usually always ready to shell out the requested money, almost before the request is made and hardly ever have the occasion to tell the child they don't have the money. At least that seems to be the case with latter-generation parents.

As I noted previously, I always used the expression, "My child is rich, but I'm poor." That was because she seemed to have gotten all of the things she needed and many of the things she wanted, even if I had to forego some of the things I wanted. If you, by your giving, made your child think you always had money, that is the reason your child thought you were rich. If the home you afforded for your family was more than adequate, if you always maintained an up-to-date automobile, if you kept better than adequate clothing on the backs of the family members and everybody went on vacation at least once a year, that's why the child thought you were rich. They are only looking at the asset expenditures. They aren't aware of the liabilities to be met.

Someday it may be eye-opening when you sit them down and tell them about your financial struggles to keep them and the other members of the family going. Tell them about the hours you may have had to work and the job you didn't like that you had to keep anyway because of their needs. Tell them about the business challenges you had and the negotiations you made with their needs in mind. Tell them about the times you had to juggle to keep the family's financial needs in the air, rather than have them fall to the ground. It may be good if they are made aware of the financial challenges you may have had as a parent, because when they become parents, they may have some of their own. Knowing these things may give them some consolation, if they ever experience similar challenges in their life.

Remember how you, as a parent, used to go about the house turning out the lights behind the child? When they get grown and in their own home, they know very well how to turn the lights out behind themselves. They may not have understood it then. Now, it may also give them a greater appreciation of who you are, and what you may have endured, in your role as a parent and provider for the family. It may also give the child a true picture of what your financial condition really is, so she or he won't be expecting you to have or be able to do what you may not be able to do. At the very least, if the child has an overabundance, she or he may not hesitate to aid in your financial well-being, rather than assume you don't need anything.

Parents are supposed to be role models for children, role models of strength, integrity and honesty and role models of success at finishing the required course. A role is more of a thing that is played than a thing that is. The role we play as parents isn't necessarily who we are as humans. We should be all of the above because they are all good, positive values. However, it takes strength to continue to uphold positive values, because the forces and conditions of life are always seeking to erode our status in many of these areas. It is always necessary to maintain a position embodying positive values. Don't ever give those up. There is some redeeming value in showing the real side of one's existence—at least at some time.

In addition to whatever else we may show or we may be, the word that ties all of these characteristics together in one neat bundle and describes us best, is "human." All of the other things we can be, but human we must be.

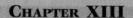

CHAPTER XIII

BUY THEM THE RIGHT TOYS FOR LIFE'S CONDITIONING

Why did you buy him such a toy?
To enhance his life or bring him joy?
I think it will throw him "out of whack."
And make you wish you could take it back.

1. WHAT IS A TOY?

A *toy* is a thing or matter of little or no value or importance, a trifle. That's one of *Webster's Dictionary's* definitions. In modern terms, this definition can't adequately describe toys. The things of today's society that are called *toys* often carry great monetary value, are of great importance and go far beyond the definition of being a trifle. In today's society, toys can be the likes of a $700,000.00 sports car, a private jet, a sixty-five foot yacht or a $28,000.00 collector's firearm. Such toys can be so important to the owner, the owner would almost live to have it or die, if he or she has to be without it.

The nature of a toy, viewed in the eyes of the owner of today, isn't defined by its size or tangible cost, but more by its worth or value in the life of the owner. The toys of life represent things that are dear to the individual, and the ownership of it should bring joy to the person's life. Many parents of today's society have taken to buying things for their child or children which they think will enhance the child's life or bring her or him joy. These things may make a child happy for a season, but in the long run, could lead to a child's undoing or even premature death.

Don't just buy toys for your child; buy her the right toys for life's conditioning. Buy those toys that will add a positive spin to her or his efforts and direction, not the things that spoil her or bring her only a fleeting moment of happiness. Clothes wear out or go out of vogue, cars become mechanical dinosaurs and are sometimes wrecked by the possessor, and false affection lasts only as long as it is being propped up.

Those parents who buy their children toys that don't enhance their life are, quite often, buying the child toys to enhance their own life. Some parents buy children toys because they are laboring under the false belief that it is what the child needs. Others buy toys because they are trying to fill a need in the child's life that they have been unable to fill with their love or presence. When you, as a parent, do this, you are not just buying things, you are unknowingly or consciously buying the child. You are trying to create your own happiness or mask your own unhappiness through the child.

Buying the child toys or buying the child creates only temporary happiness for the child and puts a constant burden on your shoulders to continue the behavior. The child will come to a point, as a child, when happiness will only be derived from things received from you, and as an adult, she or he will be continually groping for things, with the belief that her happiness lies in them. Happiness will always be an illusion, because the acquisition of one toy fuels the desire for another or for the same toy in a larger, more expensive version. You should give your child the type of toys she can and will desire to give herself as an adult and the type she can give her children as children.

The best toys you could ever give are those toys that are simple, often inexpensive, and that come with the feeling that says, "I care." They should not come with the feeling that says, "I'm giving you this because I never had it, I'm giving you this because I'm an absentee parent, or I'm giving you this to bribe you to behave properly." That is also called "buying the child." Honest things in life are either earned, bought, won, traded or given. Affection or caring comes in similar fashion. The best way to show your child that you care, or for your child to learn to care for you, is by winning your child's affection, not by buying it or trading for it. You should earn it by what you do for her, and not by what you buy for her.

Good toys are positive enhancements for a developing child's life. No toy of any type is necessary for a child's existence, although certain toys are tantamount to a child's positive physical and intellectual development. The basic necessities of life consist of food, shelter and clothing. The requirement isn't for food to do more than nourish the body, body organs and the body senses, or for shelter to do more than shield the body from the uncomfortable phases of the elements of nature, or for clothing to do more than cover the body from interacting negative elements and to speak to the norms of the society in which we live. These are life's simple requirements, but based on our ability and desire to provide, we often go far beyond the basic requirements in our ability and desire to provide. We go beyond the basic requirements, sometimes creating an overboard situation that is often called spoiling.

When we spoil children, we bend over backwards to please them in whatever area. When we bend over backwards to please them, we go beyond the enhanced basics and begin buying "toys," things of little or no value to the child's life or well-being. You should give serious thought to what you buy your child or children. Ask yourself if it is intended to make her happy or enhance her life today and in the future, or just make her happy without enhancing her life. If it only makes her happy, you failed. If it only enhances her life, you succeeded. If it makes her happy and enhances her life, you greatly succeeded.

If you buy them books, they may become thinkers; if you buy them guns, they may become violent; if you buy them wine, they may become drinkers; if you buy them sports equipment, they may become athletes; if you buy them crayons; they may become artists; if you buy them cars too soon, they may become cadavers; if you buy them birth control pills, they may engage in premature sex; if you buy them condoms, they may cause premature pregnancies; and if you take them to church, they may become Christians. You're in a position to choose to buy any one of the above, as well as many others, that are not mentioned above. However, any and all choices carry with them consequences—good or bad. The choices you make carry conditions that may go a long way to shape the child's growth pattern. The important thing is what you give, not how much of it or how expensive it is.

2. LET THE TOYS SHOW

Developing children are getting a fix on life and the things of life, through association. They're making determinations about the things of life, which they will be carrying into adulthood. They may not know which things will be good, until they reach the point of understanding which things fit into their life and how they fit. They're not even acquiring these things on their own. You, as the parent, are introducing these things into their life. So you must be mindful of the things you introduce into the child's life.

Don't set a precedent of giving the child what she or he may not be able to continue to acquire, when you're not on the scene or things such that to continue to acquire them may put her life or budget out of balance. Don't lead your child to believe (by giving an overabundance) that her life can't go on without those things. Everything you give your child should be in balance—in terms of quantity and cost.

Quality should also be of great importance, and quality doesn't always spell "designer label." Unfortunately, cost is often associated with quality—except when acquired through connective sources and outlet places. We must also be mindful of the fact that there are degrees of quality and what you give your child in terms of quality should be based on your ability to provide and the necessity of the child getting it. If you are a parent of moderate means, endeavoring to provide the best of everything for your child may be a foolish endeavor. That's like having "a champagne taste and a beer pocketbook," as the saying goes.

You should have the final decision concerning the toys your developing child will have and decisive input concerning those toys you will be buying for your adolescent child. Some young children often want items their friends have or others advertised through various media. You should look into the idea behind these items, as well as the intended motive. You should only put things in your child's life that you want to become a part of her or his life. Don't let your child demand things of you she thinks she should have. Trying to keep up with the family next door or down the street is a "no-no." If you, as a parent, get yourself locked into buying unnecessary, expensive toys, you may be setting a precedent you can't continue.

A parent can literally shape a child's future priorities by the things he or she gives the child. If you want your child to know about the Bible, buy

Bible stories for the child, when the child is at a young age. If you want your child to attend church when she is older, take her or him to church, when she or he is younger. If you want your child to recognize quality, teach her the goodness of how quality things are put together. Explain the difference between good quality and poor quality and why one should be better than the other.

If you want your child to acquire a taste for decorative art, put decorative art on the wall of the child's room when she or he is young. If you want your child to become a good reader, read to her and buy her books when she is young. If you want your child to have a taste for quality music, play it in the home when the child is young. I have witnessed the evidence over and over again that the child will grow to admire and cherish the type of music played in the home when she or he is growing up. The seed you plant in a young child will likely evidence itself in the child's life when she is older. The list of examples could go on and on.

There are certain things which are good to introduce to girls when they are young, so they will know how to handle a similar situation when they are older. There are other things that should not be introduced to boys when they are young, because these may cause them to fall when they are older. There are other things that should not be introduced to either a boy or girl, when he or she is young, because it could become a destructive habit when the child is older. Don't be too anxious to put your child in his or her own car. Let maturity set in first. Otherwise, you may end up burying the child prematurely. Don't love the child to death. Also, don't buy expensive things for the child's body that don't do anything positive for the child's head.

3. DON'T ACCEPT THE GUILT TRIP

Some parents raise their child by giving her everything she thinks she wants or needs. The child, prior to a certain age, has no idea about positive wants and needs. Some of these same parents buy the most expensive of these items. The child, prior to a certain age, has no conception of cost, and if the child is young enough, he or she will wallow in the dirt the same way in the jeans that cost $34.00 as he would in the jeans that cost $15.00, and one may destruct as quickly as the other. On the other hand, a little girl will climb the monkey bars and rip the $25.00 skirt, the same as she would the $14.00 skirt. There is nothing wrong with introducing quality to a child.

Parents should also keep in mind that price doesn't always spell quality. Some things sell because of a brand name, which may or may not spell quality. When it comes to price and quality, a parent should only go for the higher-priced items, if they can afford them, especially when the child is between the ages of birth and maybe nine or ten years of age. At that age, the child doesn't even know the difference, and if she does, she has to accept them anyway, because she or he isn't paying for them. There is no redeeming value in paying more than you can afford for a child's clothing.

When children begin to approach the pre-teen years, they will really begin to notice their peers and compare. During this time, you should begin teaching your child the facts of economic life. You should let the child know that you are the father or mother, not the parent next door, the one down the street or the one across town. You should also let the child know that not all parents are created equal when it comes to economic means. If you're doing the best you can and it's not adequate in the eyes of the child, don't permit the child or the circumstances to give you a guilt complex or make you feel badly about what you are unable to do. Even in situations where you, as a parent, may be able to do more for your child, it is not always wise to go overboard in purchasing overly expensive items. One reason is that things which come easily tend to lose their worth in the hands of the recipient. The level of appreciation for the thing tends to wane quicker.

Another reason is that some children may begin to think they need these things for their very survival. God forbid! One day the family may hit hard times and not be able to continue the pattern. At that point, the child may not readily understand and accept the changed state of existence. In addition, if you raise a child, and give her or him these unnecessary, expensive toys, what's going to happen when the child gets out on her own? She may not be able to continue this life-style on the means available at the time, and could very well turn to doing unscrupulous things to support the prior life-style you, the parent, afforded her or him. In some instances, girls marry individuals that neither can afford to nor desire to support the prior life-style given by the parents. Caring children don't drive parents to providing things beyond the parent's means, but you must teach them to be caring about your ability to do or not to do.

When we were growing up, the manner in which our parents related to us and raised us motivated us to feel and show compassion for them in their inability to afford certain things they may have desired to give us, and our compassion moved us to address their plight. We actually felt sorrowful and loved them even more because of their vulnerability. The modern-day generation of children seems to feel disdain for their parents, when they can't give them what they want.

Parents should not set children up to think they can have anything they want, even if the parent or parents don't have the means to supply it. The parent that sets this type of precedent may need to resign herself or himself to live with that for the rest of that child's life, even after the child or children have reached adulthood. Some children will argue at the parent's deathbed over material things they desired to get from the parent or over things they may have wanted and the parent failed to give them—for whatever reason. Some will remain angry at you long after you have been put in the grave. A child raised to get every requested desire feels she or he can go to the parent at anytime and get what she or he wants.

As parents, we decided early on, it would be clearly understood, I nor my child's mother would subject ourselves to any demands. We stuck by our precedent of "Don't ask for things we are aware that you need. If we can afford them, you will have them." As for other things, that was left to our discretion. We were parents who were in charge of our child and of raising her. We knew what she had and were aware of most of her needs. If there was something we may not have been aware of, after it was brought to our attention, we addressed it in the appropriate manner.

We were "on top of our game." We knew what our child had. We virtually knew of every skirt, sweater, blouse, shirt, jean, coat and pair of shoes and were probably aware of the socks. We weren't absentee parents who didn't know what our child was buying and bringing into the house. We either bought what she had or were aware of what she bought and knew who or what was given to her. At least this was so when she lived under our roof.

Should not parents know? If they are minding the store, they will surely know. Those things are tangible. You can see them with your eyes. However, some things are looked upon, but not seen.

4. But Why So Much?

Some parents give the child so much until, at some stage, the child may come to accept those things as a part of everyday existence. In many instances, the child believes he or she can't do without those things. Sometimes the parent or parents are made to continue doing this until the child is grown and moves out of the house or until the child gets married and beyond. There have been occasions in which the child got into a marital relationship, and (because of other obligations) couldn't afford the luxury of living in a style previously afforded by a parent. The child pursued an affair on the side for the benefit of the things the outside relationship afforded. In many instances, that led to friction in the family and often led to broken marriages. This can especially be true if the child is a female. Society tends to feel that if a husband takes money and things from an outside relationship, the female giving the things is no good, and if a wife takes money and things from an outside relationship, she is no good.

Don't set your daughter up for a possible life of misery, because many girls, when they are picking their mates, are picking them based on the size of their bank account or on the size of his potential for success. On the other hand, they sometimes marry the good-looking poor man, and once they get past the good looks, the reality of it all sets in. The reality is often expressed in the words of the old saying, "Her husband keeps her barefoot and pregnant." In the life of many women (after marriage) that saying can virtually be taken literally. In many situations, the husband has little concern with affording the life-style given by the parent. He didn't promise the daughter that. The girl bought his good looks, not his deep pockets. If the man she chooses has an "ego problem," he may get joy and feel a bit more secure in reducing his wife (your daughter) to an impoverished state. That often becomes a means of controlling her.

The best lessons your child can learn aren't the lessons learned by what you put on her body, but by what you put in her head. The outside appearance, as is often said "is only skin deep." The outside appearance often creates a false sense of self-esteem. If a child's sense of self-esteem is built upon how well he or she dresses, how expensive the sneakers or how fast the car you bought can go, the child may have very little to go on.

Have you ever seen a child wearing clothes that weren't so expensive but neat and clean? And did you notice that the child was bright, articulate and always had the correct answer when called upon by the teacher? Do you remember the other child, who was so well-dressed and never knew the correct answer? I remember children like that, because I went to school with some of them.

There seems to be a system of checks and balances in existence in life. That system tends to compensate for what may be lacking in one area. The person who doesn't hear well has extremely keen vision, or sometimes the person that doesn't see well has an extremely good sense of hearing. So it could very well follow that the child whose parents could not afford to dress him or her so well didn't get recognition for his dress, so he strived to be recognized in other areas. Sometimes he was recognized for his athletic prowess or even as a bully.

The latter is a negative and a direction you should steer your child away from. Another child may be recognized for her intellectual prowess. That's a positive you can steer your child toward. Push that in a child, and she may reach a point of excellence whereby she will be able to earn money to buy all of the things you could not afford to give her. It often seems that children raised with less accomplish more, because they may have more to strive for. In addition, they seem to have a more positive value system, not built on the props that sometimes fall from under those persons who are being propped up.

5. It Isn't in the Sizzle

It's not a storm; it's just a drizzle.
It's not the steak; it's just the sizzle.
The joy of the toy will sometimes fizzle.
Be certain it's the steak, and not the sizzle.

When Celeste was growing up, she got quality clothing. I could better afford to acquire them because, being in the garment business, I got them at wholesale prices. When I bought them for her, I didn't remind her of how expensive her things were. That wasn't important. She didn't grow up with a sense of being so well-dressed that the other values weren't important. We didn't buy her expensive sneakers, like some of the other parents bought their child. We probably could have afforded to, because sneakers didn't break the bank. Our priorities didn't dictate that over something else, and we didn't want her to have a value system based on how expensive her toys were. We wanted her to have a value system based on quality and positive "head stuff," the stuff that went inside the head, as opposed to the outside. She accepted our guidance. She wasn't raised to rebel against our judgment and decisions.

Some parents bought expensive sneakers for their child, and some are yet buying them, and yet some of those parents could least afford them. The children with the most expensive sneakers weren't necessarily the smartest, nor were they necessarily the best basketball players. Some children may think having Michael Jordan sneakers will give them the ability to play basketball like him. But I don't think so. Michael Jordan's talent was *in* his head, body and feet and not *on* his head, body or feet. His talent was a natural—a gift from God—and a Michael Jordan comes along once in a lifetime.

God gives special talents to individuals strictly on an individual basis. An Arnold Palmer, a Jesse Owens, a Martin Luther King, Jr., a Bing Crosby, a Thomas Edison, an Albert Einstein, a Muhammad Ali, an Oprah Winfrey, a Florence Griffith-Joyner, a Tiger Woods (and on and on and on) comes along once in a great while. One may be able to dress like any one of them, and one may even have a resemblance to any one of them, but no one will be able to exhibit a talent like any one of them. Still, you have something of your own which was given to you by God. Use it to the fullest.

This talent may not come out of how expensive your toys were when you were growing up, unless your designer wardrobe led you to become a famous designer. Famous designers have been all over the landscape (they come and they go), but the likes of the above are one in a million. Yes, a quality sneaker may have helped Michael execute the moves his head and body determined, but without the inside stuff, the outside would not have worked. You can buy your child golf clubs like Arnold Palmer and Tiger Woods, and still he or she may never be able to play like them. You can own fashionable little tennis shorts like Venus Williams, but the outfit will not give you the talent she possesses. It's not what's on the body; it's what's in the body.

Records are broken every day, but they seem not to be broken in a lifetime using the same technique or standard of the prior record setter. On the other hand, legends are born with something inside that makes them legends. They are not usually developed through the use of exterior adornments.

6. Balanced Toys, Balanced Life

Balance should be of primary concern to a parent in considering the toys she or he should give their child. You, the parent, should be balanced in deciding which, how many and at what cost. In deciding which toys, you should give a lot of thought to the purpose for which you are buying the toy and how it may affect the child's behavior as an adult. It would be good if the toy enhances a child's self-esteem, intellect, physical well-being and relationship with God and other people. The physical and intellectual quite often are certain to enhance self-esteem, and a right relationship with God, and other people can also enhance both of these. However, physical things don't always enhance the intellect, and intellectual things don't always enhance physical well-being.

Some parents begin buying children books at an early age, and those children go on to become studious, avid readers and sometimes scholars. A child who is an avid reader will find it easier to master many of the other intellectual challenges of life from the books she begins reading. She develops an appetite for reading that will cause her to devour many other books during her grade school, high school and college years. As an adult, she will continue reading good books at every opportunity.

Some parents took their child to church when she was young, bought her Bible story books and even a child's Bible. Some of these children went on to become Christians, some, although they abandoned the direction, returned to it another day, and others abandoned it in their adult life and went off into "a far country" and died there.

Church can often be boring to a child. When some children get the chance, they leave the atmosphere of the church, vowing never to return. There is redeeming value in Christian direction, but don't give it to your child in an unbalanced amount when she is young because she may come to not want any when she is older.

Some of the type of toys we gave our daughter were decorative wall art, a self-propelled car, a boom box with earphones, books, puzzles, a chemistry set, a magic set, ice skates, a bicycle, a globe, math and vocabulary flash cards, a $50.00 bill along with Christmas presents, unceremonial clothing, basic jewelry, the likes of bangles, a basic gold neck chain, a gold birthstone ring, a quality watch and a fur jacket. There was meaning to the gift of each of these things.

When Celeste got old enough to sleep alone in her own room, we decorated it and hung some basic art on the wall. The subject matter of one of the pieces was that of a young student reading. For sometime now, Celeste has been acquiring art pieces for her own home.

When she was four or five years of age, we bought her a self-propelled, battery operated, car that went up and down the sidewalk. She got her learner's permit at the earliest possible age and learned to drive. I didn't want her to go into adulthood not knowing how to drive. She has become a good driver.

Along with books, Celeste got puzzles, different types of puzzles that gave her some sense of how things fit together. This may have had something to do with honing her mechanical aptitude. I'm sure this aptitude came in handy in some of her courses of study. She subsequently became an engineer.

A chemistry set was one of the toys she received, although she didn't spend much time with it. However, a seed could have been planted that inclined her toward scientific matters. Her chosen degree was Bachelor of Science.

She received ice skates and a bicycle, among the toys she got. As an adult, she has ridden in many bike-a-thons, raising money for charitable causes. The ice skates propelled her to become a very proficient ice skater, rising to the level of teaching ice skating at a public rink.

The globe she received gave her an inquisitive nature for places and people. That gave her a yen for traveling, and she subsequently traveled extensively. The trips took her to several continents.

The boom box probably brought her many hours of pleasure in college. I'm sure it also taught her discipline, because she was forbidden to carry it outside, except in an area that was a proper setting for the noise, and that was safe from boom box snatchers.

We bought her the Britannica Junior Encyclopedia to aid her in her studies, and it also helped her in finding answers to everyday questions. We gave her math and vocabulary flash cards to strengthen her math skills and enlarge her vocabulary. These, no doubt, aided her greatly in her reading— then and later.

In her teen years, we began giving her a piece of money, so she could get the feel of having a worthwhile bill in her possession. We didn't want any offer of any size currency to ever turn her head. By the time she got to be an adult, she had gotten sufficient exposure to money.

We began to buy her unceremonial clothing by the time she was eight or nine. We wanted to move away from the idea of dressing up for, or buying special outfits for holidays and other occasions. We wanted to get her accustomed to wearing something from the wardrobe she had on hand. The lesson was well taught and well learned, because she seems unmoved by the thought of ceremonial attire, except when she feels the occasion such as a wedding or other type calls for something different to what she may have in her wardrobe.

We bought her small bracelets and a basic gold chain, a birthstone ring and a good quality watch. We didn't want her to reach adulthood, not having had those things. She may not have known what it was all about, if she had never had them. We wanted her to be accustomed to some jewelry, so she wouldn't need to go on a gold chain binge later in life, and walk around looking like "Ms. T" or some other individual you may spot around town, weighed down with layered gold chains dripping from the neck and sporting a cheap gold ring on each finger.

I promised her that when she reached adulthood, and before she went out into life on her own, I would give her a fur coat. She decided she didn't want a mink coat. She had compassion for the little minks and, instead, wanted a blue fox. (She seemed to have no compassion for the fox.) I had a blue fox jacket made for her. I went to a furrier that was recommended to me, selected the skins and had the jacket custom made. It was beautiful, and she was very excited at the thought of owning it. This was to be the last toy I gave her, which may have had an influence on her future life.

Did it do more than make her happy? Did it enhance her life? I don't know, but I do know it is about sixteen years since then, and she has not gone out to buy another fur coat, although she could probably have more than afforded one. At the least, having had a fur could have put her at the place where she did not have a longing for something she wanted but never got.

As indicated above, a parent can virtually shape a child's priorities by the toys she or he gives the child. And, as above, there was a lesson in life related to the toys given, and looking back at our child's life, I can see that she gleaned something from all the toys she received.

When we were young, my mother bought us Bible story books. I remember becoming fascinated with stories such as Joseph and the Coat of Many Colors and Samson and Delilah. Even today, many of the Old Testament stories still hold my interest and bring me much enlightenment and enjoyment. The same can be true of exposing your child to a church atmosphere. The feeling in the atmosphere of the church is something that never leaves a child. The experience seems to follow her or him for the rest of their lives. I've heard many accounts of children hitting hard times in life, and after all else failed, they (like the prodigal son) reached back, drew on the prior personal experience, and found the way back to the sanctuary of God.

We took our daughter to church while she was growing up, and she seemed to always find her place in a house of God, and that is still true today. She now takes her daughter to church. The seed was planted in our daughter more than thirty-five years ago. The experience emerged from the exposure. You, as a parent, are picking the toys, so try to pick the ones which will impact the child's life in a positive way. It all depends on what you consider positive and what you would rather be seeing your child do or not do. The fate of your child's future may rest in the selection of your child's toys, so be very selective about choosing them.

I know a father who had a very different philosophy about alcoholic beverages than my own. He decided that he wanted to condition his daughter to be able to handle a glass or two of an alcoholic beverage without losing her balance in the company of a male companion. He believed that boys sometime tried to get girls intoxicated and then took advantage of them. He must have also believed that alcohol sometimes changes the personality and even renders a person more vulnerable. The idea was to condition his daughter to be able to handle her liquor.

Maybe he was able to accomplish his goal, I don't know. To me, the better approach would have been to teach her to refuse the alcoholic beverage in the first place. He may have been operating on the assumption that sooner or later we all seize the opportunity to sample an alcoholic beverage, and because he wanted his daughter to be protected, this was his way of doing it. The possibility of her becoming a drinker clearly worried him less than did the possibility that a man would get her drunk and take advantage of her.

This may not have been a good thing to teach his son. Boys can be authors of experimentation anyway and appear to be more willing to take on bad habits than girls. On an average, girls seem to be a bit more reserved, at least that was once the conclusion. Don't start your boys off drinking, and don't introduce them to sex by buying favors from a prostitute for them. I've heard public accounts of men who introduced sex to their son, thinking they were helping him become a man. Wrong! It is potentially dangerous, at the very least, and could prove to be one of the worst investments in a boy's future well-being. Boys will find out about sex soon enough on their own from their peers. They need not be assisted in consummating their undoing.

Don't introduce your daughter or son to mind-altering drugs of any kind. If you do, you may live to regret it for the rest of your life. Endeavor to keep them sheltered from anything that holds the potential for shattering their life. I have heard and known of many accounts of parents "getting high" with their child or children. That is so very dumb. Why would any parent want his or her child to go the way of his or her destruction? The parent may think that what is being done does not hold the potential of being destructive, but studies and time have proven overwhelmingly that anything which alters the normal pattern of thought and action is destructive. Even if you (as a parent) don't believe it, you should not take the chance, because your belief just may be wrong, and the situation you create may be irreversible.

It's a bit like what some people think about Heaven and Hell, as a potential place to spend their eternity. Some don't believe there is any such a place. Some others believe that if this "Hell" spoken of is such a bad place, a good and merciful God would never send anyone there. They're right about that. God would not send anyone there, but Satan would. Those who don't believe in Heaven don't strive to get there by the life they live. However, they're taking a big chance. Suppose they are wrong and end up going to a place they did not think existed? If they do, they will have the rest of eternity to regret the error of their unbelief. And eternity is a very long time.

As a parent, you should not be so anxious to put your child behind the wheel of his own car, especially your son. In generations past, that hardly ever happened, because most parents couldn't afford to do it anyway. Our present-day society has grown to be so affluent that it has money and doesn't know what to spend it for. If you're a parent, and the best thing you can think to do with your money is to prematurely buy your son his own car, you should re-examine your thoughts.

I say, "especially your son," because boys seem more inclined to want to be "macho" and to prove their bravado to their peers. When they lack sufficient maturity, they may be inclined to operate a vehicle in a risky manner, such as driving well over the speed limit or drag racing on public roads. There is often the desire for a boy to prove something to his associates. Sometimes the boy, as well as others among his associates, doesn't live to recognize the proof. An irresponsible child should never be put behind the wheel of a car, and especially not his own.

Most parents think their son is responsible. But just because they think so doesn't make it true. Some parents have no idea what their son is like when he is out from under their watchful eye. Many parents who thought their son was responsible and bought him a car ended up buying him a casket shortly afterward. Many sons get the car and speed off down the highway at an excessive speed and/or under the influence of alcohol or drugs. The parent didn't even know the son did drugs. My, what a pity it is!

So don't subject your child to the possibility of being one of those statistics. Try waiting a bit until he gets to be really responsible. Give him more time to mature and prove himself to be responsible. As a parent, sometimes you are better off not buying your child that car. Put your money into an investment and maybe by the time he is mature enough, you will be able to buy him a Corvette, rather than an Impala. Save your money, and save his life.

In telling the story about our child's toys and how they may have helped her to become or not become, some may say it looks like the child was a "perfect robot" child. Not so! They're wrong. Celeste wasn't perfect and didn't turn out to be perfect either; nor did she have perfect parents. If she functions like a robot, she is certainly charging her own batteries and supplying her own energy for her movements, directing her own controls and not relying on anyone to get her going—except God.

She has her faults and acts independently. However, what I may consider a fault may just be my opinion of how it should be or how she should do it. Who's to say that an act (if it appears to be positive) contrary to another's opinion is a fault? We, as her parents, have our opinions, and she has her own, of which she is entitled. We can conclude with reasonable certainty that she gleaned much from the toys we supplied her as she was growing up. She shows it in how she lives and what she buys or does not buy.

It's strange to watch children and listen as they come more and more toward developing in the direction of your positive or negative teaching. Intelligent children come to realize and accept the things which are positive and life-enhancing. My child said to me some years ago, "Dad, I hope you're around when we have children, so you can help teach them the same things you taught me." Recently she said, "I remember you taught me not to be a follower, and if anything dumb was going on, I had better be leading the crowd in the dumb behavior." It's amazing how some things stick out in their minds. That remark had been uttered to her some thirty years ago.

Even with my daughter's imperfections, I would take her over most of what I witness in children parented in the recent three generations, because, as compared to them, my daughter's organization, discipline, work ethics, direction, parenting and behavior seem to speak volumes over what I'm seeing. I'm not saying this because she is my daughter, nor do I propose to predict what she will do tomorrow. That's up to her, and I may have no control over it. I can only speak on how we sent her out from our household into her adult life. I can only speak of the "now."

Teach them the right things, and buy them the right toys. If they act wisely, they'll find a way to make them fit into the pattern of their life. The right direction steers a child toward positive goals. The "right toys" give a child the right conditioning to live life and choose those things that enhance life, not those things that impact life in a negative way.

CHAPTER XIV

DON'T INTERFERE IN THEIR LIFE, BUT ALWAYS CONDEMN WRONG BEHAVIOR

You might be your child's savior,
If you condemn her wrong behavior.
It matters not that she is grown,
And living her life on her own.
Given words of advice from a sage,
A course can be changed at any age.

1. THROWING THEM TO THE WOLVES

Do you think your child has reached an age at which you should stop condemning her or his unacceptable behavior? Behavior is considered acceptable or unacceptable based on good morals and positive values. If your answer to the above question is yes, you must also think that you (the parent) will reach an age at which you will stop worrying about your child or reach an age at which you will no longer be deeply saddened by an untimely death or by some other unfortunate circumstance short of death that may befall your child.

The time when you come to feel that it's not your business to speak out against your child's negative behavior is the time when you relinquish your parental influence and subject your child to her or his own destruction or ruin. Adult children get out of line, at times, just as juvenile children do, and sometimes the only influence that may help bring them back is someone close to them, such as a parent, another close relative, the law or life. Running afoul of the law can stigmatize your child for life. On the other hand, life teaches a hard lesson, and the lesson has no respect of person. Wherever the ax falls, that's where it cuts. So would you not want to help your child (juvenile or adult) avoid having to learn life's harsh lessons?

The way to help her or him avoid the harsh lessons of life is to aid her or him in steering clear of those things that bring on harsh circumstances or to steer clear of situations, which could cause negative life responses. There are hundreds (if not thousands) of instances of individuals, caught up in unfortunate circumstances of life that could have been avoided, if they had been advised against going to certain places or engaging in certain activity. Individuals have lost their lives as a result of being in the wrong place at the wrong time. Some could have avoided being there, and some could not. Those who could have avoided being there did not exercise right judgment in their decision to go to a particular place, even after knowing they should not have gone there. Often one thinks the decision made was all right to make, but the negative results prove otherwise.

When I was growing up, there occurred a circumstance involving the daughter of a neighbor who was fatally injured because she was in the wrong place at the wrong time. She was at or near the premises of another neighbor. An argument ensued, and the victim met an untimely death as a result. She should not have been there.

Similar situations are being repeated over and over again every day, with varying repercussions and results. There are other instances, which come to mind, of individuals dying from fires or gunshot or in legal or illegal social settings. I can recall an instance in which more than a hundred individuals died in a fire, while partying in an illegal social club. A disgruntled individual torched the place, in an effort to get even with his girlfriend. It turned out that the girlfriend was not even there at the time, but more than a hundred other individuals were, and they all lost their lives.

Based on what was reported in the newspapers, some of the attendees had been advised in the past against frequenting that particular establishment. Those who died didn't listen to this advice and warning. Some, who were not there, may have been absent from the place as a result of advice and warnings. Many of those who were there and many of those who were not, were adults. Some of them had parents, or other guardians, who dared to interfere in their life by speaking against and condemning wrong behavior. Some of those absent from the club at the time of the tragedy may have had their life spared because of instructions or advice from parents or other guardians. Adult children aren't always on track and need advice sometimes from a parent. Their behavior is sometimes wrong. You should not interfere in the life of your adult child, but you should always condemn wrong behavior.

One of the most celebrated murder cases of the 1990s involved the murder of two individuals, and the murder of one of those individuals may have been the result of his being at the wrong place at the wrong time. The father of that victim mentioned, at the trial involving a civil suit, how close he and his son were, implying that it was not only a father and son relationship; it was also a buddy and pal relationship. If this was indeed so, they may have confided in each other concerning things of a very personal nature.

If the son had been involved in an ongoing relationship with the woman who died with him, he may have confided this to his father. After all, the female was the former wife of a noted celebrity. The father may or may not have advised the son against keeping company with that particular woman or against a relationship such as they may have had. On the other hand, the father may have thought it to be neat and encouraged it. After all, the female was no slouch when it came to good looks and attracting attention. She had also been the wife of somewhat of a "social giant." As far as the records showed, the son was unmarried, and so was the woman at the time. Considering the reputation of the female involved, the father should have advised the son against any such relationship with her. Not that her reputation was so bad, but it was troubled. That father's advice could have saved his son's life.

How often parents listen to and encourage children in activities that are potentially troublesome, dangerous and wrong, rather than speaking out in condemnation. They may not see the possible negative consequences down the road. They may only be looking at the "now." However, wrong behavior is wrong behavior—today or tomorrow. Parents should speak out against it at any time, regardless of the fact that the child is grown.

A TABLESPOON OF LOVE, A TABLESPOON OF DISCIPLINE

Another instance comes to mind concerning the brutal murder of several women in the New York City area in 1995. When something of this nature occurs, the first suspicion points to drugs or some other illegal activity. Early on, it was concluded that there was no connection to any illegal activity and that none of the individuals had anything to do with drugs. However, when all of the facts were in, it came to light that one or two of the murdered women were casual drug users, and one of them owed money to the low-level drug dealer who murdered them. At least one of the other women who were murdered just happened to be in the wrong place at the wrong time. Parents should be advising their adult children against what they may be thinking of doing or places they may be thinking of going that could have an adverse affect on their health and safety.

Parents are very often aware of the activities of their adult child or children, and very often know that some or all of the activities are wrong, but they don't always speak out against them. They may feel the adult child knows what she is doing or feel that, as a parent, he or she should not interfere in the life or living of the adult child. Such conclusions may be misguided. Your adult child doesn't always exercise right behavior. Reaching adulthood does not imply the ability or desire to always exercise right behavior. As a matter of fact, adults are just as inclined to exercise wrong behavior as are children, because they feel they are only restricted by their personal desire to do what's right or wrong. Parents' intentions should be to steer a child or children away from wrong behavior, so as to make their own life free of trouble and challenge. They may not always be thinking of the possible harm that can come to the child in the future.

Are you a parent who enjoys ill-gotten gain, while ignoring wrong behavior? You know your son's job doesn't pay him that kind of money, the kind needed to acquire the things he has and to give you the money he is giving you. You're not even sure your son has a regular job. He has not even given you details of where he works and what he does. Every week he comes by in his $54,000.00 automobile and places three or four hundred dollars in your hand. You smile, and then you're spending the money as fast as you get it, not giving any thought to the possibility that someday you may need it to get him out of jail or to buy him a suit, a casket and a cemetery plot.

He has no suit right now. He's a "street hustler," who deals drugs and lends money at loan-shark rates. His style isn't "suit stuff." Can you remember what he wore as a child? You could never get him to wear a tie, not even to his grandmother's funeral. Remember how he never wanted to do any hard work? All the other kids had summer jobs, and your son would just hang around the house, waiting for you to get paid. He remembers that and is now paying you back with easy, ill-gotten gain. He likes easy money and that's how he is earning it. He nor you is thinking about his tomorrow.

You are accepting the spoils and asking no questions. You have the feeling he is doing something that is illegal, but you choose not to "rock the boat," for fear of cutting off your rent money and meal ticket. Accepting ill-gotten gain from your child is another way of endorsing his negative behavior. You're not saying to the child, "You should stop that." You're saying it's okay, because you are benefiting from it.

Ill-gotten means acquired by evil or illegal means. When you encourage this type of behavior, by accepting the spoils obtained by these means, you could be paving the way for your child's untimely death, your untimely death or (at the very least) a brush with the law for you, for your child or for the both of you.

Many parents are like you. They are recipients of money from fraud, theft, gambling, gun running, drug smuggling and sales, illegal sale of cigarettes, prostitution, trafficking in human cargo, pornography and any number of other illegal or immoral activities perpetrated by their child. The parents who guide their child around wrong behavior as a means rather than an end are the type of parents who would be less likely to speak out against wrong adult behavior. Those who teach the child against wrong adult behavior, because they love him or her and recognize that it is wrong to do wrong, will be more likely to speak to their child (even as an adult), when they see him exercising wrong behavior. That is an indication the parents care about the child and want to save him or her from the destructive forces of life, which can come about through wrong doing.

Don't throw your child to the wolves. When you ignore his wrong behavior, you're casting him out, to be subjected to the elements and whims of life. Life offers exacting and grievous punishment upon individuals who habitually do it wrong, and the end results can be utter destruction.

Those parents who buy birth control pills for their daughters are unnecessarily encouraging sexual activity. Instead, they should be admonishing the child to avoid this type of activity ... until the proper time comes for her to engage in it. Those parents who refuse to speak out against their son's or

317

daughter's socialization with multiple partners are encouraging promiscuity, and this can lead to dire consequences. Some parents think it's "cool" when the son brings home the different accounts of Sally, Susan, Dana, Taisha, Michele and Lana. Some of the parents probably remark to themselves how desirable their son must be. They don't even know how easy these girls are to get. They would sleep with anyone's son without much persuasion. In many instances, the parent doesn't tell the son that this is wrong behavior and that he needs to settle down to seeking the one he is likely to marry. They don't tell the son to keep his organ in privacy, where it belongs, because he could be destroying the life of someone's daughter, just as some other boy could destroy the life of his sister.

Some sons tell their father of their sexual pursuits, and the father often smiles and nods his acceptance and approval. However, when the son comes over to reveal the fact that he has a very serious disease or illness resulting from his promiscuity, the smile suddenly turns to a frown, and the countenance suddenly takes on the burden of sadness and despair. That is somewhat of a parallel of a parent watching a little one exercising despicable behavior and smile because she thinks the child's antics are cute. She doesn't realize the child is introducing her to her future, out-of-control son or daughter. This parent is probably looking at a child who will be unmanageable tomorrow and always in trouble, a child whose bad social behavior could kill him.

2. THEY'RE STILL CRYING OUT FOR DISCIPLINE

After a child reaches adulthood, becomes independent and self-supporting, you would normally think your job, as a parent and director of your child's behavior, has ended. In some parent-child situations, that would be a true statement, and in others, it would not be. Your child is likely to reach adulthood with ways, habits, desires and behavior patterns similar to those she had or exercised in her childhood. As parents, we must remember that the transition from childhood isn't a state or stage at which an off-track or out-of-control child is likely to undergo a miracle transformation from sinner to saint, from a selfish brat to a giving angel, from lazy to industrious, from untidy to "neat freak," from brash to polite, from brawler to lady or gentleman, from a consistent lawbreaker to law-abiding citizen, from one who runs the streets to a homebody, or from one nobody could control to one who is under control. If any of these labels fit your son or daughter as a child, he or she will likely not have outgrown them as an adult, unless his life becomes impacted by the love of God, and it executes a change in his behavior and desires. Otherwise, the only thing certain and promised upon reaching adulthood alive, is a chronological age of eighteen, twenty-one or whatever the accepted age may be.

Adulthood is not guaranteed to mature a child, just as old age is not guaranteed to mature an adult. Some senior citizens are still dragging themselves in and out of dance halls, nightclubs and gambling dens, thinking they are still young and ignoring the wrinkles upon their brows and the slowed pace of their step. Sometimes the circumstances and troubles of life wake children up or sober them. Some children reach adulthood drunken with the elixir of laziness, brashness, rebelliousness and experimentation. They take the negative baggage into adulthood that you handed them in their childhood. He or she doesn't take on a new countenance. He crosses the threshold of time with all of his established ways still intact.

I have frequently heard parents say, "This child is begging for a whipping." In essence, the parent was saying that the child's behavior was one that begged for someone to say something before the forces of life did something. If you're a parent, when the forces of life come down on your child negatively, the results may bring you a lot of heartache. It's unfortunate, but a few true observations are probably certain: if you watched your son or daughter self-destruct as a child, you're likely to sit on the sidelines and watch him or her self-destruct as an adult. On the other hand, it is fair to say that a child under control will probably be an adult under control.

Life is not the *Alice in Wonderland* or *Cinderella* pageant. Your adult son or daughter is not likely to be (as an adult) something he or she was not as a child. As a parent watching your child growing up, you will get somewhat of an accurate picture of the type of adult he or she will become. If you are a parent who had it all together because of the way your parents raised you, but mistakenly failed in raising your child, be prepared for the need to interject your opinion or advice in your child's life from time to time. The adult child may or may not listen. If the child does listen, your advice may someday help him or her avoid serious mistakes and trouble, and that advice may well save his or her life.

There are many misdirected things which occur or are about to occur in the life of our adult children, and quite often we are aware of them. It's not a parent's responsibility, nor is it proper for a parent to interfere in the life of an adult child, but it is proper and maybe expedient to advise a child against wrong behavior. Some of the common problem areas that have been instrumental in bringing down your adult children include alcohol abuse, drug abuse, hanging out in the wrong places or with the wrong people, gambling, frequently changing sex partners, mistreating spouse or children or exercising beliefs or behavior that are so far from the mainstream they would be labeled radical or cultist. When you, as a parent, witness any of these things taking shape, don't pass them off by saying your child is grown and knows what he or she is doing. That is not always the case. Some children are grown, but they don't yet know what they are doing. When you see something, say something. Sometimes the adult child will not listen, but for each one that does, that may be a life or family saved.

I often reflect on a CD I listen to from time to time which has a song on it entitled, "King Heroin." It's a musical account of a daughter who was seeking the fun of the fast life and bright lights. This type of tale has been told over and over again, and the point of the tale could relate to anyone's daughter. As the song goes, the daughter was preparing to leave home and go out on her own, to see the world and have a lot of fun. There was nothing wrong with going out on her own, if it was time for her to do so. What was troubling was the motive behind her going out on her own. She didn't say she was going out on her own to seek a respectable job, continue her studies, and, if God directed her to a suitable mate, to marry and raise a family. What was her motive?

The mother advised her, even pleaded with her, not to go at that time, but her response to her mother was, "Mother, I'm old enough to know." The story told by the song is that she got hooked on cocaine at one of those fun parties she was seeking. Subsequently, her travels took her from one big city to another, still in pursuit of more parties and brighter lights. She was constantly seeking a new "high," one that would take her higher than she had even been before.

As time and circumstances would have it, her mother came to the point of dying and called for her daughter. But the daughter's drug entanglement prevented her from reaching her mother quickly. The daughter tried, but the heroin monkey was so heavy on her back, she couldn't get there in time. In fact, she died before ever reaching her mother. Her lifestyle had killed her and probably killed her mother as well. She had tried to help the child avoid the tragedy by advising her against what she was about to do, but her advice may have been too little and too late. As a parent, don't wait until it is too late before you speak out. Speak out as soon as you see your child leaning toward a behavior or association with any type of destroyer of character and body.

3. Character and Life Destroyers

Alcohol abuse and drugs are definite character destroyers. If you drink or do drugs with your adult child, you're not only endorsing the behavior; you're also encouraging it and may be hastening your child's demise. Alcohol abuse isn't the result of a glass of dinner wine, if one so desires, for that doesn't alter the personality. The ideal for some is to refrain from indulgence of any kind, lest it becomes an uncontrollable habit.

Street drugs in any form are destructive to the mind and the body. Prescription drugs may be necessary and unavoidable, but abuse of prescription drugs is known to exist. You should advise your child to avoid, at all cost, drugs which are not medicinal, but purely social. The end of the road for a drug abuser is very short and is certain to destroy the partaker. We cannot say "may destroy" or "can destroy"; it will destroy. There is absolutely no doubt about it.

Some of the clubs your adult child or children are frequently visiting are as deadly as a 357 Magnum. All types of wrong behavior and bad people congregate there. They may be fun—if that is your child's idea of having fun. But along with the fun to be had in some of those clubs are individuals spoiling for confrontation, drugs of all types and other contraband that may be peddled and can cause your child's demise.

Quite often, children frequent such places to meet people and have fun. But some of the potential acquaintances in those clubs frequent them often, meeting people and changing partners. Some of these individuals come with dates and are ready to kill another person for even looking at his or her date in the wrong way. It's a dangerous world out there these days. Your child cannot be too careful and, as a parent, you can never give too much good advice. Being in some of those clubs is definitely being in the wrong place. Some are unlicensed, overcrowded, firetraps and are often targets for vengeful individuals.

Who your child associates with can affect her life as much as where she or he goes. What about the many accounts of individuals being with the wrong people, at the wrong place and ending up in jail as an accomplice to a crime, or dead from the association? When your adult child's associate looks, sounds and appears to be of questionable character, you should voice your opinion. The few words expressed could save many tears. I'm sure the father of the young man killed in California, along with the celebrated female victim, wished he had given him some different advice, especially if he had the opportunity to do so.

Don't be afraid or hesitate about talking to your child concerning questionable behavior, because of the fact that you may have been where you're advising your child not to go or have done what you're advising your child not to do. It's like talking to an individual about salvation and allowing God to change his or her life. Don't let the individual make you feel guilty by telling you about your past. The most important thing should be the fact that you don't go there anymore and don't do that anymore. One is better reformed later than not reformed at all.

Who can better advise a person about a place than the one who has been there? Who can better advise a person about a behavior than one who has done it? As I may have quoted in another chapter of this book, the saying goes, "You can't lead where you don't go, and you can't teach what you don't know." Who can better tell a person about the pitfalls and hurdles that can be encountered along the road of life than those who have traveled the road?

A parent's qualifications to advise about life comes from having lived life. We are all about something today that we were not about yesterday, or we're at some place today where we were not yesterday. That can be for the better or for the worse. If it's for the better, then you're well advised to tell others, so as to help them avoid the worse. We were all once sinners, including the minister, who is now admonishing others to abstain from sinful behavior. Every parent was once a child, and every master was once an apprentice. Every expert was once a novice, and every teacher was once a student.

There are many things that some of our children have taken up that are licensed and publicly sanctioned, but still they lead to no good end. One such thing is gambling. There is nothing good that can come out of the institution of gambling. It probably ruins more lives than it benefits. It enriches the public coffers, but doesn't come back to benefit the people as was promised. Some may benefit from it, but others ultimately lose. No one can win money unless someone else loses money. Gambling may benefit education or the Native Americans or anything else, but it more often takes money out of the pockets of those who can least afford it. Poor people can't afford to subsidize the cost of education and the cost of the Native American dilemma. When one steps up to the slot machine or sits down to the black jack table, no one walks over to her or him and asks if she can afford to lose the money.

I'm not convinced that the gambling money intended for education and for addressing the Native American dilemma is even getting to the problem it is intended to address. The expense of those needs should be borne by someone, but not by those who can least afford them. That's why we should advise our children against the habit of gambling. Those who leave their money in the casinos of the world and with the collectors of lottery ticket money are paying for other people's jobs and ingratiating the state and city officials who process the lottery monies. They're also paying dividends and buying stock for those with ownership in the casinos. The problem goes even deeper.

Yes, I know you can't tell your child not to gamble, because you are also a gambler. If you are one of those who never gambled or one of those who stopped gambling, tell your grown child it is a losing proposition, a dead-end street. At the very least, it is a blight on their faith in God, because God is not the author of chance. God knows all things certain—without a doubt. If you believe in God's power to bless you and provide for your needs (as you say you do), gambling questions that belief, because you're not waiting for God to do what He has promised you He would do. You're endeavoring to help Him out, and He doesn't need your help. What He has to do, He can do without the help of anyone.

Also, gambling has the possibility of impoverishing your child's future, as well as your family's, because more often than not, the losses far outnumber the winnings. In addition, there always exists the opportunity for gambling to become an addiction, and anything addictive is destructive.

Another form of destructive behavior is the mistreatment of one's spouse or child. As a parent, you should not sit idly by and watch your child mistreat his or her spouse or child. There is a law in place these days that carries punishment for spousal abuse and child abuse. I admit, it needs more teeth in it, but it does exist. When you witness your son abusing his wife or your daughter abusing her husband, tell him or her that it is negative, unacceptable behavior. Don't allow him or her to convince you that the abused spouse deserves it. No adult (or child) deserves to be abused. If you cannot overcome your disagreements, then leave each other alone.

God hates abuse and, as a parent, you should hate it also. If your son or daughter engages in it, you should not hesitate to speak against it, because it simply is disgustingly negative behavior. Don't take the attitude that it's none of your business. All acts of wrong behavior are somebody's business. It's especially your business, if your child is engaging in it. If your child goes to jail for spousal abuse, will that be your business? Will you stop loving him? Will you go to jail to visit him? Will you simply ignore his being in jail and say it's not your business? If it were your son or daughter, how would you like it if she or he was being abused by his or her spouse? That may not be your business either, but it sure would not make you happy, unless you're not a normal parent.

I can recall the dilemma of an old friend of mine, whose son's girlfriend would virtually have him in tears, and the mother would be in tears over the son's dilemma, but she couldn't do anything to help her son in his circumstances. She was helpless. I wonder if the shoe had been on the other foot, if she would have felt the same.

My mother was not the interfering kind, but she was quick to tell her son or daughter not to mistreat his or her spouse. She would be quick to say, "Son, don't treat your wife [or husband or daughter or son] that way." All of the positive actions that parents take can have a positive impact on families. Shouldn't societies be all about families? Isn't the whole of all mankind all about families? Most of the problems of families in the world today have to do with what parents did or did not do, and the world is not going to get better until parents get better.

Parents' "hands-off" attitude has been and continues to be one of the main ingredients in the social and moral decline in America and the world. No one would dare to say that there is nothing wrong with America, and no one would dare to say that there is nothing wrong with our world. Parents make families, families make neighborhoods, neighborhoods make towns and cities, towns and cities make states, states make countries, and countries make up the world family. Good parents make good families, and good families produce good citizens, who can make good government, which can help bring about a good society.

Many of the ills of our society today have come about because the silent majority watched rather than acted. Those who failed to act had to accept the decisions or actions of those who refused to remain silent. Silence is consent. If you disagree with an action, the only way your disagreement can be known is if you say something. When you look around at all the things you may not like in your children, your family, your neighborhood, your government and the world and say, "I don't like that," ask yourself if you requested it. If you didn't ask for it and you didn't say anything against it when you had a chance, you may as well have requested it. Silence is consent.

Did you ask for all of the things you see wrong in your child? Did you speak out against them when they were taking shape? Don't wait and wish. If you don't speak out at the first opportunity, the time of the next opportunity may be too late.

Are you sick and tired of reading stories and witnessing accounts of mass suicides? Are you tired of hearing parents tell agonizing stories of having lost their son or daughter to some "far out" cult movement? Do you wonder what happened? Do you say to yourself, "What did the parents teach that child or what did they not teach that child?" They taught some of the same things you taught and didn't teach some of the same things you didn't teach either. They saw some of the same signs in their child you see in your child and dismissed them as having no meaning, just as you're doing right now. They said, "My child is grown and has enough sense to think for herself," and you're saying the same thing. They stood by and watched, never saying a word and eventually, the smart adult who could think for herself had become a member of a cult movement and lost her life.

Children should never be too smart or too grown for you to give them input and advice. If they refuse to listen, because they are smart enough and grown enough, the only thing you can do is to leave them in the hands of God and resign yourself to whatever possible consequences.

Sometimes you can see these things coming. When you see your child developing behavior patterns and discussing newly formulated beliefs that are so far off mainstream as to be considered radical or cultist, that's the time to begin speaking out against where the child seems to be going. Don't pass it off as your child being grown and knowing what she or he is doing. It is said that there are three to five thousand cults in this country. The number goes far beyond the wildest imagination of any of us, especially when we are naïve to cult existence and influence.

Some of these cults are attracting your adult children through very subtle and unsuspecting means. Some use the Bible and its influence to gain a sense of credibility, but they all operate by means of psychological programming and mind-bending. They all must keep their adherers separated from families, traditional ideas and thoughts. When you see your adult child pulling away from you, losing the desire to be around you and not allowing you to be around her or him, start getting suspicious and start taking whatever available action you can take to find out if your child is still in the mainstream or leaning toward a cult.

More than just a few parents have watched their adult children and, in some cases, their adult grandchildren run off to cults and never return alive. Some of those adult children had more going for them than just the basic ability to exist and allowed someone, not half their equal in intelligence, to program them and steal their minds. Some were well trained, highly-skilled university graduates, but there was something missing that you (as a parent) failed to give them when they were children. The simple instruction not to follow other people in their thoughts and behavior may have made the difference.

The "Moonies," Heaven's Gate, Jonestown and the Branch Davidians all had more than their share of the above individuals. Yet, the Heaven's Gate and Jonestown adherers succumbed to a mass suicide pact, led by obviously deranged individuals. Their followers went to early graves, to the grief of many parents. The Branch Davidians suffered a fate equally devastating by putting themselves in a position to be killed *en masse*. They appeared to have invited the tragic end they suffered. The government could have responded in a different manner, but maybe the behavior of the cult induced that response by the government.

Some of the parents may have gotten involved in advising the child or children against the direction she or they were headed and prevented them from suffering the fate of those who failed to heed the advice. Others could have heard from parents and didn't listen. Other parents may have taken the usual position, "My child is grown and intelligent enough to make her own decisions." Those who said this were wrong. The child may have been grown enough to make intelligent decisions and dumb enough to make a misguided decision that cost her or his life. So whatever help you can give your child, grown or not, in an effort to steer her or him away from a direction which may be fraught with disastrous consequences, give it. If it goes unheeded, at least you can say you tried. You will not have to wring your hands, lamenting the fact that you said nothing or say to yourself, "I wish I had said something."

Those of you who talk to your child continuously about bad, destructive behavior, and the child seems to be unmoved and unchanged, don't stop talking, and don't give up. Pray for the child. Don't doubt for one minute God's power to change a life and heal a spirit. However, you are also obligated to do what God requires of you. To pray effectively, you must have faith, and to have faith, you must have works.

I personally had an out-of-control temper as a child, and even as an adult. As a child, my parents controlled it with a strap. My father also had an out-of-control temper. However, he was in charge of my behavior, so I had little chance of winning in that area. As an adult, I was on my own, except for the power and goodness of God to help me change, and it did. If my mother had been alive, I'm sure she would have continued to admonish me to "calm down," as the expression goes.

I've heard, over and over again, the testimonies of young men, who continually walked a road of bad behavior. The testimony of this particular individual comes to mind. His mother and grandmother were continually admonishing him about his behavior. They both prayed for him continually, but he didn't seem to change. Subsequently, he became a drug dealer, with some twenty-nine people working for him, as the story goes. Later on, he became a drug addict, with nothing working for him. He degenerated to one of those homeless, street people, the type whose clothes are nasty and stink. He was one of those you would feign to go near, never mind touch.

One day he came to a soup kitchen for food and was introduced to the love of God. His mother and grandmother had already passed away. He accepted Christ in his life and is now a very changed individual. His life is like the change from night to day. This isn't just a story I heard. I know the individual, and I know the soup kitchen where he was introduced to God and His love. So, keep telling your child about her or his wrong direction. Even if the child doesn't change until later, it will be better for him or her not to have changed at all. Don't be moot on your adult child's bad behavior. Your child can be three or thirty-three, eight or eighty-eight, but if it's wrong, say so. Don't interfere in his or her life, but always condemn bad behavior.

CHAPTER XV

DON'T HOLD YOUR CHILD FOREVER IN YOUR ARMS, BUT KEEP YOUR ARMS FOREVER OPEN

Teach her and nurture her, and then let go
Of the hand of your child, so she can grow,
To be independent and survive on her own,
Against life's tests that aren't always known.
But keep arms open, if she needs an embrace,
After getting weary from running life's race.

1. BREAKING UP AND LETTING GO

A man's ego and natural instincts tell him that after marriage, his wife should be listening to him rather than to her father. I guess it is also true that a woman's instincts tell her that her husband should be listening to his wife rather than to his mother. Both ego and instincts mirror the way things should be after a couple marries. Since this is a normal trend of thought and expectation, the first order of business for a husband, prior to the marriage or certainly immediately thereafter, is to break the bonds of the so-called "daddy's girl" myth, if, in fact, this was the type of relationship the new bride had with her father. How quickly and how completely the bond is severed depends on the strength of character of the new husband and the size of his ego.

On the other hand, some husbands were so-called "mama's boys" prior to taking a wife. How quickly and how completely his bond with his mother is broken depends on the efficiency of the wife at doing the things for her husband he thought only his mother could do and the personal feeling of security of the husband in his ability to survive without his mother's guiding hand. One should not be surprised if the daughter's husband-to-be and her husband afterward, exert strong influences in getting the daughter to distance herself from her father's ideas, guidance and assistance in any and all matters she sought her father's input on in the past.

For the effect to be complete, or as near complete as the husband desires, he may seek to keep her away from her father (especially) and also her mother—as much as possible. This is especially true if the new wife had a strong influential father, who the daughter may have looked up to and respected. That little form of jealousy in the husband tells him that his wife should only listen and pay attention to him. As the scenario unfolds, you may begin to see your daughter less, because the husband fears the more frequently the wife visits her parents, the more likely she is to be influenced by their thinking, rather than by his. However, this should be expected. Be prepared for it, and accept it. This is all a part of the "letting go" process.

After some marriages, it is said: "I didn't lose a daughter, I gained a son," but after other marriages, some fathers seem to actually lose the daughter and maybe not gain a son. However, you can't hold the child forever in your arms, but you can keep your arms forever open for the child. When you begin to see evidence of the above taking place, you, as a father, should begin to step back and gradually (or at whatever pace you can) let go of the child. That is what you are supposed to do. As long as the husband treats her well and with respect, provides for her needs and the needs of the family, there is no reason for you to think you need to hold onto your child in any area of directing, influencing or providing. When God gives her a husband (and hope and pray that God gave him), He gives him to be and to do the things that the father did for her before.

The Bible admonishes a wife to forsake mother and father and cleave to her husband. If her husband is doing things properly, you should leave all matters concerning his wife (your daughter) to him to take care of. If he doesn't want her around her parents as frequently, for fear of undue influence, you should learn to miss her and go about your life. If her husband fails or shirks any of his responsibilities and she or they need your help, have your arms open for them, and lend the support she or they may need and request. Otherwise, get a life and go about the business of living it without your child's everyday presence.

Don't get into a habit of telling your daughter she needs a new dress or telling your son he needs a new suit, some new furniture or food in the refrigerator. That may be seen as "meddling." Those are areas that should not be left to your judgment, as a parent. What a parent may think a child needs isn't always what the child thinks she or he needs. If she or they think they need any of these things, she may let you know. If they're ashamed to let you know, the need probably isn't urgent enough for them to give it consideration. Allow them to work out their own priorities, as they feel necessary.

2. YOUR CHILD'S SAFETY AND WELL-BEING

There is an instance when a parent (especially a father) must interfere in the affairs of his daughter, whether requested or not, and that instance is when the husband is abusing his wife (your daughter). You would be very foolish, if you love your child, and you would be less than a father, if you could sit on the sidelines while your daughter is being physically, verbally or economically abused. I have seen nothing biblical or anything in rules of social behavior and conduct that condones the physical, verbal and economic abuse of a wife. Some societies turn a deaf ear and a blind eye to such behavior, but civilized society should have progressed far enough to not allow this type of behavior to be sanctioned.

I have seen nothing written that stipulates or implies that a parent should never involve himself in the affairs of his daughter's household under any condition or sit idly by while his child is being abused, and in some cases, even killed. What type of father could you be if you wouldn't have the guts or the backbone to prevent, or to put a stop to, abusive behavior against your daughter by her husband? You should take whatever means necessary to get to the root of and stop such behavior, even if it holds the possibility of your going up against the law. Better an abusive husband dead, than your daughter, if it comes to that.

As I reflect on this, I'm thinking of the scene in the old movie "The

Godfather," where the daughter was constantly being battered and beaten up by her husband. The brother didn't like it and eventually had the husband killed. Violence should always be a last solution to anything. Often, fathers or brothers are abusive males themselves and don't find it expedient to attempt to stop abuse against the daughter or sister. Do you fit this category? If you are an abusive husband, you should discontinue this type of behavior, because what goes around often comes around. It is difficult for the "pot to talk about the kettle" and difficult for you to tell your daughter's or your sister's husband to refrain from the type of behavior you are also guilty of.

On the other hand, could you be a cowardly father or brother, who lacks the guts to stand up to a cowardly man? Remember, only cowards beat women. Real men don't beat women, because there is no challenge in going up against a noncompetitive force. Most females are incapable of defending themselves against the strength of a man, short of the use of deadly force. What kind of sport is it to fight someone who is incapable of fighting back? Regardless of the fact that women desire to be equal, they're usually not equal in strength and physical conditioning. They can be equal in their ability to think and learn and make money and perform some tasks and in many other areas, but usually all are not equal in their ability with men in all physical aspects.

Men (for the most part) are stronger, just by reason of conditioning and physical adaptation. God meant it that way, because man was created to take the lead in directing and providing for his family. If the husband and wife are both employed, and a third job is needed to provide for the family and make ends meet, the man should be the one to take a second job. If someone needs to get up early and start the fire or turn on the heat, the man should take the initiative, unless by reason of physical incapacitation or scheduling inconveniences, it would be more expedient for the wife to do it. If a grizzly bear is at the front door, the man should answer the door. The man should be at the forefront in performing any and all tasks, unless, by reason of a physical condition, he is unable to do so. The Bible speaks of the wife, or woman, as the weaker vessel, and it is true. A woman is not meant to be beaten and battered and physically abused by any man. It is cowardly and wrong behavior, and whenever and wherever it exists, it needs to stop.

I can recall the evening my daughter's husband-to-be came to talk with me concerning his desire to marry her. I knew from observation how he had treated her, in the time they had been friends. I knew he was a quality young man from a quality family, but I felt I didn't really know him well yet. I expressed to him the possibility that the person I knew was not the real person. Often we know of a person, but don't really know the person. I asked him if there was a side of him that had not, as yet, surfaced. He suggested that there was not. Then I said to him, "If you're the type of man who believes in hitting your wife, or you think you might be inclined to exercise that type of behavior in the future, you should not marry my daughter, because that is one area of behavior which is strictly 'off limits' with me. A man is likely to have a very serious confrontation with me if he hits my child." He said that his grandfather, who raised him, taught him that such was not proper behavior. I was comfortable with that position, and I guess he was comfortable with my position.

In the cases of spousal abuse, more fathers need to begin taking charge of their daughter's life, in situations where she may be in the hands of an abusive husband. If they don't, they may one day see her killed at the hands of this type of man. There is too much of that type of behavior in our society today, and it has gotten completely out of hand, just as so many other social ills. The law isn't tough enough, orders of protection are not being enforced, and abusive men are still going about their business of wreaking physical havoc on helpless women. When you witness accounts of women being doused with gasoline and set on fire, women being stabbed multiple times, or pregnant women being bludgeoned to death, it is high time for fathers and brothers to take charge where the law seems to be turning a deaf ear.

Women are being slain before they can be rescued from abusive situations. Abusive men aren't respecting judges' orders of protection. Some of these brutes virtually smirk at the law. This is still somewhat of a "man's world," and so many men are guilty of this behavior that it often becomes difficult for one man to condemn another. Our society needs to get better. We need to get back to a society that possessed some semblance of law and order and respect and tolerance and then live and let live. I want my daughter and sisters alive, don't you?

No cowardly man's life is worth the life of my daughter or sister. If you want to rescue your daughter from physical harm or even death, you had better wake up and take action (as a father) early on, to prevent even the possibility of your daughter entering into that type of relationship. Some women don't even know the men they marry or enter into a relationship with. They're often looking only at the "window dressing." Some of the men are fresh out of mental institutions or jail cells and have not been and may never be rehabilitated. Others are products of abusive childhoods and know no other form of behavior. Fathers had better start teaching their daughters to do their homework, because what they see isn't always what they get.

No male, never mind how violent or crazy, is beyond the ability to be subdued, by a force equal to his desire or intention. But situations need not even come to these types of conclusions. Your daughter need not even marry a man who is inclined to abuse her. No woman deserves it, and no father should allow it. It is true that sometimes girls don't listen, but we must try and continue to try to get the point over to them. Men—real men— won't allow a man to beat up on his daughter or sister. If her behavior or attitude is such that the man feels inclined to physically abuse her, it is time for him to separate himself from her or seek to get counseling for her as well as himself. As a father, you must insist on her husband taking that path—if he is abusive. If he doesn't, you, your son or your brother or any other male that has a cause for concern about her safety and well-being should get in between her and this abusive male.

I find it virtually impossible to believe that a normal, rational woman desires to be beaten, and if she is not normal or rational, she doesn't belong in a relationship that will cater to this type of abnormal desire in the first place. Maybe someone should seek to get her out of it, before tragedy sets in, and it is declared to be too late. The woman who gets joy or pleasure out of being beat up (if there is indeed such a woman) is a woman who is psychologically ill. If such a woman is your daughter, you need to be forth- right at getting immediate help for her. If her husband accommodates her in these abnormal requests, he also needs psychological help. We must all be aware of the fact that there is much going on in our present society that is unacceptable but has crossed the line bordering on normally acceptable behavior.

Just because our society accepts this behavior doesn't mean it's correct. If our society is correct in what it is willing to accept, there would be no need for writings such as this that point out grossly misdirected behavior and directions for addressing it. Hundreds, if not thousands of other writ- ings thrust in front of us on a daily basis also seek to address many of the ills of our society. Trust me, our society today isn't completely whole and well.

With the high percentage of certain ethnic groups having gone through the prison gates, that tells me and many others there is something drastically wrong in our society today. With the high percentage of children committing suicide, that tells me and should tell others there is something definitely wrong in our society today. With the hundreds of thousands of registered and unregistered child molesters, that should tell all of us something is wrong in our society today. The type of cases put before jurisdictional, as well as before the Supreme Court, tells me something is wrong in our society today. The rash of crimes committed in the highest levels of government tells me something is wrong in our society today.

Much more can be said about the direction of behavior in our society today. We need not be so accepting of the types of negative behavior that were frowned upon in yesterday's society. Any reasonably intelligent individual, having only a modicum of morality, would consider some of today's social norms to be completely "off" and unacceptable. Maybe the majority of those in our society have gone off in the wrong direction. When you see behavior you think is "off," it probably is. If it is being exercised by your daughter, get help for her. When you witness a certain type of unconventional behavior in your child, you should, at least, address the issue. If you see it surfacing in your daughter's relationship with her husband, talk to her and him and put a stop to it immediately. If you don't, the situation will only get worse.

In addition to physical, spousal abuse, there are other forms of spousal abuse such as verbal spousal abuse. The comments above, as well as others that may follow, are primarily directed toward men who abuse their wives, because an individual who displays himself as a man is less than a man if his self-esteem is so low that he would permit his wife to speak to him or treat him in any manner she so desires. If a man has lived and acted in such a manner as not to deserve better respect from his wife, then he has failed as a husband. Every real woman wants a real man, but the man has to earn the respect by what he says and by what he does. A wife's respect for her husband isn't automatic by virtue of the fact that he is called a man. Along with the physical makeup that identifies him (on observation) as a man, must be the way he speaks and performs in accordance with what would normally be expected of a man.

Husbands, respect for you, as a man, has much to do with the way you influence your wife in your role as a man. You should have godly influence, born out of selflessness, compassion and conviction. Your first concern should be about the well-being of your wife and your family. Show them that you care; show compassion. Compassion goes a long way and carries a great deal of influence. It has been properly said: "People don't care how much you know until they know how much you care." As Dr. Charles Stanley remarked in his Priority Profiles, "The people that most influence us are usually the people who care for us." You, as a man, must have a strong conviction toward right behavior as it relates to all things, and especially to your wife and family.

Since we are on this subject, you must have a compelling conviction to transcend wrong motives which yield wrong behavior. All types of abuse upon a wife have the end result of destroying her self-esteem, and if your need is to make your wife look small so you can look big, you have an ego problem that requires immediate attention. In this case, do something about your life so you can feel better about who you are. When you feel good about who you are, you will have no need to put your wife down.

What can you do to feel good about yourself? You can do any number of things: seek God and His guidance. He has the power to even make a "nobody" feel like somebody. You can go back to school and learn something new or take up a trade or hobby that can give you a greater sense of accomplishment. Rise above the desire to put your wife down to build yourself up. You're less than a whole man when you do this.

Don't verbally abuse your wife by telling her she's stupid or dumb or make her think she can't do anything right. That destroys her self-esteem and can be as devastating to her as physical abuse. I've witnessed many such instances of this type of abuse, and one in particular comes to mind.

This man's wife was bright, articulate, attractive and pleasant. As far as I could see and observe, she was a good wife and mother and took good care of her family. However, he was constantly bombarding her with remarks, the type of which makes a person feel less than what her potential could yield. Eventually she began to think she was no more than what her husband thought and said she was, a helpless woman who needed him and simply could not survive without him. This was probably just what he wanted to make her think, so she would never think of being able to exist independently of him.

He succeeded at that ... until his wife went out to work and came to realize that she had the ability to support herself and her children—if need be. Eventually she was given the task of overseeing many of the financial affairs of the family. She did such a fine job that she, as well as her husband, came to realize she could prudently handle the family's financial well-being. Later on, a financial crisis came, and she stuck to the task of making financial ends meet and helping to guide the family through the crisis, by tightening the purse strings in whatever way necessary. These crises and the way she handled them, brought her to a point of equal recognition with her husband, after many years of "put downs" and verbal abuse.

Men, don't let another man do this to your daughter or sister. When you observe the manner in which your daughter's husband speaks to her, and if it borders on what might be considered verbal abuse, nip it in the bud. As her father and as the adopted father of her husband, due to marriage, sit down with him on the matter and give some matter-of-fact advice concerning the same. As a man, don't succumb to the desire to do this to your wife. Don't allow bad behavior to destroy a good wife. Proverbs 18:22 says, *"He who finds a wife finds a good thing"* (NKJ). Therefore treasure her; don't abuse her.

Another form of abuse is economic abuse, which sometimes comes about when the husband deprives himself, as well as his spouse, of economic well-being, because he is either too lazy, lacks ambition or is too frugal to provide a state of meaningful economic existence for his wife and/or family. At other times, economic abuse comes about when the husband takes a selfish approach, sees after his own needs and desires and takes no interest in the economic well-being of his wife and/or family.

I am reminded of a situation in which the wife worked, and her husband demanded that she bring her paycheck home to him, to spend and distribute as he saw fit. She was often deprived of desired necessities, while he did with the money what he pleased to do, basically selfishly looking to his own well-being. This was not only a case of economic abuse, it was also a case of verbal abuse, because he would threaten her with dire consequences if she failed to do what he instructed her to do. He would talk to her in such a way as to keep her in fear and under his control. She was very attractive, and when she went out in public, the heads of all the men usually turned her way. This husband was probably insecure and felt that controlling his wife was the only means of keeping her to himself.

This, by far, isn't the only case of its type. Behavior of this type happens every day in our society, but wherever it exists, it should not be tolerated. Neither God nor society made man master over a woman's earnings. Don't allow any man to treat your daughter or sister in that manner. It is dehumanizing and wrong behavior. Don't sit quietly by and acquiesce, while your child is being subjected to this type of treatment. For those women who see a similar scenario taking shape in their lives, wake up. This is controlling, and it will ultimately get out of hand.

There is nothing wrong with both husband and wife bringing their money home and putting it in the same pot, for both to jointly decide how it is to be dispersed. No reasonably intelligent woman, who is smart enough to earn a paycheck, needs a man to tell her how to spend it, unless she can have the same input in telling him how to spend his earnings. Any woman who is smart enough and ambitious enough to earn money is also smart enough to help decide how to spend it.

Some husbands are sole "breadwinners" in their household and hold the economic purse-strings like Scrooge's great-grandfather. This type of husband acts as if he is down to the last penny he has and will ever have. The wife lives virtually in rags, and in some cases where there are children, none of them have sufficient, serviceable clothing. The husband goes about lowering the heat and/or air conditioning, making the family sit in discomfort at all times. He will turn out the light while you're reading by it and turn off the television while you're watching it, or he will tell you, "That is enough television watching; it's time to turn it off," as if no one else should have any say in the matter.

He buys the cheapest, off-brand groceries, when he does buy, and requires the family to make do, until the next grocery shopping date. He buys the cheapest furniture and furnishings, balks on allowing his wife to go to the doctor when the cost comes out of his pocket, never takes the wife and family out for any form of recreation, never goes on a decent vacation, and refuses to get necessary repair work done on the house ... until it is almost beyond repair. He either doesn't have money to do these things or is too tight-fisted to spend the money. Does this sound like someone you know or have known?

In any case, there is no excuse for this to be a continuous state of existence in your household. This is economic abuse. Your husband doesn't want you to go out to work, for fear of some other man waking you up (if only in promises) to a better side of life. The neighbor sees you leaving the house in your cheap, inadequate attire, looks at your beauty, and says you deserve better. But your husband fails to provide adequately for your well-being. Even when you work, you are unable to get beyond these circumstances, because your money doesn't go far enough toward bettering the conditions. Your husband requires you to contribute more than your share for the upkeep of the family. You are unable to keep a decent pair of hosiery, your coat is five years old and is the one your mother gave you, you must buy the cheapest clothing, you are ashamed to invite anyone over to your house because of the condition it's in, and your husband fails to do anything more to help make ends meet.

You see your neighbor's wife walk out of a neatly kept, well-furnished home, dressed in an attractive, up-to-date outfit, get into the family car and go about her business. Your family has never owned a new car, because your husband only buys used cars and drives them until the doors fall off. It isn't so much that you want to keep up with the "Joneses"; you feel you also deserve at least a meaningful economic existence. Your husband tells you that you must make it on whatever his one job provides, because he refuses to do anything else; otherwise, you can work as much as you want to.

You work overtime, but that still isn't enough, because all of that and more is needed for the home and the children. He refuses to paint the house or hire a painter, so if you want it done, you must do it yourself. He gives you a fixed amount of money from his pay and tells you to "work a miracle." Your condition is nothing less than economic abuse.

I'm not saying a wife needs three fur coats, forty pairs of shoes and dresses and suits in the closet with the tags still on them, but I'm saying a wife needs a solid, basic "get by" wardrobe, which (at the least) should consist of two quality up-to-date dress coats for wearing with brown or black attire, a decent acceptable work coat and a serviceable casual coat. A decent wardrobe would, at the very least, have in it a pair each of quality leather (not "pleather") shoes in black, brown, tan, navy, white and patent leather. She needs at least two pairs of quality, dress leather boots, a pair of rainy weather boots and a pair of cold weather boots. She needs a dress raincoat and an everyday raincoat, and at least three pairs of serviceable, everyday shoes that she can wear to work and when she goes shopping. She also needs accessories to adequately compliment the above, such as dresses, sweaters, blouses, belts, scarves, slacks (if she wears them), jackets, feet accessories and an adequate reserve of quality hosiery.

No woman should have to leave home everyday with runs in her stockings, simply because that is all she has. She should not have to put on a pair with runs in the heels over a pair with the toes out. If she goes to business, she should have at least two quality up-to-date business suits. They need not be from Brooks Brothers, but she should certainly be able to go to one of the upscale discount houses to buy them at less than regular retail. I'm not suggesting that she would not be able to get by on less than the above, nor am I suggesting that it would be sinful to have more than the above—if it doesn't negatively impact the budget and compromise more important priorities. Priorities and their place in a budget are what govern.

A wife needs to be able to go out for basic grooming of her hair and nails on a regular basis. If she has the time and ability to groom her own nails, that is acceptable and can free the budget for other things. No woman needs to walk around with unsightly nails and unmanaged hair. The husband and the budget must allow for proper grooming. It would be sensible and positive if a wife can go for periodic skin-care treatments, if her skin can benefit in a positive way from obtaining it. This will enhance the way you feel about her, as well as the way she feels about herself.

A case comes to mind about an occasion where two gunmen went in to stick up a bar. The gunmen ordered everyone to strip down to their underwear. It was in the winter. I guess they did this so nobody would be able to chase after them. Then they ordered everyone to lie on the floor. As the story goes, one of the ladies had on underwear so ragged, the man holding the gun began laughing. As a husband, would you want this to be your wife? I can't say who is to blame for this situation. It may or may not be the husband's fault, or the lady may not have even had a husband. But if she didn't have adequate, serviceable undergarments, she had either economically deprived herself or been economically deprived by her mate.

Your wife and family don't need to sit in a cold house in the winter or a hot house in the summer because you are too frugal or can't afford to supply comfortable climatic conditions in the house. Your wife and family should not be subjected to sitting in the dark or have the television unnecessarily turned off to save electricity. I know this happens in some households.

When I was a child, my father went about the house turning off the lights. As I reflect on it, his behavior may have been justified, because he only required you to turn off the lights before you left a room. In this case, it may have been warranted because we didn't own stock in the utility company. In other cases, it may be extreme behavior.

When a husband fails to provide the basic comforts and conveniences, he is economically depriving his family and failing to adequately fulfill his responsibilities as a husband. If you (the husband) can't afford it today, do something about it so you may be able to afford it tomorrow.

I remember a discussion I was having one day concerning how expensive things were. I was speaking to a person who was earning about $100,000 a year, when I was earning about $20,000. I remember him being short of his needed cash flow from time to time and having to borrow from a couple of better-off associates in his office. His remark to me, when I mentioned how expensive things were, was: "Don, it's not that things are so expensive; it's just that you can't afford them." He said, "When I need money, I need $10,000, and when you need money, you may need only $100, but it is all relative, because it can be just as difficult for you to come up with the $100 as it is for me to come up with the $10,000."

No father wants to entrust his daughter to a spouse who will not adequately provide for her well-being because he is either too lazy, lacks the ambition or is too frugal. How many cases can you recall in which the husband never adequately provided for his wife, and when he passed away, he left sufficient money, and it wasn't until then that the wife could begin to enjoy the basic necessities and wants of life? We need not deprive our families of the basics needed for comfortable, everyday existence, in an effort to save for a rainy day. We may die before the rain comes, and where we're going after we die, we can't take anything with us.

Yes, we should be prudent and put away something for a rainy day, because rainy days do come upon us. But saving all is just as extreme as saving none. It is the other extreme. God wants us to have balance in our lives. Extreme behavior is unacceptable in any and all forms and is also self-defeating.

Husbands, don't economically abuse your wife. Provide for her well-being. If you love her, you should want to bring a smile of joy to her life. If she's your wife, she deserves it. Do whatever it takes, legally, to provide economic well-being for her and the child or children—if you have any. If it means getting a second job, do it, as long as it doesn't take away quality time needed with the family. If you find it difficult to work out the two-job scenario, you may want to do a home-based business, which can subsidize your income and still give you quality time with your family.

All of the types of abuses mentioned above are bad and should not have to be tolerated in a marriage. Physical abuse should never be on anyone's agenda, nor tolerated under any condition, because it can ultimately lead to serious problems and sometimes death. No one should ever forget the infamous O.J. Simpson case. This isn't to say that he was innocent or guilty. The jury has already spoken on that point, but there is reason to presume that some physical abuse had taken place. We don't know for certain, but we do know that two people lost their lives, families were shattered and the economic costs ran in the tens of millions of dollars. There is also reason to believe that verbal abuse was present. This runs a somewhat equal parallel to physical abuse, and the type of vocalizing that can lead to verbal abuse can also lead to physical abuse.

There are flared tempers in both cases. Flared tempers can lead to anger, and anger can lead to physical confrontation. Husbands, avoid this type of behavior. Fathers, refuse to accept it. Your daughters don't deserve it. Men who physically abuse women don't confront men, unless the odds for overcoming the man are clearly in their favor. They only abuse women, when the odds of overcoming them are in their favor.

A coward is one who acts only when the odds for success are on his side. Otherwise, he wouldn't act. Do you remember how in (the days of the old West) people frowned on the act of shooting a man in the back? It was because it constituted a very cowardly act. Real men met face to face and created their odds by being the fastest draw. In today's society, you very seldom hear of a hundred-and-fifty-pound man abusing a hundred-and-ninety-pound woman— unless he uses a knife or gun. He needs the weapon to tip the odds in his favor. However, the physical confrontation should always be off the table.

Economic abuse, although mild as compared to the other two abuses, can still have devastating effects on the mind and self-esteem of a woman and may lead to a state of depression. As is said by psychologist, depression, in its worst stage, is a very serious mental condition and quite often can lead a person to self-destruct. If you care enough to marry a lady, don't deprive her of the chance to be in an adequate state of economic stability. Don't take her from a good home or a stable economic existence and put her in a state of economic depravity. By the same token, don't take her from an economically-deprived home and continue her in that state of economic existence. A woman can do bad by herself. She doesn't need a man to help her do worse. Bring joy to your wife's countenance by enhancing her economic well-being.

3. Mother, Butt Out!

Mother, are you still buying your married, adult son's underwear and socks? What makes you think his wife isn't able to perform that chore? Even if she can't, it's not your position to continue carrying out this function long after he should have been doing this for himself. Your son should have been buying his own underwear since age fifteen, at the latest. If he was unable to do that by age fifteen, you fell down somewhere in the nurturing process. By the time most boys reach age fifteen, they are not only buying their own underwear; they are dressing themselves, and many have part-time jobs.

The mother who is still doing this for her son, who now has a wife, is interfering in his life. Even when you, the mother, give your son presents, leave the very personal type gifts for his wife to give him. When you don't, you're making two statements: (1.) You're saying that your son doesn't know how to buy these personal necessities, and (2.) Your saying that his wife isn't seeing after his needs. That can be demeaning and an insult to his wife, so, Mother, you need to stay out of it.

Allow your son to do that on his own, or let him get whatever help he needs in that area from his wife. If you were so accustomed to doing so much for him that he never had to do it for himself, you took the definition of "a mama's boy" to the outer limits. Once he gets married, he is expected to be a man, capable of buying his own underwear and making his own decisions. The role that was fulfilled prior by a mother is now expected to be fulfilled by his wife. The problems that he took to his mother to solve for him before should now be discussed and solved between him and his wife. Mothers need to leave the personal affairs of their son to the son's wife.

Don't give advice to his wife, unless she asks you for it, or unless you have something positive to say that she may not have been aware of. You need not tell the wife what to cook for her husband; he can tell her that for himself. You may be able to tell her how best to prepare it for him—if she asks you.

Don't invite your son over to discuss the personal affairs of his household; that is called meddling, and meddling in the affairs of your son's household can lead to serious rifts between him and his wife. If you persist, his wife may come to not like you very much, and her husband (your son) may come not to like the fact that his wife doesn't like his mother. This can lead to the wife not desiring to be in your company. So if the husband is ever

343

to see you, he'll have to come alone to visit, and that can also lead to conflict.

If your son loves his wife, he would probably rather keep her happy than keep you happy, because he has to live with his wife and not with you. In this circumstance, you may end up estranged from the son you love so much. So if you love your son and want to keep a healthy relationship with him and his wife, refrain from meddling in the affairs of their existence—unless and until they invite your input.

If you must add input, you are better off if the input is first sanctioned by his wife. If his wife loves and respects you, she'll make sure his relationship with you is on a right plane. Don't meddle, even in subtle ways, such as buying his underwear and socks, and giving him advice concerning the affairs of his household. Stay out of it, unless both of them ask for your input. Don't butt in; wait to be invited in.

4. If You Must, the Door Is Open

None of us knows what the tides of life will bring. None of us knows if we'll have a tomorrow, and if we do, we cannot predict what the state of existence will be like. We could be sick or well, rich or poor, up or down in our affairs. The same can be true in the life of our child or children. Once a child is married, we don't write her or him off forever and neither do we keep the room decorated the same as when she or he lived in it, in anticipation of her or him coming back to occupy it. We should not keep the money in the drawer in anticipation of the need for her to come back to get some of it, whenever she thinks she could use a little help. Of course, the same applies to your son. If he is married, you need not continue cooking his favorite dish and inviting him over to eat (without his wife) what he so enjoyed eating when he lived in your household. Your child needs to eat at his own house, and he needs to eat what his wife prepares for him—unless you invite the both of them over.

Don't continue slipping money to your daughter or son without the knowledge of the spouse, because it can cause household conflict. If a parent does it for his daughter, it could make the husband think you feel he isn't doing a proper job of taking care of her and the child or children. On the other hand, he could think she is getting money from a source representing an unethical relationship. If you (the mother) continue to financially support your son, you aren't allowing him to live up to his responsibility of being a man and a husband. You are making his life too easy, and whenever he has a financial challenge, he will run to you for help rather than do what is required of him to get himself out of that bad financial situation.

If you do this, you are sending a signal that says you really haven't let go. You're still holding your child in your arms. Don't hold your child forever in your arms, but keep your arms forever open for her or him. If your child happens to come upon hard times, by reason of no fault of her or his own doing or by reason of her or his inability to control, then you should have your arms open for her or him. Your child could come upon an unexpected financial hardship, could suffer a disabling physical condition, or could have a negative turn in domestic affairs that could leave her or him unable to cope without your help. Under these conditions, if your child needs you, open your arms to her or him. Open your door, rather than leave them outside. Open your wallet, if you can help her or him financially. Console and counsel, if help is needed in that area. If your child is sick, of course do what you can. I know that is what God would want any parent to do.

I'm sure that in some instances it may be difficult, especially when a child exercised behavior that was contrary to your moral or ethical values and advice. But if your child needs you and expresses regret for any pain she caused herself and you, pray for the child and the situation. Open your heart, your mind and your arms, and seek God's help for His direction and for your understanding. Keep your arms forever open, because you don't know when your child may need your embrace.

The End

Glossary of Slang Words and Phrases

Atomic family: Consisting of a heterosexual husband and wife.

Black eye: A thing that blights or causes negative consequences.

Baubles, bangles and beads: Part of the lyrics of a song, possibly adapted from an old musical; refers to something as being "fancy nothing."

Can't see the forest for the trees: An old sarcasm referring to a circumstance where things are so much on top of one that he or she can't see the broad scope of things around him.

Damaged goods: An old expression used in reference to a female whose virginity has been lost from a pregnancy prior to marriage.

Gift of gab: Having the ability to articulate circumstances in a manner that is very convincing.

A given: Something that must happen or take place.

Good child: A child looked upon by a parent or guardian as doing everything right, but usually is not.

Head thing: Doing something to make oneself feel exalted.

In the closet: Not openly admitted.

Keeping you: Paying or supporting an individual in his or her desired state of comfort in exchange for favors desired of the supporter.

Living in a shoebox: An old expression, the source of which I know not; it was used in our circle to denote one who had no knowledge concerning what was going on outside of his or her immediate sphere of influence.

A TABLESPOON OF LOVE, A TABLESPOON OF DISCIPLINE

Love hides a multitude of faults: A very old expression that could possibly have its roots in the Bible; when an individual cares deeply enough about another individual, he or she can see very little wrong in the countenance of the other individual.

Lose it: To lose control of a situation.

Man's world: The bad idea in a world that lifts men up and puts women down.

Mouthing off: Talking too much at the wrong time.

Off the wall: Reminiscent of individuals in an insane asylum who throws him or herself against the padded wall out of an act of conditional frustration. The individual doesn't realize the behavior could injure, so the walls are padded to prevent injury.

On top of our game: In charge and aware of what's going on at all times.

Out of it: Unaware of what's going on around you.

Out of whack: Used as expressing off-track behavior, where off-track refers to one who is misdirected.

Out to lunch: Used in reference to an individual who has shut down and ceased normal functional behavior, i.e. a person stops working when he or she is out to lunch.

Pit: Sunken deeply in a negative situation.

Regular: Accepting others as an equal.

Richie Rich: An old TV sitcom about a youthful character who was super-rich and operated in grand monetary splendor.

Suit stuff: One who wears suits and accompanying accessories such as a necktie, etc.

GLOSSARY OF SLANG WORDS AND PHRASES

Throwing down: Here it is used to refer to one who is acting out of sorts and causes a child to get in trouble.

Throwing the baby out with the water: Throwing away something perfectly good along with whatever is being discarded, as bad or useless bath water.

Tough love: To exact deserved punishment, even when you regret having to do so.

Tuffie: A coined word referring to a rough, tough, bully-type child.

Water under the bridge: An action having already taken place and the damage having already been done.

Window dressing: An out-front display to make one think there is something as good or better inside.

Wishy washy: A coined phrase referring to indecisive, flip-flop behavior.

— NOTES —

— NOTES —

– NOTES –